HUMAN CAPITAL AND ECONOMIC GROWTH

HUMAN

CAPITAL

AND

ECONOMIC

GROWTH

Andreas Savvides and Thanasis Stengos

STANFORD ECONOMICS AND FINANCE
An Imprint of Stanford University Press
Stanford, California

HD
4904.7
, S29
2009

Stanford University Press
Stanford, California
©2009 by the Board of Trustees of the Leland Stanford Junior University. All
rights reserved.

Printed in the United States of America on acid-free, archival-quality paper

Library of Congress Cataloging-in-Publication Data

Savvides, Andreas, 1957–
   Human capital and economic growth / Andreas Savvides and Thanasis
Stengos.
      p. cm.
   Includes bibliographical references and index.
   ISBN 978-0-8047-5540-5 (cloth : alk. paper)
   1. Human capital.   2. Economic development.   I. Stengos, Thanasis.
II. Title.
   HD4904.7.S29 2008
   331.1'1—dc22   2008018547

Typeset by Westchester Book in 10/13.5 Sabon

To the memory of my parents
Andreas Savvides

My family
Thanasis Stengos

Contents

Preface

This book offers a selective treatment of growth theory as it applies to the link between human capital accumulation and long-run economic growth. While the existing theoretical and empirical literature has highlighted a number of economic/political/social determinants of the long-run rate of economic growth, we have chosen to focus on a single determinant, human capital, for two main reasons. First, a number of excellent general books on the theory and empirics of economic growth exist in the literature. Treatments of individual facets of the process of economic growth are quite rare. Human capital is a complex term that eschews a simple definition and measurement and is a concept that has been investigated from a variety of perspectives by social scientists. Our intention is not to review the diversity of approaches but to concentrate exclusively on the nexus between human capital and economic growth across a large cross section of countries at various stages of economic development. In this respect in empirical applications we utilize the most frequent measure of human capital in cross-country growth research, namely the quantity of formal education each adult member of a society possesses. Second, there is intuitive appeal to the proposition that human capital accumulation (frequently associated with increasing levels of education) ought to make a country richer in the long run. Such a proposition has obvious policy implications. Despite the elegant appeal of this proposition, theoretical and empirical verification has been difficult to establish. We review the main theories linking human capital accumulation and economic growth, but the main thrust of this book is empirical evidence on this issue. We analyze and evaluate extant evidence and also contribute to the debate by providing a thorough investigation of the empirical link between human capital and economic growth using a comprehensive data set and the most recent econometric methods.

One of the main themes of our approach is that the relationship between human capital accumulation and economic growth may be characterized by the presence of thresholds that introduce nonlinear effects. The nonparametric econometric methods we use to explore nonlinearities in Chapter 9 borrow heavily from joint work with our colleagues Pantelis Kalaitzidakis and Theofanis Mamuneas, published in the *Journal of Applied Econometrics* (2006) and *Journal of Economic Growth* (2001).

The idea behind this book gestated in 2000 while we were both visiting faculty members at the Department of Economics of the University of Cyprus. Our stay there provided a stimulating academic environment in which to explore and develop the main themes behind this book. We would like to thank the members of the faculty and staff at the Department of Economics of the University of Cyprus for extending their warm hospitality during our stay. Stengos, in particular, would like to thank Pantelis Kalaitzidakis and Theofanis Mamuneas who helped him fix ideas about the process of economic growth and the measurement issues that arise in that context. Joanne Liang provided prompt and excellent research assistance throughout the writing of this book. Finally, we would like to thank our editor Margo Beth Crouppen and her assistant Jessica Walsh for encouragement and support during all phases of the preparation of this book.

HUMAN CAPITAL AND ECONOMIC GROWTH

I *Introduction*

1 Introduction to Human Capital and Economic Growth

During the last decade of the twentieth century, economics witnessed a revival of interest in the determinants of the rate of long-run growth, a revival that seemed to many economists long overdue after the emphasis on short-term aggregate fluctuations during the previous two decades. Both theoretical and empirical researchers embraced the subject with renewed fervor generating a vast literature that, itself, has been the subject matter of a number of surveys and books.[1] This ought not be a surprise given that the question at hand is one of the most fundamental questions that the discipline addresses. At the same time, it is one of the most complex issues tackled by economics, embracing not only various subdisciplines within economics, but also across other social sciences.

The subject matter of this book is the link between human capital accumulation and long-run growth. While both the theoretical literature and empirical studies have highlighted a number of economic, political, and social determinants of the rate of long-run growth, we have chosen to focus on a single determinant, human capital, for a variety of reasons. First, there is a long history of interest in human capital and growth by social scientists. In this book, we shall review briefly the historical development of the concept. During the post-World War II period, interest on this issue has concerned predominantly the contribution of human capital to the growth of per capita income. Second, human capital is a complex term that eschews a simple definition and measurement and is a concept that has been investigated from a variety of perspectives by social scientists. Our intention is not to review the diversity of approaches but to concentrate exclusively on the nexus between human capital and economic growth. In this respect the most frequent measure of human capital in cross-country comparisons of growth is the quantity of formal education each adult member of society possesses. The concept of human capital, however, is much broader, encompassing the quality of education, the general state of health of the working population, and various forms of training such as on-the-job training or other types of informal education. Including the various aspects of human capital in a comprehensive measure has, so far, proved to be intractable for a large cross section of economies.[2] We will offer a brief discussion of attempts to broaden the concept of human capital, insofar as they relate to the human capital-growth literature. Finally, there is intuitive appeal to the proposition that human capital accumulation (frequently associated with increasing levels of education in public policy discussions) ought to make a country richer in the long run. Despite the elegant appeal of this proposition, theoretical and empirical verification has been difficult to establish.

In this book we review the main theories linking human capital accumulation and economic growth. Its main thrust, however, is the empirical evidence on the issue, as has been developed during the last two decades. While theoretical developments in this area have provided very useful insights, it is our belief that empirical work provides valuable lessons for our understanding of the contribution of human capital to the process of economic growth. We analyze and evaluate the extant evidence and also contribute to the debate by providing a thorough investigation of the empirical link between human capital and economic growth using a consistent data set and recently developed nonlinear estimation methods.

1.1   An Overview of Human Capital and Economic Growth

The importance of human capital to economic well-being has historically ebbed and flowed. During the first half of the twentieth century, human capital was de-emphasized at the expense of physical capital accumulation. Theories of the time placed inordinate emphasis on the accumulation of physical capital as the key engine of economic growth. Investment in physical capital, or capital fundamentalism, came to be widely accepted as the predominant theory of economic growth.[3] During the 1960s interest in the contribution of human capital began to surface. In early contributions, the emphasis was on the contribution of human capital to a person's standard of living (income per person) and its contribution to aggregate wealth; later, emphasis shifted to its role as a contributor to aggregate economic growth. The pioneering work of Schultz (1960) and Becker (1962, 1964) contributed greatly to the swing in emphasis away from physical capital accumulation and pointed the way to a systematic study of the role of human capital. Schultz (1960) identified human capital narrowly with investment in education and put forward the proposition that "important increases in national income are a consequence of additions to the stock of this form of [human] capital" (p. 571). He went on to argue that investment in education could account in large part for the increase in per capita income in the United States.

Becker (1964) broadened the concept of human capital from that of formal schooling to include additional sources of human capital accumulation such as on-the-job training (both general and specific on-the-job training), informal gathering of information that enhances a worker's productivity, and other investments to improve "emotional and physical health." He went on to analyze the amount of investment individuals would undertake in training and the rate of return to that investment. Factors that influence the return include uncertainty and the nonliquid nature of the investment, as well as capital market imperfections and differences in abilities and opportunities. Becker and Chiswick (1966) argued that different investments in human capital and the corresponding rates of return (a result of individual maximizing behavior) determine in large part the distribution of earnings. "Institutional factors" (inheritance of property income, differences in abilities and opportunities, subsidies to education) in turn determine investments in human capital. Their empirical analysis showed that investment in formal education (the sole form of human capital for which adequate data were available) successfully explained differences in average (white male) wages across both the U.S. South and non-South and that the return to education for each schooling level (low, medium, and high number of years of schooling) was higher in the South. The variance of (the log of) earnings and years of schooling was also larger for the South. Becker and Chiswick interpreted the larger variance in schooling years in the South as an indication of less equal opportunity while the higher returns to education (at all levels) as the result of lower education levels in the South, itself the result of fewer educational opportunities.

Subsequently, interest on the economic importance of human capital lay dormant for two decades. The current resurrection in interest began with the seminal paper by Barro (1991) and its emphasis on the empirical determinants of long-run economic growth. While Barro's paper did not pertain specifically to the role of human capital, it did propel human capital (identified with formal education and measured by enrollment rates) to center stage in the economic growth process.

Shortly after the appearance of Barro's empirical investigation of economic growth, the paper by Mankiw, Romer, and Weil (1992) provided theoretical justification for the central role of human capital in the growth process. The model demonstrated that inclusion of human capital in the aggregate production function yielded income shares for the factors of production that are consistent with empirical evidence. Their augmented Solow model places emphasis on human as well as physical capital accumulation and predicts that differences in cross-country income per capita can be explained by differences in saving, education, and population growth, an assertion they verified empirically. Moreover, they derived the transition to the steady state and obtained estimates of the speed of convergence to the steady state.

The Mankiw–Romer–Weil model treats human capital as an input into an aggregate production function that assumes decreasing returns to the reproducible factors of production (physical and human capital). In another widely cited paper, Lucas (1988) focuses on the reproducible nature of human capital and the possibility of externalities generated by human capital. It is natural to speculate that knowledge accumulated by human beings (whether as a result of formal education or otherwise) would have an impact on the productivity, not only of individuals accumulating knowledge, but also their co-workers, colleagues, and others. Thus, investigators began the search for human capital externalities, a research topic which, to date, has yielded mixed evidence.[4]

Another approach to evaluating the contribution of human capital to aggregate growth is Benhabib and Spiegel (1994). Their approach follows on the traditional growth accounting methodology according to which the growth of output is determined by the accumulation of inputs and total factor productivity (TFP) growth. The point of departure and novelty of their approach is to include only physical capital and labor as (traditional) inputs and to model human capital as contributing to the growth of TFP rather than as an input to aggregate production. The contribution of human capital to TFP growth is twofold: (1) it determines the speed by which a country is able to close the gap between its level of TFP and that of the technological leader or the catch-up effect; and (2) human capital determines the pace by which a country can adapt and implement foreign technologies domestically, the imitation or endogenous-growth effect.

All the above approaches (at least in their empirical implementation by various researchers) emphasize a relationship between human capital and growth that takes various forms but is, nonetheless, linear. Motivated by theories of threshold externalities (e.g., Azariadis and Drazen 1990), several researchers have postulated that the impact of human capital on growth is nonlinear. Durlauf and Johnson (1995) divide countries into several groups based on the regression-tree methodology and show that the growth experience of the groups differs markedly. Importantly, for our purposes, the impact of education on growth depends on which group a country is a member. While the Durlauf and Johnson methodology divides countries into a small number of distinct groups, Kalaitzidakis et al. (2001) make use of recent nonparametric econometric techniques to model the human capital-growth relationship. The advantage of their methodology is that it allows the impact of human capital on growth to differ, not only by country, but also according to the time period. They find evidence to substantiate the nonlinear nature of the human capital-growth relationship.

At the empirical level, all the above studies identify a nation's level of human capital with the quantity of education possessed (on average) by each adult member of the nation's population. This is because, until recently, comparable data across countries were only available on rates of school enrollment and mean years of schooling. As data on qualitative measures of education have recently become available, several studies have considered, not only the quantity, but also the quality of education. Hanushek and Kimko (2000) use data from six international tests of student achievement in mathematics and science to derive a measure of labor quality for 31 countries. They find that the quality of education has a very large and significant effect on the growth of per capita gross domestic product (GDP) across these countries. There is no doubt that the quality of education is an important facet of economic growth and an aspect that has been relatively neglected in the literature due to the lack of data on a wide cross section of countries and time periods. This is one of the areas where, in the future, the development of statistical data will allow examination of a number of interesting hypotheses.

1.2   Objectives

This book aims to achieve several objectives. First, we review briefly the historical development of the concept of human capital. Second, we outline the various theoretical approaches to the treatment of human capital in the growth process. Where possible, we emphasize the empirical implications of the theoretical models. Third, we review the empirical treatment of human capital and economic growth. We summarize the results of the empirical literature on the link between the quantity of education and growth and discuss various other aspects including differences by gender or level of education and the quality of human capital. Where the literature allows, we draw some general conclusions and also outline controversies.

The main thrust of this book is the use of a data set to analyze consistently the various empirical approaches on the role of human capital. Through the use of consistent data we aim to evaluate the merits of various hypotheses. While the application of linear estimation techniques needs no explanation, nonlinear estimation techniques are not as widely known. Another objective is to introduce these econometric techniques. Our emphasis is clearly on the applicability of these methods to empirical research on the human capital-growth link. In a subsequent chapter, we demonstrate how these techniques can be used with the same data and nonlinear estimation methods and compare the results of linear to nonlinear estimation methods. Both approaches have their relative merits and drawbacks and we conclude by summarizing and evaluating our results.

Notes

1. Several excellent books on economic growth exist at various levels of difficulty. At the introductory/undergraduate level, the books by Gylfason (1999),

Jones (2002), and Weil (2005) deserve separate mention. At the advanced/graduate level, Aghion and Howitt (1998) and Barro and Sala-i-Martin (2004) are thorough theoretical treatments while Barro (1997) concentrates on the empirical treatment of the subject. What all these books share, however, is an all-encompassing approach to economic growth: they examine the various facets of the growth process and, by consequence, are unable to provide a thorough treatment of each aspect of growth.

2. Throughout this book our concern is with cross-country comparisons of economic growth, not the experience of one or a small number of economies. Therefore, we shall limit our discussion to studies or measures of human capital that have wide applicability across countries at various stages of development.

3. The concept of capital fundamentalism and its contribution to economic growth is analyzed by King and Levine (1994). They argue that reliance on physical capital accumulation as the source of economic growth has been misguided.

4. The papers by Barro, Lucas, and Mankiw, Romer, and Weil are indeed three of the most widely cited papers to appear in the economics literature during recent years. The Social Sciences Citation Index reveals that (as of October 2007) the Barro paper had been cited 1,075 times, Lucas 1,586 times, and Mankiw, Romer, and Weil 832 times.

2 The Concept of Human Capital: A Brief Historical Review

2.1 Introduction

The concept of human capital has a long history. The objective of this chapter is to furnish the reader with a short overview of the interpretations that have been attached to the concept over the years. It is not intended to provide a comprehensive review of the economic history of the concept. In that respect, the discussion of pre-twentieth-century contributions relies on secondary sources. We aim to provide a chronological review of the concept as a prelude to understanding the contemporary interpretation of the concept and the emphasis placed upon it by the contemporary theoretical and empirical literature. This chapter is divided into two main sections corresponding roughly to the treatment of the subject prior to and following World War II. In early discussions of the concept of human capital, the emphasis was almost entirely in relation to a person's standard of living (as measured by income per person) or human capital's contribution to aggregate income or wealth. Only in the post-World War II period, and more precisely the last two decades, has the role of human capital as a contributor to economic growth come to the fore.

2.2 Human Capital: Early Historical Interpretations

The treatment of human beings as a form of capital goes back at least to Adam Smith.[1] Spengler (1977) discusses the nature of human capital in Smith's *Wealth of Nations*. Smith considered that in addition to buildings, machines, and land improvements the concept of "fixed capital" should also include "the acquired and useful abilities of all the inhabitants or members of the society. The acquisition of such talents, by the maintenance of the acquirer during his education, study, or apprenticeship, always costs a real expense, which is a capital fixed and realized, as it were, in his person" (p. 32). The reward to this "real expense" is in terms of a higher return, much like that on any other form of capital: "the work which he learns to perform, it must be expected, over and above the usual wages of common labour, will replace to him the whole expence of education, with at least the ordinary profits of an equally valuable capital" (p. 33).

According to Smith, one source of human capital was experience gained as labor became more specialized according to the principle of the division of labor. In advanced societies (England), employment opportunities, especially for young children, increased the opportunity cost of education thereby leading to widespread ignorance: "the torpor of his mind renders him, not only incapable of relishing or bearing a part in any rational conversation, but of conceiving any generous, noble, or tender sentiment, and consequently of forming any just judgement concerning many even of the ordinary duties of private life" (p. 34). On the other hand, in underdeveloped societies (Scotland) the lack of employment opportunities allowed for education in basic literacy skills. A second source of human capital was education, either formal in schools and universities or through apprenticeships. The main question, according to Smith, was who should bear the cost of education (the state or the individual), even if education provides benefits to society beyond the individual acquiring the education. He concluded that for some education (e.g., basic literacy to prevent the adverse effects of division of labor or to prevent "cowardice, gross ignorance, and stupidity"), it was necessary for provision by society at large, if the contributions of the immediate beneficiary of this education were inadequate to cover the expense. Smith argued that the cost of human capital was 'excessive' because (1) apprenticeships were too long and could be completed in a much shorter period; (2) were a disincentive to work because apprentices had to wait for a long time to benefit from it; and (3) "robbed a man of the property he had in his own labor and bodily skills" (p. 35). Various market distortions resulted in the suboptimal use of the services of human capital. These included corporation privileges, poor and settlement laws, wage regulations, and subsidization of professional education (e.g., clergy, teachers, lawyers, physicians, and "that unprosperous race of men called letters;" Spengler, p. 36). The removal of these distortions would imply disappearance of differences in income that do not reflect differences in human capital investment.

According to Kiker (1966), in addition to Smith, other writers, including Friedrich List and Johann von Thünen, acknowledged the importance of incorporating human beings in the concept of capital. The reason for its inclusion was that raising and educating human beings entails a real cost, which raises productivity and thus adds to national wealth. Two main methods were used to estimate the value of human capital: capitalizing the value of net (i.e., excluding personal living expenses) future earnings into perpetuity at the market interest rate and the total cost of rearing a human being to a specific age.[2] Various writers carried out estimates of the total value of a nation's human capital as a means to gauging the economic power of a nation and also to exhort improvements in health (through higher expenditures) as ways of increasing human capital and national wealth. For example, Nicholson provided an estimate for the United Kingdom in 1891 and found that the value of the stock of "living" capital was five times the value of the stock of physical capital; Barriol, for France in 1908 and countries at different levels of economic development; Huebner, for the United States in 1914 (the human capital stock was between six to eight times the value of conventional capital) and Woods and Metzger for the United States in 1920 (Kiker 1966). Measurements of human capital have also been undertaken in order to estimate the cost of World War I, the value of immigration into the United States, the loss from preventable illness and death, and the return to education (especially tertiary education).[3]

The inclusion of human beings in the concept of capital was not universally accepted. Alfred Marshall in his *Principles of Economics* considered the notion that human beings are part of capital as "unrealistic" because human beings are not marketable. On the other hand, in the *Nature of Capital and Income*, Irving Fisher includes human beings as capital because they satisfy the definition of capital, that is, "useful appropriated material object" (Kiker 1966, p. 487). Whether Marshall considered the inclusion of human beings in the concept of capital and the importance attached to it appears to have been a subject for debate.[4] On the whole, though, there is general acknowledgment that the lack of emphasis on human capital in the pre-World War II period can be traced back to the acceptance, by most economists, of Marshall's notion of capital. Thus, Schultz (1960): "A serious fault in the way capital is treated in economic analysis has been the omission of human capital; had economists followed the conception of capital laid down by Fisher, instead of that by Marshall, this omission, so it seems to me, would not have occurred" (p. 572).

The most comprehensive application of the human capital concept during the pre-World War II period was Walsh (1935). His focus was on one aspect of human behavior as capital formation: expenditures to acquire education, where such expenditures are made for purposes of profit maximization and these expenditures respond to much the same economic motives that lead to investment in physical capital. Therefore, he considers only post-secondary education because the purpose of education at the primary and secondary level is to "provide political and cultural education in the widest sense" (p. 256), while expenditures by an individual and his or her parents for post-secondary education are based on economic criteria. Moreover, by the time a person engages in post-secondary education there is an opportunity cost to the additional years of education in terms of foregone earnings, costs that are unimportant in the earlier stages of education.

Walsh attempted to determine the profit-seeking nature of these expenditures by calculating the discounted value of average earnings of men in various educational groups and comparing it to the cost of various levels of training to determine whether the two are equal. He used five different sources of data and provided extensive data on median earnings by age and education; all but one referred to the earnings of men. His calculations showed that, for education beyond the secondary level, the return to education exceeded the cost of education (for men) in every case. He interpreted this as a condition of market disequilibrium: whereas in an "ordinary" competitive market the supply of this form of capital would increase, and the return would fall to meet its cost, this market was imperfect because parents with excess savings were unwilling to finance the education of other children. College-trained men constituted a "non-competing group" (p. 27). He reached the same conclusion for women, but the discrepancy between return and cost was smaller; this he ascribed to the lower opportunities for women for employment. He concluded that the supply of women graduates was about what it should have been on economic criteria.

For professional training, Walsh found that for three degrees the cost exceeded the return (MA, PhD, and MD) and for three the cost was less than the return (BBA—Bachelor of Business Administration, a professional degree taken in business school beyond the BS or BA degree, LL.B, and engineers). For all six professional degrees, however, there was a positive relationship between cost and return, a finding he interpreted as an indication of a "profit-seeking, equalizing market" (p. 279). He conjectured that for the MA and PhD degrees, the cost exceeded the return because these degrees mainly lead to teaching jobs and other benefits: "the contacts in college teaching are pleasant and stimulating. There is opportunity to do work that is looked upon as central in building the 'good life.' There is the long vacation and the opportunity to travel" (p. 279). For medicine he offered the altruistic motive as an explanation. In sum, when nonmonetary compensation was taken into account the return would approximate the cost in these three cases. For engineers the cost was roughly in line with the return. For business degrees the excess return could be rationalized because as a new discipline there is excess demand for the new profession. For lawyers the excess of return over cost, which was substantial, was presented as a puzzle. He hazarded a guess that, within professional groups, lawyers constitute a non-competing group. Walsh concluded that professional training (with the possible exception of lawyers) should be treated as similar to other capital and included, as such, in calculations of national wealth.

2.3   Human Capital: An Eclectic History of Post-World War II Contributions

The pre-World War II period can be characterized by general discussions of the concept of human capital and, on the whole, neglect of the concept in public policy discussions. The general sentiment was a reluctance to apply economic analysis to treat investment in human beings as capital formation. Where there was discussion, the purpose was not to identify and measure the contribution of human capital to the level of per capita national income or its growth. Rather, as Kiker (1966) points out, the motives behind the study of human capital were: (1) to demonstrate the power of a nation; (2) to determine the economic effects of education, health investment, and migration; (3) tax policy; (4) to determine the cost of war; (5) to promote life and health conservation and to bring out the significance of an individual's economic life to the family and nation; and (6) to arrive at fair decisions in courts about compensation for injury or death.

Interest in the economic significance of human capital was awakened in the late 1950s and early 1960s primarily through the writings of Theodore Schultz and Gary Becker. In a seminal paper (Schultz, 1960) and in his presidential address to the American Economic Association (Schultz, 1961a), Schultz set out to dispel any "moral" hesitation economists may have had in studying education as a form of investment in human beings. The role of education had been perceived as that of enabling the nurturing of "competent and responsible citizens" rather than for its investment value. He argued that the economic role of education in no way belittles its important role in the formation of citizens; rather, it is additional to its "cultural" contribution. He discussed the role of human capital in accounting for the "unexplained" portion of increases in national income, that is, after accounting for the growth of inputs. Education is the main form in which human beings invest in human capital. Schultz estimated the contribution of education in terms of the opportunity cost of attending school (foregone earnings) and the direct cost of resources used to provide for schools. The two main issues treated were the contribution of human capital accumulation to increases in national income and the "rate of return" to the decision to invest in education.

In undertaking these calculations, Schultz (1960) first estimated that, for the United States in 1949, high school students gave up about 11-weeks equivalent of the average earnings of workers in manufacturing and college students the equivalent of 25 weeks. With these estimates and estimates of the average weekly earnings in manufacturing for 1900–1956 (at 10-year intervals), he calculated the annual foregone earnings of high school and university students in current prices (after adjusting for unemployment).[5] He also calculated the value of inputs to elementary and secondary schools and universities by summing net expenditures and the implicit value of physical property. By adding the two (foregone earnings and value of resources; no foregone earnings were estimated for elementary school) Schultz arrived at the cost of education. One "surprising" result was that, for high school, foregone earnings represented more than half of the total cost for all years and this was also the case for university education for most of the years (except for 1930 and 1940). Taking all levels of education together, foregone earnings accounted for 26 percent of total costs in 1900 and 43 percent in 1956. He noted that during this period inputs into education increased much faster than for physical capital formation. If the resources into education are treated as investment in human capital, he conjectured that the rate of return on this form of investment must have been higher than that on physical investment to induce the much larger rate of resource accumulation in education.

During the first half of the twentieth century, the cost of resources going to different levels of education increased absolutely and also relative to each other. Four conclusions emerged from Schultz's calculations: (1) elementary education accounted for 5 percent of physical capital accumulation in 1900 and for 9 percent in 1956;[6] (2) the cost of secondary education rose much faster during the period, from 2 percent of physical capital formation in 1900 to 13 percent by 1956;[7] (3) for university education the trend was similar to secondary education: it accounted for 2 percent of physical capital formation in 1900 and for 12 percent by 1956 and (4) resources devoted to education increased much faster than resources devoted to physical capital formation: for all three levels they accounted for 9 percent of physical capital formation in 1900 and for 34 percent in 1956.

Schultz (1961a) took up again the reluctance of economists to tackle improvement in skills, knowledge, training, or internal migration as forms of investment in human beings in his 1960 presidential address to the American Economic Association. He argued that the concerns about "free men are first and foremost the end to be served by economic endeavor; they are not property or marketable assets" and "the mere thought of investment in human beings is offensive to some among us" (p. 2) were unwarranted. According to him, J.S. Mill was wrong to claim that "people of a country should not be looked upon as wealth because wealth existed only for the sake of people." Schultz highlighted three early historical contributions to the consideration of improvements in education, skills, and so forth, as part of capital: Smith, von Thünen, and Fisher. Yet the prevailing view among economists was that of Marshall: while from a theoretical point of view investment in human beings can be considered as capital, such consideration was not feasible from a practical viewpoint. Therefore, human labor was treated as manual work and no account for differences in ability or skills was necessary by economists.

According to Schultz, consideration of human capital can explain some puzzles in economic growth. First, the observed tendency for the capital–income ratio to fall during growth can be explained because the concept of capital included only physical and excluded human. Proper consideration would show a constant ratio and, therefore, human capital had been increasing relative to both physical capital and income. Second, the "unexplained" component of income growth (after taking account of increases in man-hours worked, physical capital, and land) had been increasing in the United States. Possible explanations were increasing returns to scale and improvements in the quality of (nonhuman) inputs. Schultz, however, argued that those were unimportant compared to human capital accumulation. Third, large increases in real earnings of workers could be explained as return to investment in human capital. In addition, the rapid post-World War II recovery that caught economists by surprise (given the destruction of physical capital) could be rationalized when account was taken of the importance of human capital to economic growth.

Schultz considered, next, the measurement of investment in human capital. Expenditures to accumulate human capital are a natural candidate, notwithstanding the problem of distinguishing between expenditures for consumption and investment purposes. The yield of investment in human capital in terms of higher earnings is another possibility. He identified five categories of activities directed at improving human capital: (1) health facilities and services; (2) on-the-job training; (3) formally organized education at the primary, secondary, and higher levels; (4) study programs for adults not organized by firms; and (5) migration of individuals and families to adjust to changing job opportunities. Schultz commented on health, on-the-job training, and formal education. He referred to estimates of investment in education from his earlier (Schultz, 1960) study and also estimated that between 1900 and 1956 the stock of human capital rose by a factor of 8.5 while reproducible nonhuman capital rose by a factor of 4.5. Finally, he estimated the "unexplained" component of the increase in U.S. national income between 1929 and 1956 to be 60 percent of the total; of that, human capital accumulation accounted for 30–50 percent.

In conclusion, Schultz raised two important policy issues: First, should the returns from public investment in human capital accrue to the individuals in whom it is made? He argued that public investments in human capital should be seen as a redistributive device and that expenditures on education promoted this goal. Second, assistance to "underdeveloped" countries should redirect attention from the formation of nonhuman to human capital.[8]

Schultz's exhortations were followed by Weisbrod (1961) who called for calculating a capital value on people as productive assets in monetary units. Weisbrod pointed to a number of important reasons: population and immigration policy, public health, highway construction and flood control policies, and educational and vocational rehabilitation policies. He measured the value of human capital as the discounted expected future stream of earnings net of consumption and discussed the conceptual difficulties in measuring both expected future earnings and consumption. Earnings were computed from median earnings by age adjusted for employment and probabilities of being alive at various ages. Consumption was measured as the marginal family consumption or the increase in family consumption as a result of increase in a family member. He used two values for the discount rate: 10 percent (return to private capital) and 4 percent (cost to the federal government of long-term borrowing). The present value calculations (human capital values) showed a unimodal distribution with respect to age with a peak at 30 years (10% interest rate) and 27 (4%). The distributions were calculated both gross and net of consumption.[9]

Weisbrod calculated the average value of a male human being as an asset over his lifetime both gross ($17,000 and $33,000 at 10% and 4% discount rates, respectively) and net ($13,000 and $26,000, respectively). He used these to obtain aggregate (male) human capital values for the United States in 1950: gross ($1,335 and $2,752 billion at 10% and 4%

discount, respectively) and net ($1,055 and $2,218 billion, respectively). He compared these estimates to the value of tangible assets and reproducible tangible assets in 1949: $881 and $729 billion, respectively. The estimates for human capital seemed impressive (especially when one considers that only male human capital was measured) and were consistent with labor income exceeding property income. Weisbrod argued that public policies to raise human capital (education, health and safety, etc.) were neglected at the expense of those aimed at raising physical capital. Moreover, public policies should have been targeted at those in the 25–40 age range with the highest human capital values.[10]

The intense interest in human capital during this period culminated in a conference on "Capital Investment in Human Beings" sponsored by the Universities-National Bureau Committee for Economic Research in December 1961. The conference brought together the major researchers in this area and the proceedings were published in a special issue of the *Journal of Political Economy*. In the introduction to the special issue, Schultz (1962) pointed out that investment in human beings is important because its large magnitude changes the usual measures of saving and capital formation. It also changes the structure of wages and salaries and the amount of earnings relative to property income. Investment in human capital offers some answers to questions and hypotheses in three areas:

1. *Economic growth*: When account is taken of human capital investment, the ratio of all capital to income has not declined but has remained roughly constant over time. The ratio of physical capital to income has been declining but the ratio of human capital to income has been rising. This consideration offers a clue to the puzzle about the increase in the unexplained part of national income: it comes out of the increase in the stock of human capital.

2. *The structure of earnings*: The economic capabilities of man are predominantly a *produced means of production* (italics in the original). Therefore, except for some inherited abilities (which are pure rent) differences in earnings can be explained by differences in investment in human capital. The structure of wages is fundamentally a function of investment in schooling, health, on-the-job training, searching for information about job opportunities, and migration, and

3. *The personal distribution of income*: Assuming that an increase in human capital relative to physical increases earnings relative to property income and that more equitable investment in human capital results in more equitable distribution of earnings, then investment in human capital was the factor principally responsible for the reduction in inequality of personal income in the United States.

The implication of this hypothesis is that income transfers, progressive taxation, and the distribution of private wealth were relatively weak instruments in bringing about changes in the distribution of income (compared to human capital investment).

Schultz was mainly concerned with the first issue: investment in human capital as a source of economic growth. In general, the labor input had been mismeasured because increases in its quality had not been accounted for in its various forms: schooling, learning on the job, advances in health, information about the economy, and migration (the last one on the presumption that a human resource in an inappropriate geographic location is less productive than one in the appropriate location). He referred to his earlier (1961a) paper to point out that those estimates that ignored the quality issue arrived at an observed growth of output much higher than the growth of inputs. Considerations of quality could explain, in large measure, the growth of the United States during the previous three decades.[11]

Schultz argued that capital formation as a percent of net national product was about the same in 1929 as in 1957 at 26 percent, but the share of human capital in the latter period was greater. In 1957 investment in "reproducible tangible wealth" was $25.5 billion and investment in human capital was $40.5 billion ($21.9 billion educational capital of the labor force and $18.6 billion on-the-job training of the males in the labor force). The reasons for the increase in the educational quality of the labor force were not clear and despite the increase in quality the rate of return to schooling had not decreased. Finally, some forms of investment in human capital (e.g., some benefits from health and education) could not be captured in terms of higher earnings and were difficult to measure.

Weisbrod (1962) argued that one of the benefits from education that does not show up in terms of productivity (and measured earnings) but is captured by the student is a "financial option return" or "the value of the opportunity to obtain still further education" (p. 108). For example, high school students discover a talent that they pursue via college education or college students pursue further college education. Moreover, some of the benefits of investment in education are not captured by the individual or his or her immediate family; that is, they are external to the student undertaking the investment. These are in terms of benefits to neighbors and taxpayers, both of them in relation to the place of the residence of the person making the investment. In addition, there are employment-related benefits that go to co-workers and employers of the person making the investment.

In his contribution to the special *Journal of Political Economy* issue, Becker (1962) sets forth a theory of investment in human beings and the relation between earnings, the rate of return, and the amount invested; a theme he followed up in a major work (Becker, 1964). Becker and Chiswick (1966) touched on the neglect by economists of discussion of the issue of the distribution of income because of a lack of economic theory able to explain differences in income distribution across regions, countries, or time. They stressed the importance of investment in human capital as a determinant of the distribution of income. After individual i has made investments in human capital of various forms $(j = 1, \ldots, m)$, his or her earnings (E_i) are given by

$$E_i = X_i + \sum_{j=1}^{m} r_{ij} C_{ij} \qquad \text{EQUATION } \mathbf{2.1}$$

where C_{ij} is the cost of the jth investment, r_{ij} is the return to the investment, and X_i is the "effect" of the original human capital on earnings.

The novelty of their approach was that the amount invested by individuals is determined by optimization behavior so that the individual maximizes economic welfare: a demand curve for investment is determined by the marginal return on additional funds invested and a supply curve by the marginal "interest" cost of the investment. The equilibrium point determines the total return from the investment; that is, the $r_{ij}C_{ij}$ term in 2.1. The supply curve is upward sloping because the cost of financing education (through gifts, parental contributions, reduced consumption, loans, etc.) increases with additional investing. The demand is downward sloping because of diminishing marginal product of additional investment. The intersection of these curves for each individual would determine the interpersonal distribution of earnings. The correlation between supply and demand conditions also determines the interpersonal distribution of income.

Becker and Chiswick provided the first regression estimates of earnings on years of schooling for white males aged 25–84 in the South and non-South United States, separately. They estimated the return to schooling for low (<8 years of schooling), medium (8–12), and high (>12) levels of education. The return to schooling was higher for males in the South at all levels of education as was the variance of the logarithm of earnings and the variance in years of schooling. They speculated that the higher inequality in schooling in the South was due to the lower opportunities for schooling even for whites (the supply curve), and the higher returns to schooling were due to the lower level of schooling in the South. They also estimated returns across the 50 U.S. states and found that schooling explained 12 percent of the distribution of earnings within each state and about a third of the differences in earnings across states.[12]

The writings discussed in this section serve to give a flavor for the historical treatment of the concept of human capital and the concerns associated with the definition of the concept. They form the basis of a number of themes taken up in subsequent chapters. For example, Mincerian wage regressions that estimate the return to an additional year of education (discussed in Chapter 6) take up the theme of the return to education discussed here. Along with developments in the theory of economic growth during the same time period, the issues discussed in this chapter formed the basic conceptual framework on which various theoretical models of the contribution of human capital to economic growth have been built. The following chapter offers an overview of the main recent theoretical contributions to the human capital–economic growth literature.

Notes

1. Walsh (1935) and Kiker (1966) mention that, perhaps, the earliest attempt to measure the economic value of human beings was in the late seventeenth century by Sir William Petty. He attempted to calculate the aggregate value of human labor in order to be included in an estimate of aggregate wealth. He accomplished this by capitalizing the total wage bill (national income minus property income) at the market interest rate.

2. Kiker (1966) presents details on the method used by Louis Dublin, Ernst Engel, William Farr, Alfred Lotka, Sir William Petty, and Theodor Wittstein.

3. A more extensive treatment of the return to education, in a historical perspective, will be provided in the following section.

4. See the exchange between Blandy (1967) and Kiker (1968).

5. Schultz acknowledged the problems associated with using figures for 1949 to apply to the first half of the twentieth century.

6. As mentioned earlier, the estimate ignored foregone earnings by elementary students that, most likely, were very important during the early part of the period and would also be important for a low-income economy.

7. He emphasized that more than half of the value of resources was due to foregone earnings; he argued that in low-income economies that had begun to experience increases in secondary enrollment by mid-century, most of the costs of education were in the form of foregone earnings.

8. Shaffer (1961) raised three objections to the treatment of education as investment in human capital: (1) it is impossible to separate education expenditures for consumption and investment purposes; (2) determination of a specific return to a specific investment in human capital is not possible; and (3) the concept cannot be used as the basis for formulating policy, private or public, and added that it is "gaining in favor among 'liberals' who apparently intend to utilize it as a rationalization of federal aid to education" (p. 1031). In his response, Schultz (1961b) acknowledged the concerns but argued that in no way do these diminish the importance of the concept.

9. The calculations showed positive and small values for a newborn male child and negative values for elderly (> 65 years at the 4% rate). Given that the net discounted value of males at birth is positive (under either interest rate), Weisbrod concluded that population growth in the United States would lead to economic growth (increased value of output minus consumption). On the other hand, Enke (1960) argued that, for India, the present value of future net earnings of a newborn was negative and therefore population control would lead to increased growth.

Weisbrod made the point that, if this were the result of consumption exceeding marginal productivity at all ages, then public policy measures to improve health and reduce death rates may be counterproductive with regard to economic growth. On the other hand, where marginal productivity exceeds consumption, as was the case in the United States, health programs would have a beneficial effect on growth.

10. As an example, Weisbrod considered the detection and treatment of tuberculosis where the cost was lower than human capital values except for the very young and very old. Therefore, such investment in health would be highly profitable: for instance the rate of return to the detection and treatment of tuberculosis in a male age 50 with average earnings profile is 700% over cost ($16,000 net future earnings at 10% interest rate relative to a cost of $2,000).

11. According to Schultz, several economists had argued that improvements in human capital are a main source of economic growth. Kuznets argued that four-tenths of the increase in income per worker was due to interindustry shifts in labor (migration). Schultz estimated that human capital investment accounted for one-fifth of economic growth between 1930 and 1957.

12. Estimates for other countries (Canada, Israel, Mexico, and Puerto Rico) also showed that higher income inequality was associated with higher returns to education and higher schooling inequality.

II   *Theoretical Research on Human Capital*
        and Economic Growth

3 Theoretical Models of Human Capital and Economic Growth

3.1 Introduction

Modeling the role of human capital in the economic growth process has presented several challenges. The Solow–Swan model of neoclassical growth has afforded a convenient point of departure from which to analyze the contribution of human capital. The reemergence of interest in long-run growth, as manifested in models of endogenous growth, has provided an alternative departure point. Following on these two general approaches, a substantial theoretical literature has developed during the last two decades that is the subject of this and the following chapter. The objective of these chapters is to provide a rather eclectic and concise treatment of the theoretical literature on the human capital–growth link with the emphasis on the empirical implications of the various theoretical contributions. Thus, by deliberate omission, this book will not review models that have provided many useful theoretical insights that, nonetheless, are difficult to subject to empirical testing given the available (at present) data.

In this chapter we begin with a brief overview of the main characteristics of the basic growth model, the Solow–Swan model with exogenous technical change. Later sections offer a more detailed picture of its mechanics, as well as its extension that allows for human capital to enter explicitly as an input in the production function; this has become known as the *human capital-extended Solow model* as developed by Mankiw, Romer, and Weil (1992). The Solow–Swan model is considered to be the workhorse model of growth theory and is the main benchmark against which alternative and more refined models are gauged. In its basic form the model describes a situation where there is zero growth (of per capita income) in equilibrium (steady state) and offers insights into why this is the case and how an economy can achieve alternative steady states characterized by positive growth rates. The main assumptions that underlie the model are: (1) a production function that displays diminishing returns in the factors of production (capital and labor) and admits constant returns to scale, that is, the case where doubling all inputs will double output (or the production function is homogeneous of degree one); and (2) saving by households is a constant proportion of their income. Hence, output is determined from the production side when firms maximize their profits taking as given the constant portion of output that is saved by households and used for capital accumulation. The model predicts that with diminishing returns there can be no long-run economic growth and the economy will stagnate at its zero growth dynamic equilibrium.

Even though the assumptions of the model are quite restrictive, the model itself is very useful in demonstrating the mechanics that allow economies to grow (or stagnate) in the long run. In the framework of the Solow–Swan model, countries with higher savings rates will have a higher per capita income in equilibrium than poorer countries, but will have zero economic growth. The model concludes that there can be no long-run economic growth, even though different economies may differ in terms of their equilibrium per capita income. The reason it fails to produce long-term growth lies in the nature of the neoclassical production function characterized by diminishing returns to its inputs. Let us, for the moment, assume that physical capital accumulates at a rate faster than the rate at which labor grows. In that case the marginal product of capital will fall as the newest capital increment will produce less output than the one before. In other words, as capital accumulates faster than the growth of the labor force its return will fall and beyond a certain point additional capital accumulation will not be profitable. Capital accumulation will then slow to the point where capital and labor grow at the same rate. In that case, due to constant returns to scale, output will also grow at the same rate and as a result per capita income stops growing and becomes stagnant.

It becomes apparent that the impediment to economic growth in the Solow–Swan model is diminishing returns. Hence, for growth to take place there has to be a way to overcome diminishing returns so that the productive inputs accumulate over time. In the benchmark Solow–Swan model this is accomplished through the introduction of exogenous technical progress. The main message from the simple model is that accumulation of capital alone, without technological progress, cannot act as a source of economic growth because at some point diminishing returns will set in and the economy will stop growing.

Within the context of the Solow–Swan, or neoclassical, model to overcome diminishing returns that act as a break on growth, technological change (technical progress) is introduced and is assumed to be exogenous. Technological improvements over time lead to overcoming diminishing returns as inputs (labor) become more and more productive. An alternative extension of the Solow–Swan model is to introduce additional inputs. In this case it is an additional form of capital, human capital, or the stock of knowledge that is used in production. The introduction of this form of capital does not change the main findings of the model. However, human capital can be turned into an important tool for the generation of sustained (endogenous) economic growth, as we will explain in the following chapter.

In an exogenous technological progress framework, technology is assumed to grow at an exogenously given constant rate. This is quite restrictive as an assumption, yet it illustrates the mechanism that produces sustained growth and can be relaxed in more sophisticated and complex models of endogenous growth. The main difference is that the labor input that in the simpler version corresponds to the physical capabilities of human beings for production is now measured in terms of effective labor units, a concept that incorporates the effectiveness of labor in production. Technical progress produces labor savings as labor units (effective labor) become more productive, a process known as *labor-augmenting technical progress*. In contrast to the benchmark version of the Solow–Swan model where all variables were expressed in "simple" labor units (per worker), all variables in this version are expressed in terms of effective labor units. In equilibrium, capital per effective labor unit is constant but not capital per unit of labor (the capital–labor ratio). In this case, the capital–labor ratio will grow at the same rate as technological progress because of the labor savings that arise from the implementation of new technologies at a constant exogenous rate. In other words, the original diminishing returns in the Solow–Swan model that resulted in zero growth are now offset by the constant rate of technical progress. In equilibrium, income per effective labor unit is constant and, for this to happen, income per capita has to grow at the same rate as the exogenous rate of technical progress. In this chapter we will discuss in greater detail the mechanics of the model with exogenous technological progress while the benchmark basic Solow–Swan model is treated quite extensively elsewhere.[1]

An alternative, and one might say, unsophisticated way to get around the issue of diminishing returns is to assume a production function that is not subject to diminishing returns. This is what the so-called *AK* model does by assuming that output is a linear function of physical capital. This constant proportions production function is an observation borne by evidence for developed countries where the ratio of capital to output is constant and approximately equal to three in the long run. An economy that is characterized by such a production function will accumulate physical capital continuously without experiencing diminishing returns. An implication of this model, however, is that economies that differ in their initial conditions (different initial capital–labor ratio) will grow at different rates indefinitely and will never converge. In this chapter we will discuss the mechanics of this model as well.

In our general overview so far, the only form of capital considered is physical capital that is accumulated through investment in machinery and equipment. In the human capital-extended Solow–Swan model of Mankiw, Romer, and Weil (1992), in addition to physical capital, human capital also enters the production function. This form of capital is also accumulated through knowledge acquisition and new technical skills and ideas that are used in production. The return to physical capital is given by its marginal product, which in a competitive economy equals the interest rate. However, the return to human capital is more difficult to measure and it is connected with the anticipated reward that people who engage in human capital accumulation (education) expect in the future. If human capital is added as another input in the neoclassical production function subject to diminishing returns and constant returns to scale, the results are qualitatively similar to the model without human capital. Here, the source of growth is again exogenous technological progress. The only way that human capital can act directly as a source of sustained economic growth is to help counter the diminishing returns that plague the neoclassical production function. This is achieved, though, in the context of endogenous growth models that we will examine in the following chapter.

Finally, in this chapter we discuss briefly a concept that is of great importance in theories of long-run economics, that of convergence. In general, convergence measures the path that some variable takes toward a particular value of interest. If it approaches this particular value then the variable converges, whereas if it tends to go further away it diverges. In the context of growing economies, convergence measures the degree to which the income per capita of poorer countries approaches that of the richer countries (or an average of that). In other words, convergence tries to measure the "catching up" that poorer countries have to do in order to reach the level of development of the richer countries, or the degree to which the distance between the two sets of economies, as far as per capita income is concerned, increases or decreases over time. Reducing this distance does not necessarily mean that poorer countries have become richer in absolute terms because it may simply result from a fall in per capita income of both rich and poor, with the richer countries experiencing a more severe reduction in their living standards. The same idea can be applied to regions within a country or different states within a union of countries, such as the European Union.

We can distinguish between two types of convergence: absolute and conditional convergence. Absolute convergence deals with transition dynamics to the steady state, and more particularly with initial conditions. A country with a low initial capital–labor ratio will converge faster to its equilibrium, compared to a country with a higher initial capital–labor ratio. As long as capital displays diminishing returns, an economy that starts off with lower capital–labor levels will accrue higher returns and grow faster compared to an economy starting with higher capital–labor levels, because in that case it will suffer more immediately from diminishing returns. Hence, the process by which a poor economy grows faster than a rich one, without conditioning on any of their respective characteristics, is known as *absolute convergence*. Empirically, there is very little evidence in support of such a convergence process.

In the context of the neoclassical model with exogenous technological progress, the implication is that not all economies, but economies with similar characteristics (savings rates, population growth, and depreciation rates), end up at the same equilibrium with identical per capita income. In this case they differ only in their transition to the common equilibrium. This transition will be characterized by differences in their capital–labor ratio: countries that start off with a higher capital–labor ratio will tend to grow less than countries that start from a lower ratio as diminishing returns set in. Convergence, in this context, measures a process that applies to countries with similar characteristics that differ only in their initial conditions that take them to their steady state (dynamic equilibrium), or a single country at different positions away from its steady state. Convergence deals with transition dynamics only and concerns the convergence speed to the steady state of a single economy, or the common steady state of a homogeneous group of countries with exactly the same characteristics. That speed will be higher the further away an economy finds itself from its long-run equilibrium. This process of convergence is known as *conditional convergence* because it considers the transition to equilibrium after taking into account the characteristics of different economies.

Conditional convergence implies that, conditional on their characteristics, economies will converge faster to their steady state the further away they are from it. Conditional convergence is a weaker form (compared to absolute) of convergence in that only economies with similar characteristics under certain conditions (diminishing returns) converge to the same equilibrium. However, the presence of conditional convergence does not imply absolute convergence, as it may well be the case that richer countries grow faster than poorer.[2]

By its very nature, the theoretical treatment of human capital is rather complex. The concept includes, not only the role of education and on-the-job training, but also the importance of differences in ability, attitudes, and outlook that individual human beings bring to the production process as they attempt to improve their economic lot and, by extension, that of society at large. The various theoretical models in this and the following chapter aim to capture these characteristics. The remainder of this chapter provides a (non-exhaustive) taxonomy of main models of human capital that are built around the assumption of exogenous technical change. In Section 3.2 we discuss the workhorse model of growth theory, the neoclassical Solow–Swan model, and the incorporation of human capital in that model. Section 3.3 reviews the extension of the neoclassical model that allows the saving rate to vary over time, the Cass–Koopmans–Ramsey model. Finally, Section 3.4 offers an initial evaluation of the endogenous treatment of human capital, beginning with the AK model, and is a precursor to the endogenous growth models of Chapter 4.

3.2   The Neoclassical Model with Human Capital

3.2.1   The Basic Solow–Swan Model

The workhorse model of growth theory is the Solow–Swan model according to which output is determined by a neoclassical aggregate production function and technological progress is labor augmenting. Output at time period t, or $Y(t)$, can be written as

$$Y(t) = F\{K(t), A(t) \cdot L(t)\}$$

EQUATION 3.1

where $K(t)$ is the aggregate stock of physical capital stock, $A(t)$ is a technology index, and $L(t)$ is the labor force input. In the neoclassical framework, labor, $L(t)$, captures the physical (physiological) attributes of human work whereas technology, $A(t)$, incorporates skills, abilities, knowledge, and so forth that enhance the ability of labor to produce.[3] The production function exhibits constant returns to scale so that in intensive form it is

$$\tilde{y}(t) = f(\tilde{k}(t))$$

EQUATION 3.2

where $\tilde{y}(t) = Y(t)/[A(t) \cdot L(t)]$ is output per effective unit of labor and similarly the effective capital–labor ratio is $\tilde{k}(t) = K(t)/[A(t) \cdot L(t)]$. The Solow–Swan model assumes that saving is a constant function of income and that the capital stock depreciates by a constant rate. Invoking the equality of saving and investment in physical capital, in equilibrium we have[4]

$$\dot{K} = s_K Y - \delta_K K$$

EQUATION 3.3

where $\dot{K} = dK/dt$,[5] $s_K = S_K/Y$ is the constant saving ratio, S_K is aggregate saving used for physical capital formation purposes, and δ_K is the constant depreciation rate of physical capital. The labor force is exogenous and grows at a constant rate that is given by $g_L = \dot{L}/L$. In the basic Solow–Swan model, technological progress is exogenous so that the technology index grows at a constant rate given by $g_A = \dot{A}/A$. Exogenous technological progress is perhaps the single most scrutinized aspect of the Solow–Swan model and one that has been the launching pad of a whole research line. The ultimate objective of this research is to look into the forces that determine long-run technological progress; a line of investigation that has led to the development of a whole genre of modeling that can be conveniently referred to as endogenous growth models. This is a subject that we return to in Chapter 4.

The definition of the effective capital–labor ratio, $\tilde{k}(t) = K(t)/[A(t) \cdot L(t)]$, serves as the basis for the fundamental equation of the Solow–Swan model, an equation that, in conjunction with 3.3, introduces a time element into the model. Differentiating $\tilde{k}(t)$ with respect to time and using 3.3, and the definitions of labor growth and technological progress, it follows that:

$$\dot{\tilde{k}} = s_K \tilde{y} - (g_A + g_L + \delta_K)\tilde{k}$$

EQUATION 3.4

The economy converges to a steady-state level of effective capital–labor ratio that, from 3.4, is equal to:

$$\tilde{k}^* = s_K \tilde{y}/(g_A + g_L + \delta_K)$$

EQUATION 3.5

In order to investigate the properties of the steady state, we assume that the aggregate production function is Cobb–Douglas and exhibits constant returns to capital and efficiency labor. Therefore, 3.1 and 3.2 can be written as

$$Y(t) = K(t)^\alpha [A(t) \cdot L(t)]^{1-\alpha}$$

EQUATION 3.6

and

$$\tilde{y} = \tilde{k}^{\alpha}$$

EQUATION **3.7**

where α is the output share of physical capital. From 3.5 and 3.7, the steady-state level of the (efficiency) capital–labor ratio and (efficiency) income per worker are equal to:

$$\tilde{k}^* = \left(\frac{s_K}{g_A + g_L + \delta_K}\right)^{1/(1-\alpha)} \quad \text{and} \quad \tilde{y}^* = \left(\frac{s_K}{g_A + g_L + \delta_K}\right)^{\alpha/(1-\alpha)}.$$

EQUATION **3.8**

The discussion above has been framed in terms of efficiency units. Income per worker, the variable measurable by national income accounts, or $y(t) = Y(t)/L(t)$, can also be found by noting that $y(t) = A(t) \cdot \tilde{k}(t)^{\alpha}$. From 3.7 and 3.8, the steady-state income per worker (in logarithm) is:

$$\ln y^* = \ln A^* + \left(\frac{\alpha}{1-\alpha}\right)\ln s_K - \left(\frac{\alpha}{1-\alpha}\right)\ln(g_A + g_L + \delta_K)$$

EQUATION **3.9**

As will be discussed in subsequent chapters, estimation of this specification has yielded an estimate of the numerical value of the output elasticity of physical capital, (α).

3.2.2   Transition Dynamics in the Basic Solow–Swan Model

In the steady state, output and capital per worker ($y = Y/L$ and $k = K/L$) grow at the same exogenous rate, g_A, and therefore the steady-state level of capital and output per *effective* worker in 3.8 is constant. In the Solow–Swan model the growth of output per worker is exogenous and, in the absence of technological progress ($g_A = 0$), is equal to zero.

The transition dynamics of the Solow–Swan model can be found by linearization of the transition path around the steady state. First, we note from 3.4 and 3.7:

$$\frac{d\ln\tilde{y}}{dt} = \frac{\dot{\tilde{y}}}{\tilde{y}} = \alpha\frac{\dot{\tilde{k}}}{\tilde{k}} = \alpha\left[\frac{s_K\tilde{y}}{\tilde{k}} - (g_A + g_L + \delta_K)\right]$$

EQUATION **3.10**

The first-order Taylor approximation of $d \ln y(t)/dt$ around the steady-state value of (efficiency) output is:

$$\frac{d \ln \tilde{y}}{dt} \simeq \frac{d \ln \tilde{y}}{dt}\bigg|_{\tilde{y}^*} + (\ln \tilde{y} - \ln \tilde{y}^*)\left(\frac{d\left(\frac{d \ln \tilde{y}}{dt}\right)}{d \ln \tilde{y}}\bigg|_{\tilde{y}^*}\right) \qquad \text{EQUATION } \mathbf{3.11}$$

Because in the steady state the growth of efficiency output is zero, the first term in 3.11 is zero. The derivative in the second term is:[6]

$$\frac{d\left(\frac{d \ln \tilde{y}}{dt}\right)}{d \ln \tilde{y}} = (\alpha - 1)s_K \frac{\tilde{y}}{\tilde{k}} \qquad \text{EQUATION } \mathbf{3.12}$$

Before evaluating 3.11 at the steady state, we note that 3.7 and 3.8 imply that $\tilde{y}^*/\tilde{k}^* = (g_A + g_L + \delta_K)/s_K$. Therefore, substituting 3.12 into 3.11 and evaluating at the steady-state value $(\tilde{y}^*)$ yields:

$$\frac{d \ln \tilde{y}}{dt} = (1 - \alpha)(g_A + g_L + \delta_K)(\ln \tilde{y}^* - \ln \tilde{y}) \qquad \text{EQUATION } \mathbf{3.13}$$

Around the steady state, the growth rate is given by 3.13 and the speed of convergence to the steady state is $\lambda = (1 - \alpha)(g_A + g_L + \delta_K)$.

The solution to the differential equation in 3.13 is:[7]

$$\ln \tilde{y}(t) = (1 - e^{-\lambda t}) \ln \tilde{y}^* + e^{-\lambda t} \ln \tilde{y}(0) \qquad \text{EQUATION } \mathbf{3.14}$$

Therefore, the average growth rate of income per worker between period τ and $\tau + \upsilon$ can be written in discrete form as:[8]

$$\frac{1}{\upsilon}\left[\ln\left(\frac{Y}{L}\right)_{\tau+\upsilon} - \ln\left(\frac{Y}{L}\right)_\tau\right] = \frac{1}{\upsilon}[g_A \upsilon + (1 - e^{-\lambda \upsilon}) \ln A_\tau + (1 - e^{-\lambda \upsilon}) \ln \tilde{y}^*$$
$$- (1 - e^{-\lambda \upsilon})(Y/L)_\tau] \qquad \text{EQUATION } \mathbf{3.15}$$

The average growth rate between period τ and $\tau + \upsilon$ can be found by substituting the steady-state income level (from 3.8) into 3.15 to yield:

$$\frac{1}{\upsilon}\left[\ln\left(\frac{Y}{L}\right)_{\tau+\upsilon} - \ln\left(\frac{Y}{L}\right)_\tau\right] = \frac{1}{\upsilon}\left[g_A \upsilon + (1 - e^{-\lambda \upsilon}) \ln A_\tau\right]$$
$$- \frac{1}{\upsilon}(1 - e^{-\lambda \upsilon})\left(\frac{Y}{L}\right)_\tau + \frac{1}{\upsilon}(1 - e^{-\lambda \upsilon})\frac{\alpha}{(1 - \alpha)} \ln s_K$$
$$- \frac{1}{\upsilon}(1 - e^{-\lambda \upsilon})\frac{\alpha}{(1 - \alpha)} \ln(g_A + g_L + \delta_K) \qquad \text{EQUATION } \mathbf{3.16}$$

According to this formulation, the average rate of growth of income per worker depends on the initial technology level, the initial level of per capita income, the share of income devoted to physical capital accumulation and exogenous model parameters: the average growth rate of technology and labor force, and the rate of depreciation. In empirical implementations of 3.16, the initial technology level has been modeled by country- and time-specific effects and special attention has been devoted to the inclusion of the initial level of income per worker to obtain estimates of the speed of convergence to the steady state. These issues will be addressed in greater detail in subsequent chapters.

3.2.3   The Solow–Swan Model with Human Capital: Mankiw, Romer, and Weil (1992)

In an influential paper, Mankiw, Romer, and Weil (1992) extended the Solow–Swan model to consider the role of human capital. The extended model assumes that the aggregate output function includes three inputs: physical capital, human capital, and labor measured in efficiency units. In the Mankiw, Romer, and Weil framework, human capital contributes directly to production. The production function exhibits constant returns to scale in the three inputs but diminishing returns in the reproducible inputs (physical and human capital). Therefore, 3.1 and 3.6 are replaced by

$$Y(t) = F\{K(t), H(t), A(t) \cdot L(t)\}$$
$$= K(t)^{\alpha} H(t)^{\beta} [A(t) \cdot L(t)]^{1-\alpha-\beta} \qquad \text{EQUATION } \mathbf{3.17}$$

where $H(t)$ represents the stock of human capital in period t and β is the output share of human capital. As before, we define variables in efficiency terms so that the equivalent of 3.7 is

$$\tilde{y}(t) = \tilde{k}(t)^{\alpha} \tilde{h}(t)^{\beta} \qquad \text{EQUATION } \mathbf{3.18}$$

where $\tilde{h}(t) = H(t)/[A(t) \cdot L(t)]$. Once more the (constant) share of output devoted to physical capital formation is s_K. Moreover, a constant portion, s_H, of output is devoted to human capital accumulation. In addition to the equation for physical capital accumulation in 3.4, human capital accumulates according to:

$$\dot{\tilde{h}} = s_H \tilde{y} - (g_A + g_L + \delta_K)\tilde{h}$$

EQUATION **3.19**

By assumption, the rate of depreciation for the two reproducible inputs is the same. The steady-state level of efficiency physical capital is given by 3.5 and the steady-state level of efficiency human capital is:

$$\tilde{h}^* = s_H \tilde{y} / (g_A + g_L + \delta_K)$$

EQUATION **3.20**

Using 3.5, 3.18, and 3.20, we arrive at the steady-state levels of human and physical capital

$$\tilde{k}^* = \left[\frac{s_K^{1-\beta} s_H^{\beta}}{(g_A + g_L + \delta_K)} \right]^{\frac{1}{1-\alpha-\beta}} \quad \text{and} \quad \tilde{h}^* = \left[\frac{s_K^{\alpha} s_H^{1-\alpha}}{(g_A + g_L + \delta_K)} \right]^{\frac{1}{1-\alpha-\beta}}$$

and the steady-state level of efficiency income as:

$$\tilde{y}^* = \left[\frac{s_K^{\alpha} s_H^{\beta}}{(g_A + g_L + \delta_K)^{(\alpha+\beta)}} \right]^{\frac{1}{1-\alpha-\beta}}$$

Equivalently to 3.9, the steady-state level of income per worker can be expressed as:

$$\ln y^* = \ln A^* + \left(\frac{\alpha}{1-a-\beta} \right) \ln s_K + \left(\frac{\beta}{1-a-\beta} \right) \ln s_H$$
$$- \left(\frac{\alpha+\beta}{1-a-\beta} \right) \ln(g_A + g_L + \delta_K)$$

EQUATION **3.21**

While 3.21 expresses the level of income per worker in terms of the share of output devoted to physical and human capital formation, Mankiw, Romer, and Weil point out that it can also be expressed in terms of the (steady-state) level of human capital by substituting for s_H and rearranging to obtain:

$$\ln y^* = \ln A^* + \left(\frac{\alpha}{1-a} \right) \ln s_K + \left(\frac{\beta}{1-a} \right) \ln \tilde{h}^*$$
$$- \left(\frac{\alpha}{1-a} \right) \ln(g_A + g_L + \delta_K)$$

EQUATION **3.22**

The distinction between 3.21 and 3.22 concerns the extent to which the empirical measure of human capital approximates more closely investment in human capital, as in 3.21, or the stock of human capital, as in 3.22. As will be explained in subsequent chapters, the expression in 3.22 corresponds more closely to the measure of human capital that is frequently used in empirical work: average years of schooling of a country's population or work force.[9]

The extended Solow–Swan model exhibits the same steady-state properties as the basic model analyzed in the previous subsection. The transition dynamics of the augmented model follow those of the basic model. Equation 3.10 becomes

$$\frac{d \ln \tilde{y}}{dt} = \alpha \frac{\dot{\tilde{k}}}{\tilde{k}} + \beta \frac{\dot{\tilde{h}}}{\tilde{h}}$$

$$= \alpha \left[\frac{s_K \tilde{y}}{\tilde{k}} - (g_A + g_L + \delta_K) \right] + \beta \left[\frac{s_H \tilde{y}}{\tilde{h}} - (g_A + g_L + \delta_K) \right]$$

so that

$$\frac{d \ln \tilde{y}}{dt} = -(\alpha + \beta)(g_A + g_L + \delta_K) + \alpha s_H \left(\frac{\tilde{y}}{\tilde{k}} \right) + \beta s_H \left(\frac{\tilde{y}}{\tilde{h}} \right)$$

The first-order Taylor series approximation is as in 3.11 and the derivative in the second term is now equal to:

$$\frac{d \left(\frac{d \ln \tilde{y}}{dt} \right)}{d \ln \tilde{y}} = (\alpha - 1)s_K \frac{\tilde{y}}{\tilde{k}} + \beta s_H \frac{\tilde{y}}{\tilde{h}} + \left[s_K \frac{\tilde{y}}{\tilde{k}} - s_H \frac{\tilde{y}}{\tilde{h}} \right] \beta \frac{d \ln \tilde{h}}{d \ln \tilde{y}} \qquad \text{EQUATION \textbf{3.23}}$$

Before evaluating 3.23 at the steady state, we note that $\tilde{y}^* / \tilde{k}^* = (g_A + g_L + \delta_K)/s_K$ and $\tilde{y}^* / \tilde{h}^* = (g_A + g_L + \delta_K)/s_H$. Evaluating 3.23 at the steady state and substituting these we have (noting that the third term in 3.23 is zero at the steady state):

$$\frac{d \left(\frac{d \ln \tilde{y}}{dt} \right)}{d \ln \tilde{y}} \bigg|_{\tilde{y}^*} = -(1 - \alpha - \beta)(g_A + g_L + \delta_K) \qquad \text{EQUATION \textbf{3.24}}$$

Using 3.24 and the Taylor approximation in 3.11 we have:

$$\frac{d \ln \tilde{y}}{dt} = (1 - \alpha - \beta)(g_A + g_L + \delta_K)(\ln \tilde{y}^* - \ln \tilde{y}) \qquad \text{EQUATION \textbf{3.25}}$$

Equation 3.25 represents the convergence to the steady state where, by comparison to 3.13, the speed of convergence is now $\lambda = (1 - \alpha - \beta)(g_A + g_L + \delta_K)$.

Comparable to 3.16, the average growth rate in per capita income between period τ and $\tau + \upsilon$ is now:

$$\frac{1}{\upsilon}\left[\ln\left(\frac{Y}{L}\right)_{\tau+\upsilon} - \ln\left(\frac{Y}{L}\right)_{\tau}\right] = \frac{1}{\upsilon}[g_A\upsilon + (1 - e^{-\lambda\upsilon})\ln A_\tau]$$

$$-\frac{1}{\upsilon}(1 - e^{-\lambda\upsilon})\left(\frac{Y}{L}\right)_{\tau} + \frac{1}{\upsilon}(1 - e^{-\lambda\upsilon})\left\{\frac{\alpha}{(1-\alpha-\beta)}\ln s_K\right.$$

$$\left. +\frac{\beta}{(1-\alpha-\beta)}\ln s_H - \frac{\alpha+\beta}{(1-\alpha-\beta)}\ln(g_A + g_L + \delta_K)\right\} \qquad \overline{\text{EQUATION 3.26}}$$

The growth rate can also be expressed in terms of the (steady-state) level of human capital by substituting for s_H to arrive at:

$$\frac{1}{\upsilon}\left[\ln\left(\frac{Y}{L}\right)_{\tau+\upsilon} - \ln\left(\frac{Y}{L}\right)_{\tau}\right] = \frac{1}{\upsilon}\left[g_A\upsilon + (1 - e^{-\lambda\upsilon})\ln A_\tau \frac{1-\alpha-\beta}{1-\alpha}\right]$$

$$-(1 - e^{-\lambda\upsilon})\left(\frac{Y}{L}\right)_{\tau} + \frac{1}{\upsilon}(1 - e^{-\lambda\upsilon})\left\{\frac{\alpha}{(1-\alpha)}\ln s_K\right.$$

$$\left. +\frac{\beta}{(1-\alpha)}\ln \tilde{h}^* - \frac{\alpha}{(1-\alpha)}\ln(g_A + g_L + \delta_K)\right\} \qquad \overline{\text{EQUATION 3.27}}$$

Equation 3.27 shows that the determinants of the long-run growth of income per worker are the initial level of income, the (steady-state) level of the human capital stock, the share of income devoted to physical capital accumulation and model parameters: the growth of the labor force, the rate of technological progress, and the depreciation rate. Estimation of the specification in 3.27 has formed the basis of a number of empirical studies that will be reviewed in subsequent chapters.

3.3   The Cass–Koopmans–Ramsey Model: An Introductory Exposition

One of the main simplifying assumptions of the Solow–Swan model is a constant savings rate: s_K and s_H are constant over time. However, it is more plausible to assume that the savings rate is not constant but is determined endogenously through the optimizing behavior of households. In this context, households choose their lifetime consumption (and savings) by maximizing their utility subject to a lifetime budget constraint. Firms, on the other hand, choose the levels of capital and labor they use in producing output in order to maximize profits. This framework has become known as the *Cass–Koopmans–Ramsey (CKR) model* after the work of Ramsey (1928) that was followed by Cass (1965) and Koopmans (1965). This model arrives at a Pareto optimal decentralized equilibrium, since a social planner maximizing social welfare would arrive at the same equilibrium outcome. In this context, a social planner is a fictional character who possesses all the powers to achieve the best possible outcome for all members of society. If a decentralized economy attains the same equilibrium, then the decentralized economy achieves Pareto optimality because it is not possible to improve the welfare of a single person without reducing the welfare of someone else. If there is a divergence between the equilibrium outcomes achieved by a social planner and the decentralized economy, the latter does not attain a Pareto optimal solution and there is room for intervention by a policy-making authority to improve welfare.

One of the main findings of the CKR model vis-à-vis the Solow–Swan model with a constant savings rate is that the optimal capital–labor ratio will be higher in the latter case. This is to be expected because households in a CKR environment save less than what they would in the Solow–Swan model. This happens because future consumption does not yield the same utility as present consumption due to the presence of a discount factor. This calls for less "sacrifice" in terms of foregone consumption and consequently less savings and a lower level for the equilibrium level of per capita income and capital–labor ratio than in the Solow–Swan model with a constant savings rate.

Consumer-optimizing behavior can be also used in the context of an *AK* model, where output is a constant function of the capital–labor ratio. In that case there are no diminishing returns and the economy attains sustained positive growth (in contrast to zero growth in a model without exogenous technical change). The equilibrium outcome here is also Pareto optimal, as discussed in Section 3.4.

The overall conclusion is that relaxing the assumption of a constant savings rate and adopting consumer-maximizing behavior does not lead to qualitatively different equilibria outcomes from the Solow–Swan model.

As long as there are diminishing returns, there will be no growth in the model, unless one introduces exogenous technological change. Similarly, in the context of the AK model, whether households maximize utility or not will lead to a constant growth rate. The difference between the two setups is that in a CKR environment the optimal level of per capita output in long-run equilibrium will be lower than that in a Solow–Swan environment. This is due to the discount factor that penalizes future consumption and produces lower savings and consequently lower capital accumulation relative to the case of constant savings. However, an important characteristic of the decentralized economy described by the CKR model is that it is Pareto optimal.

According to the skeletal CKR model, consumers maximize lifetime utility from consumption taking into account preferences for consumption over time and the trade-off between present and future consumption. The representative infinitely-lived household has $L(t)$ members and family size is expected to grow at the rate g_L so that $L(t) = e^{g_L t}$ (where we have normalized initial household size to unity). As in the Solow–Swan model, labor, $L(t)$, is related to the physical attributes of work. The lifetime utility function of the representative household is

$$W = \int_0^\infty u\left(c(t)\right) L(t) e^{-\rho t} dt = \int_0^\infty u(c) e^{g_L t} e^{-\rho t} dt \qquad \text{EQUATION } \mathbf{3.28}$$

where $c(t) = C(t)/L(t)$ is consumption per household member, $u(.)$ is the instantaneous utility function with $u'(.) > 0$ and $u''(.) < 0$, and ρ is the rate of time preference. The economy is characterized by identical infinitely-lived consumer/producer households. Therefore, lifetime utility is maximized subject to the constraint that consumption plus investment equals net income or

$$\dot{k} = y - (g_L + \delta_K)k - c = f(k) - (g_L + \delta_K)k - c \qquad \text{EQUATION } \mathbf{3.29}$$

where $k = K/L$ and production is characterized by a homogenous of degree one function $y = f(k)$. The optimal level of consumption is chosen by maximizing the Hamiltonian

$$\Re = u(c)e^{-(\rho - g_L)t} + v[f(k) - (g_L + \delta_K)k - c] \qquad \text{EQUATION } \mathbf{3.30}$$

where the co-state variable v is the shadow price of investment. The first-order conditions for maximization are given by

$$\frac{d\Re}{dc} = 0 \implies v = u'(c)e^{-(\rho - g_L)t}$$

EQUATION **3.31**

$$\frac{d\Re}{dk} = -\dot{v} \implies \dot{v} = -v[f'(k) - (g_L + \delta_K)]$$

EQUATION **3.32**

where $u'(c)$ and $f'(k)$ are the first derivatives of the utility and production function, respectively. The transversality condition

$$\lim_{t \to \infty} e^{-(\rho - g_L)t} vk = 0$$

ensures that capital cannot be accumulated forever without consuming it, or consumers desire to run down their capital stock to zero at the end of their lifetime.

Differentiating 3.31 with respect to time and substituting into 3.32 we arrive at the Euler equation:

$$f'(k) - \delta_K = \rho - \left[\frac{u''(c) \cdot c}{u'(c)}\right]\frac{\dot{c}}{c}$$

EQUATION **3.33**

The Euler equation portrays the familiar equality between the (net) return to saving/investment and consumption. The return to saving (the left-hand side of 3.33) requires no explanation. If $\dot{c}/c > 0$, the right-hand side shows that households sacrifice some present consumption for future consumption for which they have to be compensated. This compensation is captured by a return on saving that is sufficiently higher than the rate at which they discount future consumption (ρ). The term in the brackets is the compensation because $-\{u''(c) \cdot c/u'(c)\} > 0$ given that $u''(.) < 0$.[10]

In order for a steady-state path to exist where both the net return to saving and growth of consumption are constant, the elasticity (the term in brackets in 3.33) must be constant. The most common utility function employed in the literature that satisfies this property is a member of the isoelastic class of utility functions

$$u(c) = \frac{c^{1-\sigma} - 1}{1 - \sigma}$$

EQUATION **3.34**

where $\sigma > 0$ such that $\sigma \neq 1$. In 3.34, σ is the elasticity of marginal utility for this function.[11] Using 3.34, the Euler equation becomes:

$$\frac{\dot{c}}{c} = \frac{f'(k) - \delta_K - \rho}{\sigma} \qquad \text{EQUATION } \mathbf{3.35}$$

According to the CKR model, the growth rate of consumption depends on model parameters: the marginal product of capital, the depreciation rate, the rate of time preference, and the intertemporal elasticity of substitution.

As in the Solow–Swan model, the CKR model can be extended to consider the possibility of labor-augmenting technological progress by defining, as before, $\tilde{k}(t) = K(t)/[A(t) \cdot L(t)]$ and $\tilde{c}(t) = C(t)/[A(t) \cdot L(t)]$. In this case the capital accumulation equation in 3.29 becomes $\dot{\tilde{k}} = f(\tilde{k}) - (g_A + g_L + \delta_K)\tilde{k} - \tilde{c}$ where g_A is, as before, the growth of technology.[12] The growth rate of consumption in 3.35 becomes:

$$\frac{\dot{\tilde{c}}}{\tilde{c}} = \frac{f'(\tilde{k}) - \delta_K - \rho - \sigma g_A}{\sigma} \qquad \text{EQUATION } \mathbf{3.36}$$

The transitional dynamics of the CKR model are quite complex but similar in nature to the Solow–Swan model described in the previous section.[13] In the steady state, consumption, capital, and output per household member (c, k, and y, respectively) grow at the same exogenous rate (g_A) without resulting in the net marginal product of capital declining below the rate of time preference (ρ) in 3.35, if $g_A = (1/\sigma)[f'(k) - \delta_K - \rho]$. Moreover, in the steady state there is no growth in consumption, capital, and output per effective household member; thus, in 3.36, $\dot{\tilde{c}}/\tilde{c} = 0$. These results are the same as the Solow–Swan model with constant savings ratio. Unlike the Solow–Swan model, however, the convergence speed is a rather complex function of the model parameters so that no simple counterpart to λ in Section 3.2.2 exists.

It is worth stressing the Pareto optimality nature of the equilibrium outcome. The equilibrium growth rate in 3.36 reached by a competitive decentralized economy is Pareto optimal in the sense that a social planner with the same utility function as that of the representative private agent will also arrive at the equilibrium reached by a decentralized economy.

3.4   The *AK* Model

In the neoclassical Solow–Swan model, diminishing returns to the reproducible inputs limit economic growth. In an attempt to counteract diminishing returns, economists have turned their attention to models where the determinants of growth are endogenous and where long-run economic growth can be sustained, even in the absence of (exogenous) technological progress that is necessary for sustained growth in the neoclassical model. Naturally, these models have come to be known as *endogenous growth models* and will form the subject of the following chapter. In this section, we discuss a type of model that can be viewed as an alternative to the neoclassical Solow–Swan model in that it does not assume a neoclassical production function subject to diminishing returns. This model has come to be known as the *AK* model because it assumes that output is a linear function of physical capital. An economy that is characterized by such a production function will accumulate physical capital continuously without suffering from diminishing returns of capital. An implication of this model, however, is that economies that differ in their initial conditions (different initial capital–labor ratios) will grow at different rates indefinitely and will not converge.

AK models of economic growth assume that diminishing returns to capital are counteracted by growth in other variables so that production does not encounter diminishing returns. The nomeclature of this strand of modeling derives from the fact that production is assumed to be linearly proportional to an aggregate measure of capital, a concept that will be operationalized presently. In Section 3.4.1 we outline the basic *AK* model with a fixed saving ratio and in Section 3.4.2 we introduce an *AK* model of intertemporal optimization in the spirit of the CKR model.

3.4.1   *Early Expositions of the* AK *Model*

As mentioned in the introductory chapter, the concept of capital fundamentalism was predominant in the early post-war development literature. One of the earliest models to expound the role of capital, the Harrod–Domar model, postulated a direct relation between output and the capital stock, the constant of proportionality being the incremental capital-output ratio, or ICOR. The emphasis of the early models was on physical capital accumulation. The Harrod–Domar model assumes a fixed-coefficient production function with capital being the constraining input. In its more recent reincarnation, the model has been labeled the *AK* model

$$Y = \frac{1}{q} \cdot K = A \cdot K$$

EQUATION 3.37

where q is the ICOR, considered a constant determined by exogenous technological conditions. With a fixed saving ratio the steady-state growth of output per capita in this model is:

$$g^* = s_K A - (g_L + \delta_K)$$

EQUATION 3.38

It is clear that the *AK* model implies sustained growth of output per capita without the need to resort to exogenous technological progress. Unlike the neoclassical model, in the *AK* model an increase in the saving ratio or the level of technology will raise the steady-state growth rate.

In an early paper, Horvat (1958) emphasized the importance of introducing the concept of human capital in the technical relation in 3.37. He argued that a distinction needs to be made between investment in physical assets and in the "human factor of growth" (p. 748). Additions to the capital stock have to be absorbed by the economy and the success with which the absorption takes place depends on the human factor. Thus, the fixed coefficient in the *AK* production function (A) depends on the human factor, or $A = A(H)$. He speculated that the human factor, rather complex in nature, depends on "four basic factors (policy variables): personal consumption, health, knowledge, and economic and political organization" (p. 751). He did not, however, provide any empirical evidence to substantiate his speculation. Horvat's suggestion has been followed by more recent developments in the literature on human capital and growth that are examined next.

3.4.2   *The* AK *Model with Human Capital and Constant Saving Ratio*

A convenient way of introducing the role of human capital in the *AK* model is to assume a two-input linear homogenous function

$$Y(t) = F\{K(t), A(t) \cdot L(t)\} = K(t)^{\alpha}[A(t) \cdot L(t)]^{(1-\alpha)}$$

where all variables were defined previously: for simplicity we have assumed a Cobb–Douglas production function. In this framework, human capital is assumed identically equal to the total labor force measured in efficiency units, $H(t) = A(t) \cdot L(t)$. Therefore, the aggregate production function is:

$$Y(t) = K(t)^{\alpha} \cdot H(t)^{(1-\alpha)} \qquad \text{EQUATION } \mathbf{3.39}$$

As in the Mankiw, Romer, and Weil model of Section 3.2.3, a fixed proportion of income is invested in physical and human capital, s_K and s_H, respectively. The rate of depreciation is δ_K and δ_H, respectively. Thus, the rates of accumulation of the reproducible inputs are:

$$\dot{K} = s_K Y - \delta_K K, \quad \dot{H} = s_H Y - \delta_H H \qquad \text{EQUATION } \mathbf{3.40}$$

Population is constant and total saving is apportioned between the two forms of capital so in equilibrium the rates of return must be equal. Equating the two net marginal products we have:

$$\left(\frac{K}{H}\right)^{-(1-\alpha)} \left(\frac{K}{H} - \frac{\alpha}{(1-\alpha)}\right) = \frac{\delta_H - \delta_K}{(1-\alpha)}$$

Therefore, in equilibrium the physical–human capital ratio must be constant. Assuming the two rates of depreciation are equal ($\delta_K = \delta_H = \delta$), this equilibrium ratio is given by:[14]

$$\theta = \frac{K}{H} = \frac{\alpha}{(1-\alpha)} = \frac{s_K}{s_H} \qquad \text{EQUATION } \mathbf{3.41}$$

In equilibrium, the two savings ratios must satisfy this condition. The production function in 3.39 can, therefore, be written as:

$$Y = \theta^{-(1-\alpha)} K$$

Because θ is constant, this provides the model with its AK characterization.

In this model, as can be seen from 3.39, the rate of economic growth is a weighted average of the growth rates of the inputs. Substituting for the growth of inputs from 3.40, we obtain the following steady-state growth rate:

$$g^* = (1-\alpha)\theta^{\alpha}(s_K + s_H) - \delta$$

In the AK model of 3.39 there are constant returns to the reproducible factors of production. The model yields a sustained constant steady-state growth rate that depends on model parameters: the two saving ratios, the equilibrium physical–human capital ratio, the rate of depreciation, and the human capital elasticity of output. By contrast, the Solow–Swan model assumes decreasing returns to the reproducible factors and without exogenous technical change, the growth rate decreases as the economy approaches the steady state (where the instantaneous growth rate is zero). This is one of the basic features that distinguishes the neoclassical model with diminishing returns to models that are not subject to them.

3.4.3   The AK Model with Human Capital and Variable Saving Ratio

In this section we introduce human capital in an AK model where the saving ratio is determined endogenously via intertemporal utility maximization. In the following chapter we discuss additional models of human capital and economic growth, some of which share this intertemporal consumption maximization feature. We have, however, chosen to treat these models in a separate chapter because they highlight other aspects of economic growth such as the endogenous nature of productivity growth and the process of human capital accumulation, features not present in the AK model. The model we treat here is a simple extension of the CKR model discussed in the previous section.

As in 3.28 we assume that infinitely-lived households maximize utility:

$$W = \int_{0}^{\infty} \frac{c^{1-\sigma} - 1}{1 - \sigma} e^{-(\rho - g_L)t} dt \qquad \text{EQUATION } \textbf{3.42}$$

With the AK production function in 3.37, or $y(t) = A \cdot k(t)$ in intensive form, the constraint in 3.29 can be written as:

$$\dot{k} = (A - g_L - \delta_K)k - c \qquad \text{EQUATION } \textbf{3.43}$$

The steady-state growth of consumption in this case is:

$$g^* = \frac{\dot{c}}{c} = \frac{A - \delta_K - \rho}{\sigma} \qquad \text{EQUATION } \textbf{3.44}$$

Using the transversality condition, it can be shown (see Barro and Sala-i-Martin, 2004, Ch. 4.1.4) that the steady-state growth of the capital–labor ratio is the same as 3.44. Given the AK production function, the growth of output is also given by 3.44. It is important to note that the steady-state growth rate is constant (gives the AK model its endogenous character) and does not depend on the capital–labor ratio.

The role of human capital in this model can be introduced by interpreting K as a composite between physical and human capital, and the production function is homogeneous of degree one in the two inputs (physical and human capital):

$$Y(t) = F\{K(t), H(t)\} = K(t)f[H(t)/K(t)]$$ EQUATION **3.45**

As in Section 3.4.2, in equilibrium H/K is a constant; if this constant is equal to A, it yields the AK production function of Section 3.4.1. In this model, human capital grows at the same rate as physical capital, output, and consumption and the growth rate is given by 3.44. Therefore, the assumption of constant returns in the two inputs is sufficient to generate sustained steady-state growth.

In order to illustrate the point further, we consider the AK production function in 3.39 an economy where no distinction is made between households and producers or households carry out their own production. The investment constraints of the economy are illustrated in 3.40. Consumers/producers maximize intertemporal utility

$$W = \int_0^\infty \frac{C^{1-\sigma} - 1}{1 - \sigma} e^{-\rho t} dt$$

where for simplicity we have assumed constant population of mass equal to unity. As in 3.30, the Hamiltonian for this problem is:

$$\Re = \frac{C^{1-\sigma} - 1}{1 - \sigma} e^{-\rho t} + v[(1 - s_H)K^\alpha H^{(1-\alpha)} - \delta_K K - C] + \mu[s_H Y - \delta_H H]$$

The solution of this maximization problem yields a constant K/H ratio that, as in 3.41, is equal to $\alpha/(1 - \alpha)$.[15] The growth of consumption in this case is:

$$\frac{\dot{C}}{C} = \frac{\alpha(K/H)^{-(1-\alpha)} - \delta_K - \rho}{\sigma} = \frac{\alpha\theta^{-(1-\alpha)} - \delta_K - \rho}{\sigma}$$ EQUATION **3.46**

As in the simpler AK model without human capital in 3.42–3.44, the steady-state growth rate of physical and human capital, as well as output, is equal to the growth of consumption and is given by 3.46. As discussed in the previous subsection, the growth rate is constant and depends on model parameters. The assumption of constant returns to scale in the reproducible inputs yields sustained output growth in the steady state. This is similar, of course, to the Solow–Swan model with exogenous technical change. Furthermore, as in the case of the CKR version of the Solow–Swan model, the *AK* model with optimizing consumers also attains Pareto optimality because there are no externalities. The latter arises in endogenous growth models, a point we return to in Chapter 4.

3.5   Models of Growth and Human Capital with Exogenous Technical Change: Summary and Conclusions

In the Solow–Swan neoclassical model, the main impediment to sustained economic growth is diminishing returns. Hence, for growth to take place there has to be a way to overcome diminishing returns for the reproducible inputs. In the benchmark Solow–Swan model this is done through the introduction of exogenous technical progress. The main conclusion is that accumulation of capital alone, without technological progress, cannot act as a source of sustained economic growth, because at some point diminishing returns will set in and the economy will stop growing.

Sustained long-run economic growth can come about with technological change that is assumed exogenous. In this context technological improvements overcome diminishing returns because inputs (labor) become increasingly productive. An alternative approach is to introduce additional inputs to the two basic inputs (capital and labor). In this case we have an additional form of capital, human capital, or the stock of knowledge that is used in production. The introduction of this form of capital does not change the main findings of the model. Human capital, however, can be turned into an important tool for the generation of sustained (endogenous) economic growth, the subject of the following chapter.

An alternative way to get around diminishing returns is to assume directly a production function that is not subject to diminishing returns. This is what the *AK* model does by assuming that output is a linear function of capital. An economy characterized by such a production function will accumulate physical capital continuously without experiencing diminishing returns to capital. An implication of this model, however, is that economies that differ in their initial conditions (different initial capital–labor ratios) will grow at different rates indefinitely and will not converge.

Finally, relaxing the assumption of a constant savings rate and adopting a variable-saving environment with consumer-maximizing behavior does not lead to qualitatively different equilibria outcomes from the Solow–Swan model. As long as there are diminishing returns, there will be no sustained growth in the model, unless one introduces exogenous technological change. Similarly, in the context of the *AK* model, whether households maximize utility or not will lead to a constant growth rate. The difference between the two setups is that in a CKR environment the optimal level of long-run equilibrium per capita output will be lower than that of a Solow–Swan environment due to the discount factor that penalizes future consumption and produces lower saving and, consequently, lower capital accumulation. An important characteristic, however, of the decentralized economy described by the CKR model is that it is Pareto optimal.

The only way any input, in general, and human capital, in particular, can act as a source of sustained economic growth is when it helps counter diminishing returns in the production process. This can come about through the introduction of external economies that increase aggregate productivity and is the subject matter of endogenous growth models that we examine in the following chapter.

Notes

1. See, for example, Barro and Sala-i-Martin (2004).

2. There is no convergence for heterogeneous countries because their differences signify the presence of different steady states (long-run equilibria).

3. The assumption that technological progress is labor augmenting in the Solow–Swan model is one of necessity so as to yield a steady state for the model (a situation where all the major quantities grow at a constant rate). The proof of the necessity of labor-augmenting technology in order for the Solow–Swan model to reach a steady state is provided in Barro and Sala-i-Martin (2004).

4. In what follows, unless necessary to illustrate the nature of the model, the time indicator will be omitted for clarity of exposition.

5. Throughout this book, a dot above a variable will denote its time derivative.

6. To obtain the derivative we differentiate 3.10 with respect to $\ln \tilde{y}$ to arrive at $\tilde{y}\{(\alpha s_K/\tilde{k}) - [(\alpha s_K \tilde{y}/\tilde{k}^2)(d\tilde{k}/d\tilde{y})]\}$. Substituting from 3.7 for $(d\tilde{k}/d\tilde{y}) = (1/\alpha)(\tilde{k}/\tilde{y})$ yields 3.12.

7. The solution is found by noting that 3.13 can be written as $[d \ln \tilde{y}(t)/dt] \cdot [1/(\ln \tilde{y}^* - \ln \tilde{y}(t))] = \lambda$ so that $d \ln[(\ln \tilde{y}^* - \ln \tilde{y}(t))]/dt = -\lambda$ and $[\ln \tilde{y}^* - \ln \tilde{y}(t)] = e^{-\lambda t + c_0}$, where c_0 is the constant of integration. Substituting the initial conditions we find that $e^{c_0} = \ln \tilde{y}^* - \ln \tilde{y}(0)$. Substituting for e^{c_0} in the previous expression we arrive at 3.14.

8. As noted earlier, $\ln(Y/AL)_\tau = \ln(Y/L)_\tau - \ln A_\tau = \ln y_\tau - \ln A_\tau$.

9. While the stock of steady-state human capital per worker appears in 3.22, in empirical work it is assumed that the steady-state value can be proxied by the current value of the human capital stock.

10. Barro and Sala-i-Martin (2004, Ch. 2) show that the term in the brackets in 3.33, $u''(c) \cdot c/u'(c)$, is the elasticity of marginal utility $u'(c)$ with respect to c and is a measure of the concavity of the utility function.

11. Barro and Sala-i-Martin (2004) also show that for this function, the intertemporal elasticity of substitution in consumption is $1/\sigma$.

12. It is worth noting that the underlying (per capita) income constraint in the CKR model, given here, is the same as in the Solow–Swan model in 3.4. The difference is that saving in the Solow–Swan model in 3.4 is exogenous and is a constant fraction of (per capita) income whereas in the CKR model it is determined endogenously.

13. The details of the transitional dynamics are described in Barro and Sala-i-Martin (2004, Ch. 2).

14. The last equality is obtained by noting that if the physical–human capital ratio is constant, then in equilibrium their growth rates must be equal. Using 3.40, it follows that $s_K(Y/K) - \delta_K = s_H(Y/H) - \delta_H$. For equal rates of depreciation, $K/H = s_K/s_H$.

15. The first-order conditions for this maximization problem are $\partial \Re/\partial C = 0$, $\partial \Re/\partial s_H = 0$, $\partial \Re/\partial K = -\dot{\nu}$, and $\partial \Re/\partial H = -\dot{\mu}$.

4   Human Capital and Endogenous Models
of Economic Growth

4.1   Introduction

The main message of the AK approach discussed in Chapter 3 is that, by contrast to the neoclassical model, a sustained rate of growth is possible in the absence of technological progress. This is the case irrespective of whether the saving rate is constant (as in 3.38) or variable (as in 3.44). In both cases, an increase in the aggregate technology parameter, A, will result in a higher sustained rate of growth, a conclusion not borne by the neoclassical model. To the extent that the technology parameter depends on the *level* of human capital, as in the production function in 3.45, a higher *level* of human capital can lead to a higher sustained growth rate. One undesirable feature of the AK model, however, is the fixed-coefficient production function implicit in 3.37.

In comparison to the AK model, an implication of the Solow–Swan neoclassical growth model is that for sustained equilibrium growth there has to be a way of overcoming diminishing returns to the reproducible inputs. One way to achieve this is the introduction of exogenous technical change discussed in Section 3.2. Labor-augmenting technical change introduces the notion of effective labor units and allows per capita income and the capital–labor ratio to grow at the same rate as the exogenous rate of technical change (at a nonzero constant rate). The drawback of this approach, however, is the assumption that technical change occurs exogenously. This is quite a restrictive assumption and its reexamination has given rise to a new literature, known as *endogenous growth theories*.

In endogenous growth models the process of technical change or accumulation of knowledge is not constant and predetermined but is derived from the model's features. Accumulation of knowledge takes many forms, from accumulation of scientific knowledge that is the product of basic research to more specific types that deal with experience acquired in connection with skills that are used at the firm level. New production techniques and the implementation of new management and organizational structures are also part of this process. All these forms of knowledge accumulation exert different influences on the productive capacity of the economy. From a modeling point of view, there are two types of knowledge accumulation. One has to do with human capital accumulation, specifically education of the work force with the necessary skills and updating of skills as newer ones become necessary in the production process. Another involves new technologies applied in production to develop new products or improve the quality of existing ones. In the first category we have the "learning-by-doing" models of Arrow (1962) and of Romer (1986) and the Lucas–Uzawa model (see Lucas, 1988). In the second category we have the innovation model of Romer (1990) that focuses on the role of human capital in the development of new product varieties. In this model the stock of human capital appears as a determinant of the long-run rate of economic growth. These models yield a Pareto suboptimal equilibrium because human capital accumulation is associated with a positive externality that is ignored by individual agents. The equilibrium reached by a social planner yields higher levels of human capital accumulation because these externalities are internalized.

The learning-by-doing models arrive at a constant nonzero growth rate because the positive human capital externality overcomes diminishing returns. An individual's higher level of capital contributes to an increase in labor productivity for all workers in the economy, and the more workers (the greater the population) in the country, the higher the positive externality effect. The implication is that two countries with the same capital stock will grow differently if they differ in their population size with the more populous country experiencing higher growth. This is known as the *scale effect* and is a property of these models that has come under criticism.

From a firm's point of view, a characteristic of learning-by-doing models with external economies is that when firms maximize profits they do not take into account the social benefits that accrue from physical capital accumulation (the fact that workers as a whole become more productive), and therefore do not invest enough in physical capital accumulation; this constitutes the externality. There is scope for intervention in the form of incentives (subsidies) to spur physical capital accumulation that will increase the return to physical capital, increase its level in the economy, and reap the benefits of a more productive labor force.

There are two main conclusions of models with external economies and human capital. All forms of capital (physical or human) tend to be more productive in an environment where there are higher levels of both forms of capital. Hence, economies that possess more of both of these types of capital are in a better position to grow without resorting to introducing exogenous technological progress, because, in this case, diminishing returns are no longer as important an issue. The second conclusion is that intervention may be desirable in order to achieve Pareto optimality, something a decentralized economy cannot attain. Models of learning-by-doing and human capital formation are discussed in Section 4.2. Section 4.3 discusses the Lucas–Uzawa model, the seminal contribution on human capital externalities.

Human capital accumulation, therefore, can help eliminate the limiting influence of diminishing returns and lead to economic growth, even in the absence of technical progress. However, in the absence of technical progress, human and physical capital grow within certain bounds before hitting the "diminishing returns" wall in the long run. Hence, achieving positive growth without technical progress can only be a short-lived phenomenon. A way to achieve sustainable long-run growth is by means of continuous improvements of the production process through the adoption of new technologies and methods. These come about through the development of new (intermediate) inputs and technological improvements in the existing ones. This process, however, requires investment in research and development (R&D) that generates rents for those who pursue it. Since R&D, by its very nature, generates positive externalities (it can be used not only by those who develop it), there is a need for safeguards to be in place for these rents to accrue to the agents that develop new technologies and pay the costs. The resolution of this issue leads to patent laws that allow agents pursuing R&D to reap exclusively the benefits of their research over a given time period and, in effect, create monopolies. The presence of monopoly power, naturally, leads to non-Pareto optimal equilibrium outcomes.

There are two approaches adopted in this context. One is a model that looks at the development of new inputs that are neither substitutes nor complements to existing inputs. The second model deals with quality improvement of existing inputs that render the older ones obsolete. Both models lead to economic growth that depends on the cost of developing new inputs, for the first model, and the cost of the rate of input improvement, for the second. An important characteristic of these models is that the scale of the economy is important. Larger economies will experience higher growth rates as they are able to devote more resources to R&D and, as a result, will secure a technological advantage for themselves. By implication, growth in larger economies will tend to diverge from smaller ones. This is an empirical prediction of these models that is not borne out by evidence. It seems that on a global scale larger economies may well be the ones that undertake more research, yet this research is diffused and adopted by smaller countries that employ it more effectively.

An important drawback of these approaches to growth is their inability to allow for (conditional) convergence in per capita income. Hence, economies with similar characteristics will grow at the same rate and differences in initial conditions will persist indefinitely as two economies that differ only in their initial conditions, but are similar in every other dimension, will find their per capita income does not converge to a common long-run equilibrium. Furthermore, there is evidence suggesting that countries that produce leading technologies are not the ones that experience the highest rates of economic growth; the leaders in growth seem to be countries that emulate rather than produce new technologies. In other words, it seems economies that grow fastest adapt new technologies to their own circumstances rather than produce them, a process known as *technological diffusion*. Free access to the findings of basic scientific research, importing new technologies and technologically sophisticated new capital goods, and buying off patent rights for new discoveries are some of the channels through which technological diffusion occurs. The main ingredient of a model that captures the process of technological diffusion is that for some countries it will be cheaper to emulate technologies produced by others rather than produce their own. In that case technological diffusion may help explain, not only conditional convergence for a homogeneous group of countries, but also the phenomenon of "leapfrogging" where one country that had been a follower jumps ahead and becomes a leader as far as technological superiority goes. More importantly for the purposes of this book, technological diffusion is linked to human capital accumulation because human capital is necessary for the effective use of new technologies.

The model of human capital and technological diffusion that we discuss in detail in Section 4.4 is that of Benhabib and Spiegel (1994). This model builds on an earlier formulation by Nelson and Phelps (1966) and distinguishes between a technological leader and a follower: the former conducts research pushing the technological frontier, whereas the latter emulates and adopts the technologies developed by the leader. There is a cost in the adoption of these technologies but this cost will be lower than the cost of developing them. Human capital is the factor identified as the key to the adoption of new technologies in these models.

In the Benhabib–Spiegel model, in addition to emulating foreign technologies countries also develop new technologies but this process is not made explicit. This is done in Romer (1990) where new technologies are implemented through the use of new intermediate product varieties. According to the Romer model, human capital plays a dual role: it can be used in final production but is also the key ingredient of technological progress in the form of the development of new intermediate goods. We discuss the Romer model in Section 4.5.

There is a type of convergence in these models. The follower will have a higher growth rate than the leader until it has managed to emulate and adopt all the intermediate goods that have been developed by the leader. After that point there will be simultaneous adoption of all intermediate goods that are developed and both countries will have the same growth rate. The models allow for the process of leapfrogging in the following sense. New technologies are more productive, but for their implementation there is a need for learning-by-doing (specific human capital). At the beginning it may not be advantageous for the leader to adopt a new technology as it may not be as productive initially as existing technologies (it will have a lower initial return). For the follower this will not be the case as it typically uses older and less productive technologies. Hence, in that case, adopting the new technology with the lower initial return will be more attractive for the follower than the leader. Under the influence of human capital accumulation (learning-by-doing), productivity in the follower country will overcome that of the leader and leapfrogging results as their roles change. The role of human capital is crucial, because it not only affects the way that new technologies are developed, but also the way that they are implemented.

Technological diffusion constitutes an important channel for the transfer of technological know-how from leaders to followers. These models make apparent that technological leadership does not ensure a country's permanent advantage over its competitors, neither does being a follower exclude a country from catching up with more technologically advanced economies. A follower can exploit its comparative advantage in the adoption of new technologies (lower costs) rather than in their development.

In this chapter we explore some of the main formulations that have been proposed to model human capital within the endogenous growth process. We begin with the learning-by-doing models of Arrow (1962) and Romer (1986) in Section 4.2 and continue in Section 4.3 with one of the most popular formulations of human capital within the endogenous growth process, the Lucas–Uzawa model. Unlike other models that treat human capital as an input in a manner symmetric to physical capital (see Section 3.2.3 and 3.19, and Section 3.4.2 and 3.40), the Lucas–Uzawa formulation pays particular attention to the endogenous formation of human capital. In Section 4.4, we introduce the Benhabib–Spiegel approach (that is built on Nelson and Phelps) according to which human capital does not enter the production process directly but it facilitates the adoption and development of technology; thus, human capital is ultimately a determinant of aggregate productivity growth. As will be outlined, the two approaches in Sections 4.3 and 4.4 yield different predictions on whether the *level* or *growth* of human capital is the determinant of the long-run rate of economic growth. Finally, Section 4.5 introduces the Romer model that focuses on the role of the stock of human capital in the development of new product varieties and as a determinant of the long-run growth rate.

4.2   Externalities and Endogenous Growth: Learning-by-Doing and Spillover Effects

As a first step in the development of endogenous models of human capital, its role is introduced by exploring learning-by-doing and spillover effects in production. As in Section 3.4.2, the stock of human capital is defined identically equivalent to the effective labor force, or $H(t) = A(t) \cdot L(t)$. According to the learning-by-doing and spillover framework, the mere act of investment in physical capital by a firm generates externalities. These are: (1) Increased investment activity in physical capital by a firm enables an increase in the firm's own productivity, a concept formalized by Romer (1986). In particular, if we assume that each firm's production function is neoclassical with two inputs (physical and human capital), increased investment in physical capital increases the stock of human capital, $H(t) = A(t) \cdot L(t)$, by raising the efficiency factor $A(t)$; and (2) Knowledge is a public good and investment in physical capital by one firm increases knowledge that then spills over to other firms, raising their productivity. Investment by one firm raises the aggregate capital stock and this investment spills over to other firms in the form of learning externalities manifested in enhanced productivity.

Taking into account these considerations, the production function of a firm (firm i) is a linear homogenous function in two inputs, physical capital ($K_i(t)$) and human capital ($H_i(t)$), or

$$Y_i(t) = F\{K_i(t), H_i(t)\} = F(K_i(t), A_i(t) \cdot L_i(t))$$

$$= F(K_i(t), K(t) \cdot L_i(t)) \qquad \text{EQUATION 4.1}$$

where $K(t)$ is the aggregate stock of physical capital. The last equality encapsulates the notion that an individual firm's investment activity increases the aggregate capital stock and generates knowledge spillovers that are available instantaneously to all other firms in the economy. As a result, such investment in physical capital generates positive externalities by increasing human capital in the form of a higher productivity index, $A(t)$.

The steady-state rate of growth of consumption in this model can be found by following the procedure for the CKR model; it is that given by 3.35. In order to compute this steady-state rate, we define 4.1 in intensive form:

$$\frac{Y_i}{L_i} = y_i = \frac{F(K_i, K \cdot L_i)}{L_i} = f(k_i, K) \qquad \text{EQUATION } \textbf{4.2}$$

The last equality follows from the homogeneity assumption of the production function. Assuming a finite number of identical firms, in equilibrium all firms will make the same choice concerning the capital–labor ratio so that $k_i(t) = k(t)$. Aggregating over all firms, $K(t) = k(t) \cdot L(t)$ and from 4.2 we have:

$$\frac{y_i}{k_i} = \frac{f(k_i, K)}{k_i} = \bar{f}(L) \qquad \text{EQUATION } \textbf{4.3}$$

The first term is the average product of capital and the last term is obtained by making use of the homogeneity assumption. It must also be true that in symmetric equilibrium, aggregate output per worker (y) is given by $y = k \cdot \bar{f}(L)$. Finally, differentiating 4.3 we have:

$$\frac{\partial f(k_i, K)}{\partial k_i} = \bar{f}(L) - L \cdot \bar{f}'(L) \qquad \text{EQUATION } \textbf{4.4}$$

Using the formulation in 3.35, the optimal rate of consumption is:

$$\frac{\dot{c}}{c} = \frac{[\bar{f}(L) - L \cdot \bar{f}'(L)] - \delta_K - \rho}{\sigma} \qquad \text{EQUATION } \textbf{4.5}$$

With L constant, the growth rate of consumption is constant. The model does not display transitional dynamics: k and y also grow at the same rate as consumption in 4.5 and, thus, the model yields sustained growth in steady-state equilibrium.

The existence of externalities in this model implies that the rate of consumption reached by infinitely-lived consumer/producer households in equation 4.5 is, as one would suspect, not Pareto optimal. A social planner would take into account the impact of an individual firm's investment decision on the aggregate capital stock and also the productivity and spillover effects of such an investment. The planner would maximize intertemporal utility in 3.28 subject to the accumulation constraint in 3.29. Using the utility function in 3.34 and also 4.3, the social optimum is reached by maximizing the Hamiltonian:

$$\mathfrak{R}^S = \frac{c^{1-\sigma}-1}{1-\sigma} \cdot Le^{-\rho t} + v(k \cdot \bar{f}(L) - \delta_K k - c)$$

The first-order conditions are:

$$\frac{\partial \mathfrak{R}^S}{\partial c} = 0 \implies v = c^{-\sigma} Le^{-\rho t}$$

$$\frac{\partial \mathfrak{R}^S}{\partial k} = -\dot{v} \implies \dot{v} = v[\delta_K - \bar{f}(L)]$$

Differentiating the first of these with respect to time and using the second, we arrive at the socially optimal rate of consumption:

$$\left(\frac{\dot{c}}{c}\right)^S = \frac{\bar{f}(L) - \delta_K - \rho}{\sigma} \qquad\qquad \overline{\text{EQUATION } \mathbf{4.6}}$$

Comparing 4.5 and 4.6, it follows that

$$\left(\frac{\dot{c}}{c}\right)^S = \frac{\bar{f}(L) - \delta_K - \rho}{\sigma} > \frac{[\bar{f}(L) - L \cdot \bar{f}'(L)] - \delta_K - \rho}{\sigma} = \left(\frac{\dot{c}}{c}\right)$$

because the average product of capital is greater than the marginal product. Therefore, the competitive equilibrium growth rate is too low or, conversely, the socially optimal rate of growth exceeds that achieved by a decentralized economy. The rationale is straightforward: the social planner internalizes the externality and thus determines the growth rate of consumption based on the average product, whereas competitive producers base their decisions on the private marginal product, ignoring spillover effects.

4.3   The Lucas–Uzawa Model and Human Capital Accumulation

In his celebrated article, Lucas (1988) considers identical infinitely-lived consumers/producers that maximize an isoelastic intertemporal utility function (see 3.42). Each agent is endowed with physical and human capital, $k(t)$ and $h(t)$, respectively. The model makes two important assumptions: agents divide their time between production and schooling in the amounts $(1 - z(t))$ and $z(t)$, respectively; schooling in this model is investment that propels human capital formation. Second, production depends not only on the individual inputs of physical and human capital (what Lucas calls the *internal effect*), but also on an aggregate human capital (the *external effect*). The presumption is that all agents benefit from a higher aggregate level of human capital in terms of increased productivity, but no individual agent takes it into account in deciding $z(t)$ because individual human capital decisions have no significant effect on the aggregate measure.

In the Lucas–Uzawa model, production is a constant-returns-to-scale function in the reproducible inputs

$$y(t) = A \cdot k(t)^{\beta}[(1 - z(t)) \cdot h(t)]^{1-\beta}[h_A(t)]^{\gamma} \qquad \text{EQUATION } \textbf{4.7}$$

where A is the aggregate technology level, assumed constant by Lucas–Uzawa.[1] This production function incorporates the notion that individuals allocate a portion of their time to current production, $(1 - z(t)) \cdot h(t)$, and there is an external effect of human capital captured by the aggregate stock of human capital, $h_A(t)$. Assuming identical individual consumers/producers, aggregate human capital h_A is the summation of each individual's (i) human capital, $h_A = \sum h_i$. Much as in previous models, the constraint faced by agents is that income is either consumed or invested in physical capital accumulation so that $y(t) - c(t) = \dot{k}(t) + g_L k(t)$ or:

$$\dot{k}(t) = A \cdot k(t)^{\beta}[(1 - z(t) \cdot h(t)]^{1-\beta}[h_A(t)]^{\gamma} - g_L k(t) - c(t) \qquad \text{EQUATION } \textbf{4.8}$$

Finally, Lucas assumes that human capital accumulation is directly proportional to the share of h devoted to "education" (building of human capital)

$$\dot{h}(t) = \zeta\, z(t) \cdot h(t) \qquad \text{EQUATION } \textbf{4.9}$$

where ζ is the efficiency with which the economy accumulates human capital. This formulation captures the investment decision by individual agents in accumulating human capital.

Agents maximize intertemporal utility in 3.42 subject to 4.8 and 4.9. The Hamiltonian for this maximization is:

$$\Re = \frac{c^{1-\sigma} - 1}{1 - \sigma} e^{-(\rho - g_L)t} + v(A \cdot k^{\beta}((1 - z) \cdot h)^{1-\beta} h_A^{\gamma} - g_L k - c) + \mu(\zeta z h)$$

The first-order conditions are:

$$\frac{\partial \Re}{\partial c} = 0 \implies c^{-\sigma} e^{-(\rho - g_L)t} = v \qquad \text{EQUATION } \textbf{4.10}$$

$$\frac{\partial \Re}{\partial z} = 0 \implies v(1-\beta)((1-z)^{-\beta})Ak^\beta h^{1-\beta+\gamma} = \mu\zeta h \qquad \text{EQUATION } \textbf{4.11}$$

$$\frac{\partial \Re}{\partial k} = -\dot{v} \implies v(\beta Ak^{\beta-1}(1-z)^{1-\beta}h^{1-\beta+\gamma} - g_L) = -\dot{v} \qquad \text{EQUATION } \textbf{4.12}$$

$$\frac{\partial \Re}{\partial h} = -\dot{\mu} \implies v\{(1-\beta)Ak^\beta u^{1-\beta}h^{-\beta+\gamma}\} + \mu\zeta z = -\dot{\mu} \qquad \text{EQUATION } \textbf{4.13}$$

In deriving 4.11–4.13 we make use of the fact that with all agents identical, the average human capital level is the same for all agents so that $h_A = h$; moreover, in 4.13, individual agents do not internalize the *external* effect implied by the production function in 4.7.[2]

Differentiating 4.10 and using 4.12 we arrive at the familiar Euler equation:

$$\frac{\dot{c}}{c} = \frac{A\beta((1-z)h/k)^{1-\beta}h^\gamma - g_L - \rho}{\sigma} \qquad \text{EQUATION } \textbf{4.14}$$

In the steady state, k, h, and c grow at a constant rate and $(1-z)$ is also constant. Moreover, in the steady-state the growth of k equals that of c. To demonstrate this, we denote the steady-state growth rate of consumption by g_c^*. Using 4.14 and 4.8 we can derive the steady-state growth of k (denoted by g_k^*) as:

$$g_k^* = \frac{\sigma g_c^* + g_L + \rho}{\beta} - \frac{c}{k} - g_L \qquad \text{EQUATION } \textbf{4.15}$$

Given that in the steady state g_c^* and g_k^* are constant, 4.15 implies that the ratio c/k must also be a constant in the steady state. With c/k a constant in the steady state it must be that $g_c^* = g_k^*$. Using this equality in the steady state and 4.15, the Euler equation in 4.14 implies that

$$\ln(\sigma g_c^* + g_L + \rho) = \ln(A\beta) + (1-\beta)\ln(1-z^*) - (1-\beta)\ln k^*$$

$$+ (1-\beta-\gamma)\ln h^* \qquad \text{EQUATION } \textbf{4.16}$$

where z^*, k^*, and h^* denote steady-state values of the variables. In the steady state, g_c^* and z^* are constant; time differentiating 4.16 implies that the steady-state growth rates of consumption and capital are proportional to the steady-state growth of human capital (g_h^*) or:[3]

$$g_c^* = g_k^* = \frac{(1 - \beta + \gamma)}{(1 - \beta)} g_h^*$$

EQUATION **4.17**

To determine the rate of growth of output, we use 4.11 and 4.17 to derive the rate of growth of the co-state variables (shadow prices of k and h) as:

$$\frac{\dot{v}}{v} - \frac{\dot{\mu}}{\mu} = -\frac{\gamma}{1 - \beta} g_h^*$$

EQUATION **4.18**

To find $\dot{v}/v$ we differentiate 4.10 with respect to time:

$$\frac{\dot{v}}{v} = -\sigma \frac{\dot{c}}{c} - \rho$$

EQUATION **4.19**

Similarly, to find $\dot{\mu}/\mu$ we use 4.13 (and substitute from 4.11) to arrive at:

$$-\frac{\dot{\mu}}{\mu} = \zeta$$

EQUATION **4.20**

Using 4.17–4.20 we derive the steady-state growth of human capital as:

$$g_h^* = \frac{(1 - \beta)}{\sigma(1 - \beta + \gamma) - \gamma} (\zeta - \rho)$$

EQUATION **4.21**

In the steady state, the growth of output (g_y^*) is equal to the growth of consumption and physical capital and, from 4.17 and 4.21, is given by:

$$g_y^* = \frac{(1 - \beta + \gamma)}{\sigma(1 - \beta + \gamma) - \gamma} (\zeta - \rho)$$

EQUATION **4.22**

The steady-state rate of growth is constant and depends on model parameters; in other words, the model yields sustained steady-state growth. Moreover, sustained growth is not the result of the spillover effect from the aggregate human capital stock because there is sustained growth even in its absence $(\gamma = 0)$; from 4.22 it is equal to $(\zeta - \rho)/\sigma$. Rather, sustained growth derives from the intertemporal externality implicit in the model in 4.9: the current level of human capital has an effect on the future return of human capital and agents internalize this intertemporal externality. The model also allows the derivation of the optimal proportion of time devoted to the accumulation of human capital. From 4.21 and 4.9 it is equal to:

$$z^* = \frac{(1-\beta)}{[\sigma(1-\beta+\gamma)-\gamma]}\frac{(\zeta-\rho)}{\zeta}$$

As with the growth rate of output, it is constant and depends on model parameters. Finally, we note that in the absence of contemporaneous spillover effects ($\gamma = 0$) the growth of output is:

$$g_y^* = \zeta z^*$$

The rate of economic growth is directly proportional to the time devoted to human capital accumulation and the efficiency with which the economy accumulates human capital. An increase in the rate of human capital accumulation (or the efficiency of human capital accumulation) will increase the long-run rate of growth.

Given the spillover externality from aggregate human capital present in the model (and that private agents do not internalize), the equilibrium reached by the decentralized economy is suboptimal from the societal viewpoint. A social planner would take this externality into account when computing the marginal product of human capital. The first-order conditions for the societal maximization problem are the same as 4.10–4.13 with the exception of 4.13, which now becomes:

$$\frac{\partial \mathfrak{R}^S}{\partial h} = -\dot{\mu} \implies -\dot{\mu} = vAk^\beta(1-z)^\beta(1-\beta-\gamma)h^{-\beta+\gamma} + \mu\zeta z$$

The externality is now reflected in the marginal product of h. Equations 4.17–4.19 remain the same but 4.20 now becomes:

$$-\frac{\dot{\mu}}{\mu} = \zeta + \frac{\gamma}{1-\beta}\zeta(1-z) \qquad\qquad \text{EQUATION } \textbf{4.23}$$

Using 4.17–4.19 and 4.23 we have

$$\left[\frac{\sigma(1-\beta+\gamma)-\gamma}{(1-\beta)}\right]g_h^{*S} = (\zeta-\rho) + \frac{\gamma}{1-\beta}\zeta(1-z) \qquad\qquad \text{EQUATION } \textbf{4.24}$$

where g_h^{*S} is the steady-state rate of growth of human capital at the social optimum. Finally, from 4.9 we note that $\zeta(1-z) = \zeta - (\dot{h}^*/h^*)^S = \zeta - g_h^{*S}$. Substituting this into 4.24 and solving for g_h^{*S}, we find that

$$g_h^{*S} = \frac{(1-\beta)(\zeta-\rho)+\gamma\zeta}{\sigma(1-\beta+\gamma)} > \frac{(1-\beta)(\zeta-\rho)}{\sigma(1-\beta+\gamma)-\gamma} = g_h^*$$

where, for the right-hand side of the inequality, we have made use of 4.21. As is evident, the socially optimal rate of growth of human capital and, by consequence, production and physical capital, is higher than that of a decentralized competitive economy. This conclusion is consistent with the argument that a policy of subsidies to education is a way of closing the gap between the social and competitive equilibrium.[4] Finally, it can be shown that the time devoted to education is lower in the competitive equilibrium

$$z^{*S} = \frac{(1-\beta)(\zeta-\rho)+\gamma\zeta}{\zeta\sigma(1-\beta+\gamma)} > \frac{(1-\beta)(\zeta-\rho)}{\zeta\sigma(1-\beta+\gamma)-\gamma} = z^*$$

where z^{*S} is the time devoted to education by a social planner.[5]

4.3.1 Lucas–Uzawa and Physical Capital in the Human Capital Accumulation Function: Rebelo (1991)

The Lucas model assumes that no physical capital is required in the production function for education (human capital accumulation), as shown in 4.9; rather the only input necessary is human capital itself. Rebelo (1991) extended the Lucas model to consider an education production function that requires both human and physical capital inputs. The production of final output is similar to that of the Lucas model except for contemporaneous spillovers between aggregate human capital and productivity. Therefore, the Rebelo model replaces 4.7 and 4.9 by

$$y(t) = A_1[\phi_1(t) \cdot k(t)]^\beta[(1-z(t)) \cdot h(t)]^{1-\beta}$$

and

$$\dot{h}(t) = A_2[(1-\phi_1(t)) \cdot k(t)]^\eta[z(t) \cdot h(t)]^{1-\eta}$$

where $(1-\phi_1(t))$ and $\phi_1(t)$ are the proportion of the stock of physical capital employed in human capital accumulation and production, respectively, and A_1 and A_2 are constant technology parameters.[6] The economy is composed of infinitely-lived consumers/producers that maximize intertemporal utility. In the steady state the rate of growth of k, h, and c is the same and the agent's basic choice is the proportion of k and h to devote to production and human capital accumulation.

Rebelo distinguishes between two efficiency conditions. The first is *static* and uses the marginal value product of physical and human capital in production and in human capital accumulation to determine the optimal allocation of the existing stock of physical and human capital across the two activities. In an efficient allocation, the marginal products (measured in terms of units of physical capital) should be equal across the two sectors or

$$\beta A_1 \left(\frac{(1-z)h}{\phi_1 k} \right)^{1-\beta} = \phi_2 \eta A_2 \left(\frac{zh}{(1-\phi_1)k} \right)^{1-\eta} \qquad \text{EQUATION } \mathbf{4.25}$$

$$(1-\beta)A_1 \left(\frac{(1-z)h}{\phi_1 k} \right)^{-\beta} = \phi_2 (1-\eta) A_2 \left(\frac{zh}{(1-\phi_1)k} \right)^{-\eta} \qquad \text{EQUATION } \mathbf{4.26}$$

where ϕ_2 is the relative value of human capital in terms of physical capital. The requirement for efficiency in production is that the rate of transformation is equated across the two sectors or, from 4.25 and 4.26:

$$\frac{1-\beta}{\beta} \frac{\phi_1 k}{(1-z)h} = \frac{1-\eta}{\eta} \frac{(1-\phi_1)k}{zh} \qquad \text{EQUATION } \mathbf{4.27}$$

Therefore, in the steady state the k/h ratio is constant.

The second efficiency condition is *dynamic* and relates to the decision about investing in the two forms of capital. One unit of physical capital invested in the production sector will yield a return equal to

$$r^k = \beta A_1 (\phi_1 k)^{\beta-1} ((1-z)h)^{1-\beta} - \delta_K$$

where r^k is the marginal product of physical capital in production. An alternative investment is to accumulate $1/\phi_2$ units of human capital (with relative price ϕ_2); the return to investment in the human capital accumulation sector (expressed in units of physical capital) is (assuming an equal rate of depreciation for human and physical capital):

$$r^h = (1-\eta)A_2[(1-\phi_1)k]^\eta (zh)^{-\eta} - \delta_K + \frac{\dot{\phi_2}}{\phi_2}$$

The final term $(\dot{\phi}_2/\phi_2)$ represents the possibility of a capital gain from human capital investment. Given that in steady state the ratio k/h is constant, 4.25 and 4.26 imply that $\phi_2(t)$ is also constant. Therefore, equating the two rates of return $(r^k = r^h)$, it must be true that in the steady state:

$$\beta A_1 \left(\frac{\phi_1 k}{(1-z)h} \right)^{\beta-1} = (1-\eta) A_2 \left(\frac{(1-\phi_1)k}{zh} \right)^{\eta} \qquad \text{EQUATION } \textbf{4.28}$$

Solving 4.27 and 4.28 we find that

$$\frac{\phi_1 k}{(1-z)h} = \left(\frac{A_1}{A_2} \frac{\beta}{(1-\eta)} \right)^{\Gamma_1/\eta} \left(\frac{(1-\eta)}{\eta} \frac{\beta}{(1-\beta)} \right)^{\Gamma_1}$$

$$\frac{(1-\phi_1)k}{zh} = \left(\frac{A_1}{A_2} \frac{\beta}{(1-\eta)} \right)^{\Gamma_1/\eta} \left(\frac{(1-\eta)}{\eta} \frac{\beta}{(1-\beta)} \right)^{-\Gamma_1(1-\beta)/\eta}$$

where $\Gamma_1 = \eta/(1+\eta-\beta)$. Therefore, in steady state the physical–human capital ratios used in production and in human capital accumulation are constant and depend only on model parameters.

Substituting the physical–human capital ratios in the equation for the return to physical investment we arrive at

$$r^k = A_1^{\Gamma_1} A_2^{1-\Gamma_1} \Gamma_2^{\Gamma_1}$$

where $\Gamma_2 = \beta^{\beta}(1-\beta)^{1-\beta} \eta^{1-\beta}(1-\eta)^{(1-\beta)(1-\eta)/\eta}$. Therefore, in steady state the marginal product of physical capital is constant and does not depend on k or h. With an isoelastic utility function, the Euler equation is :

$$\frac{\dot{c}}{c} = \frac{r - \delta_K - \rho}{\sigma} = \frac{A_1^{\Gamma_1} A_2^{1-\Gamma_1} \Gamma_2^{\Gamma_1} - \delta_K - \rho}{\sigma}$$

Along the steady-state path, investment and physical–human capital grow at the same rate as consumption, and therefore the steady-state rate of growth of production is:

$$g_y^* = \max \left\{ \frac{A_1^{\Gamma_1} A_2^{1-\Gamma_1} \Gamma_2^{\Gamma_1} - \delta_K - \rho}{\sigma}, -\delta_K \right\}$$

The solution makes explicit the possibility of a corner solution with zero investment. In the case where the economy is not at the corner solution, the rate of growth is constant and depends on A_1 and A_2 and model parameters.[7]

In the Rebelo model the accumulation of human capital raises the marginal product of physical capital, and therefore encourages the accumulation of physical capital. This, in turn, raises the marginal product of human capital and thus promotes further human capital accumulation. The interconnection between the two forms of capital renders the model the property of sustained growth in steady state because, while there exist diminishing returns to each factor individually, there are constant returns to the reproducible factors together. The latter prevents the marginal product from falling while human and physical capital are cumulated and this gives the model the sustained growth property.[8]

4.4   Human Capital and Technological Diffusion: Nelson and Phelps (1966) and Benhabib and Spiegel (1994)

In their seminal contribution, Nelson and Phelps (1966) distinguish between two types of jobs: those that are "routinized" and those that require "adaptation" to change. Their main hypothesis is that productive activity requires adaptation to change and more educated workers are more prone to introduce new techniques. Education makes people more likely to innovate and "speeds the process of technological diffusion" (p. 70). Their model follows in the neoclassical tradition and assumes a labor-augmenting production function; see 3.1 where $A(t)$ is an average index of technology. In addition to average technology, they introduce the concept of the theoretical level of technology $T(t)$: this corresponds to the best-practice level that would be available if technological diffusion were instantaneous or, conversely, the universe of knowledge or body of techniques available to innovators. The theoretical level is assumed to grow exponentially at the exogenous rate ω, or $T(t) = T(0)e^{\omega t}$, where $T(0)$ represents the initial level and $\omega > 0$.

Nelson and Phelps discuss two models. The first assumes that there is a time lag between the creation of a new technique and its adoption and this lag depends negatively on the average level of educational attainment (human capital):

$$A(t) = T(t - \Omega(H)), \qquad \Omega'(H) < 0$$

$\Omega(.)$ is the lag in adoption. Therefore,

$$A(t) = T(0)e^{\omega(t-\Omega(H))}$$

and $A(t)$ grows also at the rate ω and is an increasing function of H. The marginal productivity of human capital is positive and depends proportionally on ω (for a given wage bill).[9]

The second model has received the most attention. Nelson and Phelps point out that the lag in technology adoption depends on the profitability of the innovation and that an increase in human capital does not reduce the lag instantaneously. The second model argues that technological progress ("rate at which the latest, theoretical technology is realized in improved technological practice," p. 73) depends upon human capital and the gap between the current and theoretical level of technology as follows:

$$\frac{\dot{A}(t)}{A(t)} = \Phi(H)\left[\frac{T(t) - A(t)}{A(t)}\right] \qquad \Phi(0) = 0, \quad \Phi'(H) > 0 \qquad \text{EQUATION } \mathbf{4.29}$$

The rate of technological progress is an increasing function of the *level* of human capital H and the technology gap $T(t) - A(t)$. The model yields two conclusions. First, in the long run, $\dot{A}(t)/A(t)$ will be equal to ω irrespective of the value of H. This is because if $\dot{A}(t)/A(t)$ exceeds ω, the gap in 4.29 will decrease and this will reduce $\dot{A}(t)/A(t)$ until it is equal to ω; at that point the system will be in long-run equilibrium and the gap will be constant. The solution of the differential equation in 4.29 is:[10]

$$A(t) = \left[A(0) - \frac{\Phi(H)}{\Phi(H) + \omega}T(0)\right]e^{-\Phi(H)t} + \frac{\Phi(H)}{\Phi(H) + \omega}T(0)e^{\omega t} \qquad \text{EQUATION } \mathbf{4.30}$$

Therefore, the (long-run) equilibrium path of technology is given by:

$$A^*(t) = \frac{\Phi(H)}{\Phi(H) + \omega}T(0)e^{\omega t}$$

Second, in long-run equilibrium, the technology gap is constant (both a follower country and the leading technology country grow at the constant rate ω) and depends on the level of human capital (see Figure 4.1):

$$\frac{T(t) - A^*(t)}{A^*(t)} = \frac{\omega}{\Phi(H)}$$

For an economy with a positive rate of technological progress the equilibrium gap depends positively on ω and negatively on H. Moreover, the

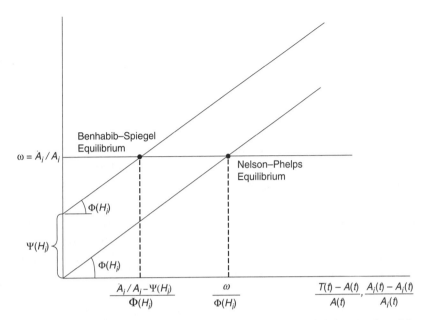

FIGURE **4.1** Long-run equilibrium in the Nelson–Phelps and Benhabib–Spiegel models
Source: Adapted from Nelson and Phelps (1966), *American Economic Review*, 56, 69–75.

elasticity of the long-run equilibrium level of technology with respect to H or $[(\partial A^*(t)/\partial H) \cdot (H/A^*(t))]$ depends positively on the level of technological progress so that the "payoff to increased educational attainment is greater the more technologically progressive the economy is" (p. 74).

Nelson and Phelps conclude by pointing out that more technologically advanced economies should build human capital relative to physical capital (because of the higher marginal productivity of human capital). Innovations generate externalities and therefore education (by stimulating innovation) would also generate externalities. This would imply that the private return to education would differ from the social rate, a conclusion reached by other endogenous growth models.

Benhabib and Spiegel (1994) build on the Nelson and Phelps formulation in two ways: they assume that convergence in 4.29 is not to a theoretical level that grows exogenously (ω) but to that of the country with the "leading" technology; second, in addition to the "catch-up" effect in 4.29, human capital also influences productivity growth endogenously because it enables a country to develop its own technological capabilities. Therefore, they modify 4.29 as

$$\frac{\dot{A}_i(t)}{A_i(t)} = \Psi(H_i) + \Phi(H_i) \left[\frac{\max_j A_j(t) - A_i(t)}{A_i(t)} \right] \qquad \Psi(0) = 0, \quad \Psi'(H) > 0$$

EQUATION **4.31**

where $i = 1, \ldots n$ is a country index. The first term represents the "endogenous" effect introduced by Benhabib and Spiegel and the second, the "catch-up" effect emphasized by Nelson and Phelps. At an initial time ($t = 0$), the leading country is the country with the highest level of technology. For the leading country, the second term in 4.31 is zero and its productivity grows at the endogenous rate. The level of technology of the leader at time t, $A_l(t)$, is given by $A_l(t) = A_l(0)e^{\Psi(H_l)t}$ where H_l is the human capital level of the leader. If initially a country i has a greater level of human capital than the leader ($H_i > H_l$ at $t = 0$), then during a finite time (τ) country i will overtake the leader and become the leader. This is because $\Psi(H_i) > \Psi(H_l)$ and for country i the second term in 4.31 is positive; therefore, $A_i(\tau) > A_i(0)e^{\Psi(H_i)\tau} > A_L(0)e^{\Psi(H_l)\tau}$. Country i will remain the leader unless another country manages to generate a higher level of human capital than the leader. A country with a lower level of human capital cannot overtake the leader because once it catches up to the leader (and the second term becomes zero) the endogenous growth component of the leader (with the higher level of H) will be higher.

Assuming that at time t country l is the technological leader, the growth of total factor productivity of country i is:

$$\frac{\dot{A}_i(t)}{A_i(t)} = \Psi(H_i) + \Phi(H_i) \left[\frac{A_l(t) - A_i(t)}{A_i(t)} \right]$$

$$= \Psi(H_i) + \Phi(H_i) \left[\frac{A_l(0)e^{\Psi(H_l)t} - A_i(t)}{A_i(t)} \right]$$

EQUATION **4.32**

The solution of this differential equation is:[11]

$$A_i(t) = \left[A_i(0) - \frac{\Phi(H_i)}{\Phi(H_i) - \Psi(H_i) + \Psi(H_l)} A_l(0) \right] e^{[\Psi(H_i) - \Phi(H_i)]t}$$

$$+ \frac{\Phi(H_i)}{\Phi(H_i) - \Psi(H_i) + \Psi(H_l)} A_l(0)e^{\Psi(H_l)t}$$

EQUATION **4.33**

The solution is very similar to that of the Nelson–Phelps model in 4.30 where the latter assumes that the endogenous component is zero ($\Psi(H_i) = 0$) and the technology of the leader grows exogenously at rate ω. As in the Nelson–Phelps model, in the long run, the asymptotic growth rate of country i is equal to that of the leader and the level of human capital affects productivity only in the transition phase. The reason is because in the limit the ratio $A_i(t)/A_l(t)$ is constant and equal to $\Phi(H_i)/[\Phi(H_i) - \Psi(H_i) + \Psi(H_l)]$; therefore, A_i and A_l will grow at the endogenous rate set by the leader and equal to $\Psi(H_l)$. As in Nelson and Phelps, the long-run equilibrium technology gap is constant and depends on the level of human capital (see Figure 4.1 where the leader is assumed to grow at the rate ω).

The Benhabib–Spiegel approach provides a reduced-form equation for the determinants of the growth of aggregate output of country i. In order to arrive at an estimable reduced-form equation, aggregate production of country i at time t is expressed as a Cobb–Douglas function, or:

$$Y_i(t) = F\{A_i(t), K_i(t), L(t)\} = A_i(t)K_i(t)^\alpha L_i(t)^\beta$$

Log–differencing the production function and combining it with the evolution of aggregate productivity growth in 4.32, we can derive the discrete growth rate of output between time period τ and $\tau + \upsilon$ as:

$$\ln\left(\frac{Y_{i,\tau+\upsilon}}{Y_{i,\tau}}\right) = \Psi(H_{i,\tau}) - \Phi(H_{i,\tau}) + \Phi(H_i)\left(\frac{A^l_{i,\tau}}{A_{i,\tau}}\right)$$

$$+ \alpha \ln\left(\frac{K_{i,\tau+\upsilon}}{K_{i,\tau}}\right) + \beta \ln\left(\frac{L_{i,\tau+\upsilon}}{L_{i,\tau}}\right) \qquad \text{EQUATION } \textbf{4.34}$$

This is quite similar to the growth accounting methodology (discussed in Chapter 6) according to which the growth of output depends on a weighted average of the growth of inputs (labor and physical capital). In addition to input growth, however, output growth depends on an endogenous growth and a catch-up effect, both of which depend on the *level* of a country's human capital. In order to estimate this reduced-form functional form, Benhabib and Spiegel make several simplifying assumptions: the $\Psi(H_{i,\tau})$ and $\Phi(H_{i,\tau})$ functions are linear in $H_{i,\tau}$, the aggregate productivity level at time τ for the leader and country i ($A^l_{i,\tau}$ and $A_{i,\tau}$, respectively) can be approximated by their respective (per capita) income levels, and the technological leader is the country with the highest income level. The reduced-form equation in 4.34 was estimated with cross-section data by Benhabib and Spiegel and subsequently by other researchers (see Chapter 6 for a discussion).

In summary, the Benhabib–Spiegel model views the country with the leading technology level as the "locomotive" that provides the engine by which other countries catch up to the leader; asymptotically all countries grow at the same rate (but as they point out, the transition period may be "extremely" long). While the level of human capital is positively related to the growth of total factor productivity as in 4.31, they caution that the effect may be masked empirically unless one controls for the catch-up effect. Countries with low levels of technology and human capital may grow faster than the leader because the catch-up effect may dominate, while countries similar to the leader (in terms of the level of productivity and human capital) may grow more slowly than the leader if the catch-up effect is insignificant compared to the endogenous growth effect.

4.5   Human Capital and Innovations: Romer (1990)

Nelson and Phelps argue that human capital determines the rate of technological progress endogenously. The role of human capital in promoting technological progress and growth is, however, not explored explicitly. Moreover, in the Benhabib–Spiegel model, human capital is a non-excludable public good and all of it can be used for innovation and catch-up purposes simultaneously. Romer (1990) notes that research and development is carried out by educated workers and concludes that a greater stock of human capital will lead to higher economic growth by virtue of its innovation-promoting effects. A portion of human capital is used in the production of final goods (similar to the Lucas model) but the remainder is employed in R&D activities. The Romer model, however, does not need to rely on externalities in the intertemporal accumulation of human capital (as in the Lucas model) to generate sustained per capita income growth, and does not treat human capital as a non-excludable good (as do Benhabib and Spiegel). In some ways, the Romer model can be conceptualized as combining the Nelson and Phelps idea that human capital is an input to the innovation process and the Lucas view of human capital as an input into the production of final goods, but differs from these in substantial ways.

In the Romer model, there is a continuum of intermediate goods and a fixed cost necessary for the production of intermediate goods. With economic growth, the size of the market expands and makes possible the production of a greater variety of intermediate goods. Because of the existence of fixed costs, these goods are produced under imperfect competitive conditions and this yields the possibility of monopoly rents in production. Such rents serve a dual role: they allow the existence of increasing returns and also reward firms for the resources devoted to R&D aimed at expanding the existing variety of intermediate products.

Romer makes a distinction between unskilled workers (L) and skilled workers or human capital (H); the stock of each is fixed. Production of final goods requires inputs of both skilled and unskilled labor but only skilled workers are employed in the development of new varieties of intermediate products. A portion of the stock of human capital is employed in the production of final goods (H_Y) and a portion in the development of new products (H_A); the total stock of human capital is given by $H = H_Y + H_A$. The production function for final output requires both skilled and unskilled workers as well as intermediate inputs according to

$$Y = H_Y^\alpha \cdot L^\beta \cdot \int_0^A x_i^{1-\alpha-\beta} di \qquad \text{EQUATION } \textbf{4.35}$$

where x_i is the input of the intermediate good i and A is the current number of intermediate inputs. The rate of intermediate product development (technological progress) requires a certain input of skilled labor or

$$\frac{\dot{A}}{A} = \xi \cdot H_A \qquad \text{EQUATION } \textbf{4.36}$$

where ξ is the efficiency with which firms generate new intermediate products. There exist spillovers in research production: the existing body of cumulated knowledge (A) is available to all researchers for use so that knowledge is a non-rival good. Knowledge is also excludable: firms must pay for the exclusive use of the new variety of intermediate product and therefore there is a fixed cost in the adoption of new intermediate product designs. This fixed cost determines, in turn, the price of the intermediate product. In the Romer model there are increasing returns because of product differentiation and research spillovers.

The price of new intermediate products is determined by the requirement that the marginal productivity of human capital in final goods and research production be equal or

$$P_A \cdot \xi \cdot A = \alpha H_Y^{\alpha-1} L^\beta \int_0^A x_i^{1-\alpha-\beta} di = \alpha H_Y^{\alpha-1} L^\beta A x^{1-\alpha-\beta} \qquad \text{EQUATION } \mathbf{4.37}$$

where P_A is the price of the intermediate product.[12] For skilled workers to be indifferent between employment in the final goods sector or the research sector, in equilibrium the marginal contribution of one unit of human capital in the two sectors must be equal. It follows that:

$$P_A = \frac{\alpha}{\xi} \frac{L^\beta x^{1-\alpha-\beta}}{H_Y^{1-\alpha}} \qquad \text{EQUATION } \mathbf{4.38}$$

The value of x produced by each intermediate firm is determined by profit maximization and each intermediate firm operates as a local monopolist. In symmetric equilibrium the output of each of the A intermediate firms is (from 4.35) equal to $H_Y^\alpha \cdot L^\beta \cdot x^{1-\alpha-\beta}$. The marginal product of the intermediate input in final production defines an inverse demand function for intermediate products as

$$p(x) = (1-\alpha-\beta) \cdot H_Y^\alpha \cdot L^\beta \cdot x^{-\alpha-\beta}$$

where $p(x)$ denotes the inverse demand for the intermediate product.[13] The intermediate firm's total revenue is:

$$R(x) = p(x) \cdot x = (1-\alpha-\beta) \cdot H_Y^\alpha \cdot L^\beta \cdot x^{1-\alpha-\beta}$$

One unit of capital can produce one unit of the intermediate product so that the marginal cost of the intermediate product is the rate of interest (r^k). Equating marginal revenue with marginal cost yields

$$r^k = (1-\alpha-\beta)^2 \cdot H_Y^\alpha \cdot L^\beta \cdot x^{-\alpha-\beta} \qquad \text{EQUATION } \mathbf{4.39}$$

from which the optimal level of x can be derived as:

$$x = \left[\frac{(1-\alpha-\beta)^2 \cdot H_Y^\alpha \cdot L^\beta}{r^k} \right]^{1/(\alpha+\beta)}$$

The value of each intermediate firm's profits is given by:

$$R(x) - r^k \cdot x = \frac{\alpha+\beta}{(1-\alpha-\beta)} \cdot r^k \cdot x$$

The discounted value of each intermediate firm's profits (over an infinite horizon) will determine the equilibrium price of the intermediate product, P_A, as:

$$P_A = \frac{R(x) - r^k \cdot x}{r^k} = \frac{\alpha + \beta}{(1 - \alpha - \beta)} \cdot x \qquad \text{EQUATION } \mathbf{4.40}$$

The equilibrium level of skilled employment in final goods production (H_Y) can be derived from 4.38 by substituting from 4.39 and 4.40 and is

$$H_Y = \Lambda_1 \frac{r^k}{\xi} \qquad \text{EQUATION } \mathbf{4.41}$$

where Λ_1 is a constant that depends on technology parameters, $\Lambda_1 = \alpha/[(\alpha + \beta)(1 - \alpha - \beta)]$.

In steady state, the growth of output (g^*) is equal to the growth of technology so that:

$$g^* = \frac{\dot{A}}{A} = \xi \cdot H_A = \xi(H - H_Y) \qquad \text{EQUATION } \mathbf{4.42}$$

The model is closed by the Euler equation derived from the preference side of the economy. Assuming isoelastic preferences and ignoring capital depreciation, from 3.35 the steady-state growth rate is:

$$g^* = \frac{r^k - \rho}{\sigma} \qquad \text{EQUATION } \mathbf{4.43}$$

Using 4.41–4.43 we find the optimal growth rate as:

$$g^* = \frac{\xi H - \rho \Lambda_1}{1 + \sigma \Lambda_1} \qquad \text{EQUATION } \mathbf{4.44}$$

The model yields a sustained growth rate that depends on model parameters and exhibits scale effects in human capital: a larger stock of human capital generates higher sustained economic growth.[14] The steady-state rate of growth also depends positively on the efficiency of research activities (ξ).

Romer (1990) demonstrates that the optimal growth rate reached by a decentralized economy in 4.44 would be lower than the social optimum. In symmetric equilibrium the capital stock is equal to the total production of intermediate goods or $K = x \cdot A$. Output in symmetric equilibrium is given by $Y = H_Y^\alpha L^\beta A x^{1-\alpha-\beta} = H_Y^\alpha L^\beta K^{1-\alpha-\beta} A^{\alpha+\beta}$. Therefore, (ignoring depreciation) the capital accumulation constraint is given by:

$$\dot{K} = H_Y^\alpha L^\beta K^{1-\alpha-\beta} A^{\alpha+\beta} - C \qquad \text{EQUATION } \mathbf{4.45}$$

The objective of the social planner is to maximize utility in 3.34, subject to the capital constraint in 4.45 and the accumulation of new intermediate products in 4.36. The current value Hamiltonian is:

$$\Re^S = \frac{C^{1-\sigma}-1}{1-C} e^{-\rho t} + \mu(\xi A H_A) + \nu\left[(H-H_A)^\alpha L^\beta K^{1-\alpha-\beta} A^{\alpha+\beta} - C\right]$$

The first-order conditions are

$$\frac{\partial \Re^S}{\partial C} = 0 \implies C^{-\sigma} e^{-\rho t} = \nu \qquad \text{EQUATION } \mathbf{4.46}$$

$$\frac{\partial \Re^S}{\partial H_A} = 0 \implies \frac{\alpha \nu}{(H-H_A)} \Lambda_2 = \mu \xi A \qquad \text{EQUATION } \mathbf{4.47}$$

$$\frac{\partial \Re^S}{\partial K} = -\dot{\nu} \implies \frac{\nu(1-\alpha-\beta)}{K} \Lambda_2 = -\dot{\nu}$$

$$\frac{\partial \Re^S}{\partial A} = -\dot{\mu} \implies \mu \xi H_A + \frac{\nu(\alpha+\beta)}{A} \Lambda_2 = -\dot{\mu} \qquad \text{EQUATION } \mathbf{4.48}$$

where $\Lambda_2 = (H-H_A)^\alpha L^\beta K^{1-\alpha-\beta} A^{\alpha+\beta}$. From 4.47, we obtain:

$$\frac{\nu}{\mu} = \xi \alpha^{-1} A^{1-\alpha-\beta}(H-H_A)^{1-\alpha} L^{-\beta} K^{-(1-\alpha-\beta)}$$

Taking logs of this and differentiating with respect to time we have:

$$\frac{\dot{\nu}}{\nu} - \frac{\dot{\mu}}{\mu} = (1-\alpha-\beta)\frac{\dot{A}}{A} - (1-\alpha-\beta)\frac{\dot{K}}{K}$$

Along the symmetric equilibrium growth path $K = x \cdot A$, or K/A is constant. Therefore, K and A grow at the same rate and it follows that:

$$\frac{\dot{\nu}}{\nu} = \frac{\dot{\mu}}{\mu} \qquad \text{EQUATION } \mathbf{4.49}$$

Differentiation of 4.46 with respect to time yields

$$\frac{\dot{\nu}}{\nu} = -\rho - \sigma\frac{\dot{C}}{C} = -\rho - \sigma\frac{\dot{A}}{A} = -\rho - \sigma \xi H_A \qquad \text{EQUATION } \mathbf{4.50}$$

because along the balanced growth path $\dot{C}/C = \dot{A}/A$. Substituting 4.47 into 4.48 yields:

$$-\frac{\dot{\mu}}{\mu} = \xi H \left(\frac{\alpha+\beta}{\alpha}\right) - \frac{\xi\beta}{\alpha} H_A \qquad \text{EQUATION \textbf{4.51}}$$

From 4.49–4.51 the socially optimal level of human capital in research is:

$$H_A^S = \frac{\xi\left(\frac{\alpha+\beta}{\alpha}\right)H - \rho}{\xi\left(\frac{\beta}{\alpha}+\sigma\right)}$$

The socially optimal growth rate is therefore given by

$$g^{*S} = \frac{\dot{A}}{A} = \xi \cdot H_A^S = \frac{\xi\left(\frac{\alpha+\beta}{\alpha}\right)H - \rho}{\left(\frac{\beta}{\alpha}+\sigma\right)}$$

which can be rewritten as

$$g^{*S} = \frac{\xi H - \rho\Lambda_3}{\sigma\Lambda_3 + (1-\Lambda_3)} \qquad \text{EQUATION \textbf{4.52}}$$

where $\Lambda_3 = \alpha/(\alpha+\beta)$.

In order to compare the private decentralized equilibrium growth rate in 4.44 with the socially optimal growth in 4.52 we note that

$$\Lambda_1 = \left(\frac{1}{1-\alpha-\beta}\right)\Lambda_3 > \Lambda_3$$

where $1/(1-\alpha-\beta)$ is the profit markup in the noncompetitive intermediate goods sector. Therefore, from 4.44 and 4.52:

$$g^{*S} = \frac{\xi H - \rho\Lambda_3}{\sigma\Lambda_3 + (1-\Lambda_3)} > \frac{\xi H - \rho\Lambda_1}{\sigma\Lambda_1 + 1} = g^*$$

Romer points out that the socially optimal growth rate is larger because there is an externality in the contribution of intermediate firms in the development of new product varieties and, second, an externality in research spillovers. The level of employment in the research sector (H_A) chosen by the social planner would be greater than the decentralized economy because, in the first instance, there are monopolistic profits in the intermediate goods sector $1/(1-\alpha-\beta) > 1$ that do not appear in the social optimum but do appear in $\Lambda_1 = [1/(1-\alpha-\beta)]\Lambda_3 > \Lambda_3$ and the decentralized equilibrium. Therefore, the social planner will choose a greater level of production of each intermediate product than the monopolist, resulting in greater value of intermediate products and greater H_A. Second, there is an intertemporal research spillover because private firms cannot internalize the future productivity enhancing effect of the development of new product varieties, and their investment in new research designs is below the social optimum. Thus, the denominator in the socially optimal growth rate replaces 1 with $(1 - \Lambda_3)$, and according to Romer (1990, p. S98) this "reflects the effect of correcting for the external effects associated with the production of new ideas." The two changes in the socially optimal rate of growth (the substitution of Λ_3 for Λ_1 and $(1 - \Lambda_3)$ for 1) "cause the socially optimal allocation of human capital in research to be higher, and this causes the socially optimal rate of growth to be higher."

4.6   Endogenous Models of Growth and Human Capital: Summary and Conclusions

The endogenous growth models outlined in the previous sections would seem to provide contradictory conclusions about the role of human capital in the growth process. The Lucas model in 4.21 and 4.22 allows for sustained growth in the steady state and the growth rate is dependent on the rate of human capital *accumulation*. In the Lucas approach, human capital is an input in the production function for final output along with physical capital and its contribution does not depend on the state of technology an economy finds itself in. A higher sustained growth rate is possible by diverting resources from final production to accumulating human capital or, equivalently, requires devoting more time to education.

In the Nelson and Phelps approach (as refined by Benhabib and Spiegel), human capital is not an input in the production of final output but rather contributes to raising the rate of productivity growth. There are two mechanisms by which human capital influences aggregate productivity growth: first, it allows a faster rate of innovation of domestic products/processes; and second it enables a country to adapt technologies developed elsewhere (by the technological leader) to domestic production conditions, achieve faster productivity growth, and ultimately converge to the productivity growth of the leader (catch-up effect). These processes occur simultaneously and depend on the current availability of the human capital stock. In this model, resources devoted to education (to build the stock of human capital) and research and development are complementary. It also follows that the current state of technology in an economy determines the marginal contribution of human capital: *ceteris paribus*, a given increase in the stock of human capital will contribute less to productivity growth in an economy closer to the technology frontier than a more distant one. Similarly, of two economies equally distant from the technological leader, the one with the larger human capital stock will innovate faster. In sum, the rate of productivity and output growth depends on the *stock* of human capital and not its rate of accumulation. The Benhabib–Spiegel model also suggests that through the catch-up effect, the impact of human capital on productivity growth may be nonlinear and, by consequence, it may be masked in empirical formulations that treat it linearly. This is an important point and we shall return to it in Chapter 5 (especially Section 5.3.2). Finally, the growth-enhancing effects of the level of human capital stock are also present in the Romer model in 4.44.

The basic question at hand is whether raising human capital contributes to raising the *level* of output or its *growth* rate. The two approaches provide a setting for contrasting hypotheses on the impact of human capital on economic growth, an issue that is ultimately empirical in nature and will be discussed in subsequent chapters. But the two approaches may not be as contradictory as would appear on the surface. Indeed, as pointed out by Aghion and Howitt (1998), they can be reconciled by considering the definition and nature of human capital. If human capital is conceived strictly in terms of the average education level of a country's population, then an increase can come about because of additional schooling at different levels: primary, secondary, or tertiary. It would seem more appropriate that primary-level schooling contributes directly to production and would approximate the concept envisaged by Lucas. On the other hand, higher-level education would more appropriately enhance innovation and adoption of technology, the contribution of human capital emphasized by Nelson and Phelps and Benhabib and Spiegel. We shall return to the issue of the definition and measurement of human capital and the different levels of education in subsequent chapters.

Notes

1. Therefore, as will be seen, the model generates sustained growth in the absence of technological progress.

· 2. The transversality conditions are $\lim_{t \to \infty} e^{-(\rho - g_L)t} v(t)k(t) = 0$ and $\lim_{t \to \infty} e^{-(\rho - g_L)t} \mu(t)h(t) = 0$.

3. Note that in the absence of spillover effects from aggregate human capital ($\gamma = 0$), the steady-state growth of h is equal to that of c and k.

4. Naturally, the conclusion is valid for $\gamma > 0$, otherwise the competitive and social equilibria are identical.

5. It can also be shown that a proportional rate of taxation would leave the steady-state rate of growth of the economy unchanged and equal to that in 4.22.

6. In the Rebelo formulation, an exogenously specified number of hours is consumed as leisure and that reduces the number of human capital available for human capital accumulation. It is ignored here because it does not have any appreciable effect on the main conclusions of the model (also see next note).

7. If we consider the number of leisure hours (Υ) in solving the model (see previous note), the growth rate of production becomes $g_y^* = \max \left\{ \frac{A_1^{\Gamma_1} A_2^{1-\Gamma_1} \Gamma_2^{\Gamma_1} (1-\Upsilon)^{1-\Gamma_1} - \delta_K - \rho}{\sigma}, -\delta_K \right\}$. In this case, the growth rate depends on the number of hours worked and "economies with hardworking agents will grow faster."

8. Rebelo was interested in demonstrating the long-run effects of a proportional rate of taxation. In this case, the physical–human capital ratio remains unchanged but the return to physical capital is lower. Unlike the Lucas model, however, the rate of growth of consumption is $\{(1-\text{tax rate})^{\Gamma_1} A_1^{\Gamma_1} A_2^{1-\Gamma_1} \Gamma_2^{\Gamma_1} - \delta_K - \rho\}/\sigma$.

9. The marginal product is $-\omega \Omega'(H) A(t) L(t) [\partial F/\partial(A(t) \cdot L(t))] = -\omega \Omega'(H) \cdot wage\ bill > 0$ for $\omega > 0$.

10. The model in 4.29 can be written as $\dot{A} = \Phi T_0 e^{\omega t} - \Phi A(t)$. The solution of this equation is $A(t) = e^{-\int \Phi dt}[B + \int \Phi T_0 e^{\omega t} e^{\int \Phi dt} dt] = e^{-(\Phi t + c_1)}[B + T_0 e^{c_1}(\Phi/(\Phi + \omega))e^{(\omega + \Phi)t}]$ where B is a constant and c_1 is the constant of integration from $\int \Phi dt = \Phi t + c_1$. By substituting for the initial conditions we have that $B = [A_0 - (\Phi/(\Phi + \omega))T_0]e^{c_1}$. Substituting for B in the above we arrive at 4.30.

11. The solution of the differential equation follows the procedure outlined in the previous note for the Nelson–Phelps model.

12. The final equality in 4.37 is obtained because in symmetric equilibrium each intermediate-goods firm produces the same amount of good i so that $x_i = x \, \forall i$.

13. The price elasticity of intermediate demand is $-1/(\alpha + \beta)$.

14. This property of the Romer model, the scale effect, has been criticized by subsequent contributions and "second generation" growth models do away with this property as it is clearly counter to empirical evidence.

5   Threshold Effects, Multiple Equilibria, and Nonlinearities in Human Capital and Economic Growth

5.1   Introduction

The models we outlined in the previous two chapters were primarily concerned with establishing the role of human capital in the process of economic growth. In contrast to the neoclassical model, endogenous models of human capital and economic growth emphasize the possibility of self-sustained growth even in the absence of exogenous technological progress. Endogenous models of human capital and growth differ on whether the level or the growth of human capital is the source of sustained growth. The overriding issue in these models is that sustained growth centers around the presence or, to be more precise, the absence of diminishing returns to the reproducible inputs and specifically, for this book, human capital. Several approaches were described in the previous two chapters that tackle the issue of diminishing returns. All these approaches, however, retain an important assumption, at least in their empirical implementation: the relationship between human capital and growth is linear, even though the channels through which human capital affects growth differ from model to model. In this chapter we discuss in detail the linearity assumption and raise the possibility that non-diminishing returns might lead to multiple steady-state equilibria or nonlinear dynamic behavior.

Drawing on the early post-war development literature on poverty traps, underdevelopment equilibria, and the necessity of a "big-push," several economists have put forward the notion that economies may find themselves in a low-growth equilibrium where a greater human capital input may not promote economic growth. Barring a structural change, economies may be unable to escape from a low- or zero-growth equilibrium. Such models allow the possibility of a nonlinear relationship between human capital and growth. In this section we review several contributions in this area as precursor to the nonlinear models of economic growth that we estimate empirically in the third part of this book. The models reviewed describe general nonlinearities in the relationship but do not provide specific nonlinear functional forms. The semiparametric econometric methods we introduce in Part III are capable of estimating general nonlinear functional forms and are well-suited to dealing with the possibility of general nonlinearities.

The nonlinear impact of human capital on economic growth typically stems from the presence of thresholds in the levels of human and physical capital. These thresholds arise as a result of physical or human capital accumulation that produces shifts in aggregate productivity. In this case one of the main premises of the neoclassical production function, concavity in its inputs, no longer holds. In the context of a single economy, physical and human capital accumulation by individual agents will confer external economies to other agents in the economy, increasing their productivity and producing in some sense "increasing returns" on an aggregate basis for these inputs. These spillover effects, if strong enough, will create nonconcavities in the aggregate production function and will result in multiple equilibria and two different levels of the capital stock will have the same marginal product. If the aggregate production function is no longer concave (diminishing returns no longer hold over its entire range),[1] different initial conditions will lead to different long-run steady states.[1] For a group of countries, thresholds through increasing returns will give rise to "clubs" where, within a club, behavior is homogeneous and members (countries that belong to this club) achieve conditional convergence, but behavior is heterogeneous between clubs. Therefore, thresholds are the main source of nonlinearity and, in our context, can be interpreted as synonymous with heterogeneity.

Nonlinearities, especially those that are created by the presence of threshold externalities in the production of human capital, can lead to multiple steady-state growth paths, including possible sustained low-growth (or low-development) "traps" where low investment in human capital (education) will discourage further human capital accumulation (acquisition of additional skills) and, hence, will result in a low-growth equilibrium state. Consequently, a group of countries with unequal initial educational endowments may never catch up to each other and the growth rate of the ones with higher endowments will diverge from those with lower initial endowments of human capital. The possibility of low-growth equilibria suggests a role for government policy in the educational sector to promote sustained high growth through policies (such as educational subsidies) that support skill acquisition and higher educational attainments. Examples of models with thresholds in human capital and low-growth equilibria are Azariadis and Drazen (1990) and Becker, Murphy, and Tamura (1990); we discuss these models in Section 5.2.

Another source of nonlinear behavior is inter-sector linkages, a concept first introduced by Hirschman (1958) and formalized and extended by Durlauf (1993). In this framework, linkages between domestic industries create sequential complementarities that, over time, affect aggregate behavior when they build up and create local spillovers that influence aggregate growth. At the same time, if the leading industrial sectors that are linked to all other domestic sectors through internal trade are very successful and take off, they help reduce production costs in the rest of the economy. This externality induces a sequence of local spillovers that push the economy, in the aggregate, to a higher sustained growth path.

From an empirical perspective, models of threshold externalities have led several researchers to postulate that the impact of human capital on growth is nonlinear. In empirical implementations Durlauf and Johnson (1995) divide countries into several groups based on the regression-tree methodology and show that the growth experience of the groups differs markedly. Importantly, for our purposes, the impact of education on growth depends on which group a country is a member of. While the Durlauf and Johnson methodology divides countries into a small number of distinct groups, Liu and Stengos (1999) and Kalaitzidakis et al. (2001) make use of recent nonparametric econometric techniques that allow the impact of human capital on growth to differ, not only by country, but also by time period. We take up this issue in Chapters 8 and 9.

A different interpretation to that of threshold-induced nonlinearities that classify countries into clubs holds that nonlinearities may not reflect different steady states but are simply differences in the timing as countries approach the steady state. According to this interpretation, all countries eventually move from stagnation to growth but this process will differ from country to country. When observed over a given time interval, these economies display differences in their growth characteristics that classify them as poor or rich because of their differing positions in the transition to a high-growth environment; examples of this approach are Galor and Weil (2000), Galor and Moav (2002), and Galor (2005).

Galor (2005) takes a very long-run view of development and argues that the transition from stagnation to growth is an inevitable outcome of the process of development. Differences across countries in the timing of the take-off from stagnation to growth have contributed to what he refers to as the "Great Divergence" and the emergence of convergence clubs. It is the recognition that the growth process is characterized by different stages of development that leads to the observed nonlinearities in the data, in which case these nonlinearities capture the differential pattern across economies in the timing of the take-off from stagnation to growth. Whatever the nature of the origins of nonlinearities, however, they are observable in the data and an empirical strategy that ignores them will run into mis-specification problems, an issue that is explored in the third part of this book.

In what follows we discuss in detail some of the main contributions to the literature on human capital and nonlinearities in growth. Threshold effects and low-growth equilibrium traps are taken up in Section 5.2. Section 5.3 discusses multiple growth regimes and the methodology of Durlauf and Johnson (1995) that has spearheaded the empirical literature in this area. This section also discusses the idea of Benhabib and Spiegel (2005) that the process of technological diffusion may result in multiple growth regimes. Both these approaches lend themselves to direct empirical tests of the nonlinear effect of human capital on growth and the empirical formulations derived from them are also discussed in Section 5.3. Finally, Section 5.4 discusses the model of Redding (1996) that focuses on the complementarity between human capital and research and development (R&D) and whose key result is also the possibility of a low-growth equilibrium trap.

5.2   Threshold Effects and Low-Growth Traps: Azariadis and Drazen (1990) and Becker, Murphy, and Tamura (1990)

Azariadis and Drazen (1990) observe that long-run growth rates exhibit persistent differences between more and less developed economies. Some low-income economies appear to be caught in low-growth equilibria and lag behind countries similar in terms of endowments. The neoclassical growth models cannot account for such persistent differences. While one can seek explanations for this stylized fact in noneconomic factors, Azariadis and Drazen propose that technological externalities with a "threshold" property are important in understanding how economies with very similar structures can exhibit marked growth experiences. They define a threshold as "radical differences in dynamic behavior arising from local variations in social returns to scale" (p. 508). The externalities they emphasize arise in the process of creating human capital. Specifically, once human capital attains a certain threshold level "aggregate production possibilities may expand especially rapidly" (p. 506). Economies that have not attained this threshold level may languish in a self-perpetuating low-growth equilibrium.

Azariadis and Drazen assume that economic agents live for two periods (young and old). The average quality of labor services ("human" capital) at time t is $h(t)$. This is the average for both young and old agents at time t; moreover, it is the endowment inherited by each young agent at t. Each young individual has access to (identical) technology that enables an increase in the supply of labor services at time period $t+1$ according to

$$h^i(t+1) = h(t) \cdot \varphi\{z^i(t), h(t)\}$$

EQUATION 5.1

where $h^i(t+1)$ is labor services supplied by individual i at $t+1$, $z^i(t) \in (0, 1)$ is the share of time invested by each agent in education and other activities aimed at increasing future labor supply, and $\varphi\{\cdot\}$ is the technology available to each agent;[2] the technology is assumed to be weakly increasing and concave in z. Individuals choose z to maximize the present value of income flows

$$(1 - z^i(t)) \cdot w(t) \cdot h(t) + [w(t+1) \cdot h(t) \cdot \varphi\{z^i(t), h(t)\}]/r^k(t)$$

where w is wage income (in efficiency units) and r^k the return to physical capital. Maximizing the present value of income with respect to z yields the familiar equality between the return to the two forms of capital (physical and human):

$$r^k(t) = [w(t+1)/w(t)] \cdot \varphi'\{z^i(t), h(t)\}$$

EQUATION 5.2

Assuming identical individuals 5.1 describes, not only the evolution of individual labor services, but also the average for the economy (without the i superscript). The economy's total labor supply at t (in effective units) is $\aleph(t) = [1 - z(t)]h(t) + h(t)$, an aggregate between young and old workers.

In period t firms produce by hiring labor services and having borrowed capital during period $t - 1$. Production is linear homogeneous and in its intensive form is given by $y(t) = A(t) f(k(t))$. Dynamic equilibrium satisfies several conditions (in addition to 5.1 and 5.2) as follows:

$$\aleph(t+1) \cdot k(t+1) = s\{r^k(t), w(t) \cdot h(t) \cdot (1 - z(t)), w(t+1) \cdot h(t+1)\}$$

EQUATION 5.3

$$r^k(t) = A(t+1)f'(k(t+1))$$

EQUATION 5.4

$$w(t) = A(t) \cdot [f(k(t)) - k(t)f'(k(t))]$$

EQUATION 5.5

$$A(t) = A\{k(t) \cdot h(t), h(t)\}$$

EQUATION 5.6

The condition in 5.3 describes the equality between investment at time t (assuming no initial capital stock investment is equal to the capital stock at $t + 1$) and saving. Saving is a function of the yield on physical capital and the income profile of the representative individual (when young and old). The conditions in 5.4 and 5.5 describe demand for the reproducible inputs and 5.6 allows human and physical capital to be "social" inputs (not controlled by individual producers).

Azariadis and Drazen show that the model exhibits a unique balanced growth path if utility is homothetic, A is constant and the $\varphi\{\cdot\}$ function in 5.1 is independent of h, or $\varphi\{z(t), h(t)\} = \overline{\varphi}\{z(t)\} \, \forall \, h(t)$. Therefore, introducing human capital into the neoclassical model in and of itself does not yield multiple equilibria. For human capital accumulation to allow for multiple equilibria and thus persistent differences in growth behavior across similar countries, there must be increasing returns to human capital accumulation: a higher *level* of human capital increases the *return* to accumulating human capital, or there are externalities in the technology for accumulating human capital. Threshold externalities in the model result from attaining a *critical mass* of human capital.

The possibility of externalities in human capital accumulation gives rise to two steady states: one corresponds to no investment in education; and one to positive investment. Therefore, economies that are quite similar in endowments may have quite different growth experiences. They assume that the training technology available to individual agents is described by the following function

$$\varphi\{z^i, h\} = 1 + \zeta(h) \cdot z^i \qquad \text{EQUATION } \mathbf{5.7}$$

where ζ is the private rate of return to investing in human capital (as in 4.9) that depends positively on h and approaches a maximum value $\widehat{\zeta}$ as $h \longrightarrow \infty$. This dependence plays an important role in the model. It introduces threshold externalities and the possibility of multiple paths of economic growth. Equations 5.1 and 5.2 are now replaced by:

$$h(t+1)/h(t) = 1 + \zeta(h(t)) \cdot z(t)$$

$$r^k(t) \begin{cases} = [w(t+1)/w(t)] \cdot \zeta(h(t)) & \text{if } z(t) > 0 \\ > [w(t+1)/w(t)] \cdot \zeta(h(t)) & \text{if } z(t) = 0 \end{cases}$$

In this case the model gives rise to the possibility of a low-development equilibrium for some $\zeta < \overline{\zeta}$ where no investment in training is undertaken in the economy ($z(t) = 0$ for all t after some finite time). A second solution is an interior equilibrium with positive investment along the equilibrium path where $\zeta(t) > \overline{\zeta}$ for all t. In this case a steady state (z^*, k^*) exists such that $z^* > 0$ and $f'(k^*) = \widehat{\zeta}$. The steady state is stable and corresponds to a growth rate of $\widehat{\zeta}z^*$. Azariadis and Drazen (1990, p. 515) summarize their argument succinctly: "multiple, locally stable balanced growth paths will exist in this model whenever individual yields on human capital rise with the average quality of labor." (as modeled in 5.7).

The model generates multiple interior equilibria if $\zeta(h)$ is a step function: $\zeta(h) = \zeta_1$ for $h < h^*$, $\zeta(h) = \zeta_2$ for $h > h^*$, and $\zeta_2 > \zeta_1$. If $\zeta(h) = \zeta_1 \forall h \in (0, h^*)$, the economy converges to a balanced growth path (z_1^*, k_1^*) provided $\zeta(h) = \zeta_1 > \overline{\zeta}$. If $h(t) > h^*$ the economy approaches a steady state where $\zeta(h) = \zeta_2$. An economy could go through multiple stages before reaching a "proper steady state." At each stage j labor quality

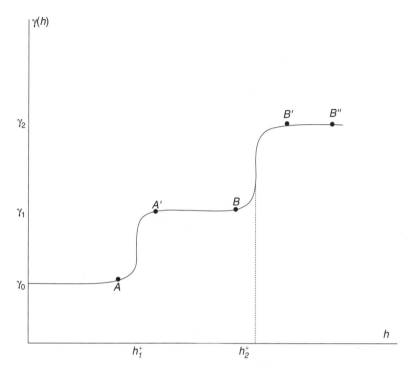

FIGURE **5.1** Threshold externalities in economic development
Source: Adapted from Azariadis and Drazen (1990), *Quarterly Journal of Economics,*
105, 501–526.

grows at the rate $\zeta_j z_j$ until it reaches the next threshold value, at which
point the economy grows very quickly and achieves a faster growth path.
The process comes to an end when "labor quality attains the highest possible value and the system settles down on the 'ultimate' stage of growth"
(p. 517). The step functional form generates the possibility of multiple
equilibria shown graphically in Figure 5.1.

Two economies on either side of the threshold, similar in terms of their
general characteristics (e.g., per capita income), would display different
dynamics so that economies to the right of the threshold (A' or B') invest
and accumulate human capital at a faster rate than those to the left (A
or B). Once two economies such as those at B' or B'' reach a particular
"stage" they converge to a balanced growth path. Azariadis and Drazen
argue that what distinguishes the two economies on either side of the
threshold is that the one to the right invests much more in human capital,

relative to its per capita income, than the one to the left. Given the level of a country's per capita income one can think of "a highly qualified labor force as a *necessary but not sufficient precondition for growth*" (p. 519, emphasis in the original).

Becker, Murphy, and Tamura (1990) also present a model of thresholds in human capital and growth that is characterized by two types of steady-state equilibria, one that is high and the other low development. Their model shares an important assumption with Azariadis and Drazen concerning returns to human capital. They assume that when an economy's stock of human capital is low there are increasing rather than diminishing returns to human capital accumulation. This is because the sector producing human capital uses skilled labor much more intensively than sectors producing consumption or capital goods. In the Becker–Murphy–Tamura model, fertility is determined endogenously and this leads to multiple steady states. The reason is that fertility determines the rate at which future consumption is discounted in an agent's intertemporal utility function. Higher fertility implies a higher discount rate that discourages future investment in both types of capital (physical and human). As a result, two possible steady-state equilibria arise: one with low levels of human capital, low return to investment in human capital, and low development; and the other with high levels and return to human capital and high development. A country's initial conditions will determine its growth experience, that is, the steady-state equilibrium to which it will converge. An economy may stagnate at the low-development equilibrium from which it is unable to escape, barring a major favorable shock.

5.3   Multiple Growth Regimes and Human Capital

5.3.1   *Human Capital and Thresholds: Durlauf and Johnson (1995)*

Durlauf and Johnson (1995) draw on the work of Azariadis and Drazen (1990) and Becker, Murphy, and Tamura (1990), as well as other work by Durlauf (1993) and Murphy, Schleifer, and Vishny (1989) that rationalizes the existence of multiple growth equilibria. They argue (p. 365) that "cross-country growth behaviour in these models is typically *nonlinear*, exhibiting multiple regimes" (our emphasis). Durlauf and Johnson base their study on the human capital augmented growth model of Section 3.2.3 but reject the assumption implicit in that model that all countries follow the same growth pattern. Instead they identify subsets of countries whose growth behavior follows the same linear model but differs significantly from each other.

Specifically, Durlauf and Johnson reject the assumption implicit in the aggregate production function of 3.17 that there exists a unique output elasticity of human capital that is constant across countries. In its stead they propose that the threshold that induces multiple equilibria (as described by the models in the previous section) is consistent with a production function that incorporates a (time-dependent) human capital threshold $\overline{H}(t)$. It follows that the aggregate production function can be written as[3]

$$Y_j(t) = K_j(t)^\alpha H_j(t)^{\beta_n} (A(t) \cdot L_j(t))^{1-\alpha-\beta_n}, \quad \begin{cases} \beta_n = \beta_1 & \text{if } H_j(t) < \overline{H}(t) \\ \beta_n = \beta_2 & \text{if } H_j(t) > \overline{H}(t) \end{cases}$$

where Y_j, K_j, H_j, and L_j represent aggregate output and inputs of country j. In their formulation countries belong to different groups depending on the value of their human capital relative to the threshold. The upshot of this proposition is that a separate human capital elasticity should be estimated for each country grouping. The groupings are determined endogenously based on regression-tree analysis. They find that the human capital elasticity differs significantly across groups. One way of interpreting this finding is as evidence consistent with the thresholds in the Azariadis–Drazen model. Therefore, it is possible to observe convergence to different steady states depending on a country's level of human capital, or the possibility of "convergence clubs." Economies go through various stages where the organization of production is constrained by human capital. When the human capital constraint is no longer binding "marginal increases in human capital will appear to have low marginal product, until an economy grows to the point where production is reorganized, creating a need for more human capital" (p. 376). Their evidence, however, is also consistent with a model where a unique steady state exists and where economies go through various stages on their way to this unique steady state.

In the second part of this book, we explore nonlinearities implied by human capital thresholds. Whereas the Durlauf–Johnson formulation allows for a single threshold, we consider the possibility of multiple thresholds as outlined by Azariadis and Drazen and shown in Figure 5.1. We use semiparametric estimation methods that allow the human capital elasticity to differ by country (and time period), not only between a (small) number of country groups.

5.3.2 Technology Diffusion and Multiple Growth Paths: Benhabib and Spiegel (2005)

The Benhabib–Spiegel (1994) model as described in 4.32 assigns a central role to human capital in technology diffusion. Implicit in 4.32 is a specific type of technological diffusion known as the *confined exponential diffusion process*. As explained in Section 4.4 if technology diffuses according to this process, followers will eventually experience a growth rate of technology that is equal to that of the leader (so the leader acts as a "locomotive") and, in the long run, each country's technology gap with the leader will be constant. Benhabib and Spiegel (2005) extend their original model to consider an alternative mechanism of technology diffusion. They argue that the alternative formulation is richer insofar as it allows not only catching up to the leader, implicit in the exponential diffusion process, but also the possibility that a country's growth rate falls progressively behind that of the leader. The latter notion is consistent with the existence of "convergence clubs" that was discussed in the previous section.

The alternative formulation replaces the exponential technological diffusion process in 4.32 with the logistic model of technology diffusion:

$$\frac{\dot{A}_i(t)}{A_i(t)} = \Psi(H_i) + \Phi(H_i)\left[\frac{A_l(t) - A_i(t)}{A_l(t)}\right]$$

$$= \Psi(H_i) + \Phi(H_i)\left(\frac{A_i(t)}{A_l(t)}\right)\left[\frac{A_l(0)e^{\Psi(H_l)t} - A_i(t)}{A_i(t)}\right] \qquad \text{EQUATION } \mathbf{5.8}$$

In comparison to 4.32 the logistic process introduces an additional term $A_i(t)/A_l(t)$, a term that determines the speed at which a country catches up to the leader. According to the logistic formulation the speed at which a country closes the technology gap (catch-up) depends, not only on a country's level of human capital, $\Phi(H_i)$, but also how far behind the leader a country finds itself, $A_i(t)/A_l(t)$. The latter "acts to dampen the rate of diffusion as the distance to the leader increases, reflecting perhaps the difficulty of adopting distant technologies" (p. 943). In general, the catch-up term in 5.8 will be slower when a country is either too close or too far from the leader and will be fastest at intermediate distances (hence the term *logistic diffusion*).

If technology diffuses according to the logistic model in 5.8, it is possible that some countries may find their productivity levels converging to the leader while others find that they diverge, that is, the possibility of convergence clubs arises. This can be seen by solving the model in 5.8:[4]

$$A_i(t) = \frac{A_l(t)}{\left\{ e^{-[\Phi(H_i)+\Psi(H_i)-\Psi(H_l)]t} \left(\frac{A_l(0)}{A_i(0)} - \frac{\Phi(H_i)}{[\Phi(H_i)+\Psi(H_i)-\Psi(H_l)]} \right) \right\}}$$
$$+ \left\{ \frac{\Phi(H_i)}{[\Phi(H_i)+\Psi(H_i)-\Psi(H_l)]} \right\}$$

Therefore, in the long run:[5]

$$\lim_{t \to \infty} \frac{A_i(t)}{A_l(t)} = \begin{cases} \frac{[\Phi(H_i)+\Psi(H_i)-\Psi(H_l)]}{\Phi(H_i)} & \text{if} \quad [\Phi(H_i)+\Psi(H_i)-\Psi(H_l)] > 0 \\ \frac{A_i(0)}{A_l(0)} & \text{if} \quad [\Phi(H_i)+\Psi(H_i)-\Psi(H_l)] = 0 \\ 0 & \text{if} \quad [\Phi(H_i)+\Psi(H_i)-\Psi(H_l)] < 0 \end{cases}$$

EQUATION **5.9**

There are several alternative long-run steady-state levels to which the technology of country i will converge that depend on the catch-up rate ($\Phi(H_i)$) and the difference in the endogenous rate between country i and the leader ($\Psi(H_i) - \Psi(H_l)$). If the follower's human capital level is sufficient so that the catch-up rate plus the endogenous rate of country i exceeds the endogenous rate of the leader or $[\Phi(H_i) + \Psi(H_i) - \Psi(H_l)] > 0$, then the productivity growth rate of country i will converge to that of the leader (the leader acts as a "locomotive") and the follower achieves a fraction $[\Phi(H_i) + \Psi(H_i) - \Psi(H_l)]/\Phi(H_i) < 1$ of the leader's productivity level. It could be, however, that the follower's human capital level is insufficient so that $[\Phi(H_i) + \Psi(H_i) - \Psi(H_l)] < 0$ and the rate of productivity growth of the follower diverges from the leader, with the follower falling continuously behind the leader.

Benhabib and Spiegel point out that the two diffusion processes identified in 4.32 and 5.8 are polar cases of a more general diffusion process. This general process can be described by defining country i's productivity level relative to that of the leader as $B_i(t) = A_i(t)/A_l(t)$, such that $\dot{B}_i(t)/B(t) = \dot{A}_i(t)/A(t) - \Psi(H_l)$. The general diffusion process can, therefore, be written as

$$\frac{\dot{B}(t)}{B(t)} = \frac{\Phi(H_i)}{b}(1 - B(t)^b) + \Psi(H_i) - \Psi(H_l) \quad \text{or}$$

$$\dot{B}(t) = \left(\frac{\Phi(H_i) + b[\Psi(H_i) - \Psi(H_l)]}{b}\right)B(t) - \frac{\Phi(H_i)}{b}B(t)^{b+1} \qquad \text{EQUATION 5.10}$$

where the diffusion parameter is $b \in [-1, 1]$. The process in 5.10 nests the exponential diffusion process in 4.32 and the logistic process in 5.8 as extreme cases when the diffusion parameter is $b = -1$ and $b = 1$, respectively. The general diffusion process is a Bernoulli equation and its solution is:[6]

$$B(t) = \left\{\frac{\left(1 + \frac{b[\Psi(H_i) - \Psi(H_l)]}{\Phi(H_i)}\right)}{1 + \left[\left(1 + \frac{b[\Psi(H_i) - \Psi(H_l)]}{\Phi(H_i)}\right)B(0)^{-b} - 1\right]e^{-\{\Phi(H_i) + b[\Psi(H_i) - \Psi(H_l)]\}t}}\right\}^{1/b}$$

EQUATION 5.11

Given that $\Psi(H_l) > \Psi(H_i)$, it follows that if either $\Phi(H_i) + b[\Psi(H_i) - \Psi(H_l)] > 0$ or $b < 0$, then:

$$\lim_{t \to \infty} B(t) = \left\{1 + \frac{b[\Psi(H_i) - \Psi(H_l)]}{\Phi(H_i)}\right\}^{1/b}$$

In this case the growth rate of the follower converges to that of the leader. On the other hand if $1 + \{b[\Psi(H_i) - \Psi(H_l)]/\Phi(H_i)\} < 0$ and $b > 0$, then $\lim_{t \to \infty} B(t) = 0$. In this case the growth rates of the leader and follower diverge with the follower falling progressively behind (and in the limit its productivity is driven to zero). In sum, the model yields the possibility of divergent or convergent growth paths that depend on the value of b and the human capital accumulated by the leader and followers.

In this general model of the diffusion process, the question of divergence or convergence is ultimately an empirical issue. Insights can be offered by estimating the empirical counterpart to 5.10. In order for this estimation to be tractable, Benhabib and Spiegel assume (as they did in their earlier model of Section 4.4) that the endogenous and catch-up functions are constant across time and take on the simple linear form $\Phi(\ln H_i) = c_{imit} \cdot \ln H_i$ and $\Psi(\ln H_i) = c_{innov} \cdot \ln H_i$. In this case the empirical counterpart to 5.10, in discrete time, is:

$$\ln\left(\frac{A_{i,\tau+\upsilon}}{A_{i,\tau}}\right) = \left(c_{innov} + \frac{c_{imit}}{b}\right)\ln H_i - \frac{c_{imit}}{b}\ln H_i\left(\frac{A_{i,\tau}}{A_{l,\tau}}\right)^b \qquad \text{EQUATION 5.12}$$

This empirical specification nests the logistic and exponential diffusion processes. The estimated values of the model's parameters, c_{imit}, c_{innov}, and b will determine whether a country's growth rate will converge or diverge from that of the leader. For $b \in (0, 1]$, the condition for convergence can be stated as:

$$c_{imit} \cdot \ln H_{i,\tau} + b(c_{innov} \cdot \ln H_{i,\tau} - c_{innov} \cdot \ln H_{l,\tau}) > 0 \quad \text{or}$$

$$1 + \frac{c_{imit}}{bc_{innov}} > \frac{\ln H_{l,\tau}}{\ln H_{i,\tau}} \qquad \text{EQUATION } \mathbf{5.13}$$

Countries whose initial (period τ) level of human capital is insufficient so that their relative human capital level $\ln H_{l,\tau} / \ln H_{i,\tau}$ exceeds $1 + [c_{imit}/(bc_{innov})]$ should find their growth rate diverging from that of the leader, with their productivity level declining over time toward zero. Given data on a country's growth rate of TFP ($\ln(A_{i,\tau+\upsilon}/A_{i,\tau})$), its human capital level ($\ln H_i$), and its relative (to the leader) TFP level ($A_{i,\tau}/A_{l,\tau}$) the empirical formulation in 5.12 can be estimated with nonlinear methods to yield estimates of the three parameters of interest. Thus, a researcher can gauge empirically, at a given point in time, how many countries would fall below the threshold level that determines convergence to the leader.

5.4   Low-Growth Traps and the Complementarity between Human Capital and R&D: Redding (1996)

Redding (1996) argues that investment by workers in training and education that increases their future human capital and investment by firms in research and development (R&D) that increases their future productivity are "strategic" complements. This paper attempts to marry the literature on human capital accumulation and endogenous growth (e.g., the Lucas model reviewed in Section 4.3) with the literature emphasizing investment in new product innovations (e.g., the Romer model reviewed in Section 4.5).[7] The paper models both worker and entrepreneurial behavior and argues that the fundamental complementarity between the two forms of investment gives rise to the possibility of multiple equilibria and also possible coexistence between a low-growth investment equilibrium and a high-growth investment equilibrium.

According to this model there exists a sequence of nonoverlapping generations (indexed by t) consisting of a continuum of workers (indexed by i) and entrepreneurs (indexed by e).[8] Workers live for two generations and maximize lifetime utility or $U(c_1(t), c_2(t)) = c_1(t) + [1/(1+\rho)]c_2(t)$, where c_1 and c_2 represent consumption of each worker when young and old, respectively. Following the suggestion by Lucas (1988), each worker inherits the average stock of human capital cumulated by the previous generation according to

$$h_1^i(t) = (1 - \delta_H) \cdot H_2(t-1) = (1 - \delta_H) \cdot \int_0^1 h_2^i(t-1)di \qquad \overline{\text{EQUATION } \mathbf{5.14}}$$

where $h_1^i(t)$ represents the human capital stock of each worker i of generation t, $H_2(t-1)$ is the aggregate human capital stock of generation $(t-1)$, and δ_H is the depreciation rate.

Much like Azariadis and Drazen (1990), young workers have training technology at their disposal that raises their productivity in the second period depending on the amount of time invested in training and education. Following the formulation in 5.1, the training technology is given by

$$h_2(t) = (1 + \zeta z^{(1-\eta)}) \cdot h_1(t) \qquad \text{EQUATION } \mathbf{5.15}$$

where $0 \leq z \leq 1$ is the amount of time devoted to education and training, $\zeta > 0$ characterizes education productivity, and $0 \leq (1-\eta) \leq 1$ is the elasticity of human capital with respect to time spent in education.[9]

Entrepreneurs produce final goods in each of the two periods according to a constant returns-to-scale production function

$$y_1^e(t) = A_1^e(t) \cdot h_1(t) \quad \text{and} \quad y_2^e(t) = A_2^e(t) \cdot h_2(t)$$

where $A^e(t)$ is the productivity of technology and $h(t)$ the human capital employed by each entrepreneur e in each of the two periods. Entrepreneurs invest in R&D in period 1 and the investment has an uncertain yield in period 2; the entrepreneur enjoys the return for only one period (at which point it spills over and becomes available to other entrepreneurs). Following the idea laid out in Romer (1990), when investing in R&D in period 1 entrepreneurs are faced with a fixed cost that is expressed as a proportion of period 1 output. If resources devoted to investment in R&D (expressed as a proportion of output and denoted by α_{RD}) exceed the fixed cost (denoted by $\bar{\alpha}_{RD}$), the investment is made in period 1 and its yield in period 2 is uncertain: there is a probability ψ of successful innovation. If investment in R&D in period 1 is less than the fixed cost

$\bar{\alpha}_{RD}$, the probability of successful innovation is zero. The probability that an entrepreneur innovates in period 1, denoted by π, is therefore equal to:

$$\pi = \begin{cases} 0 & \text{if} \quad \alpha_{RD} < \bar{\alpha}_{RD}, \quad 0 < \bar{\alpha}_{RD} < 1 \\ \psi & \text{if} \quad \alpha_{RD} \geq \bar{\alpha}_{RD}, \quad 0 < \psi < 1 \end{cases}$$

EQUATION 5.16

Finally, successful innovation in new technologies allow human capital to increase its productive services by $\kappa > 1$.

Workers and entrepreneurs are matched one to one so there is no unemployment in the model. Production surplus is divided between entrepreneurs and workers in proportions $(1 - \beta)$ and β, respectively. Wages per unit of human capital for firm i are therefore equal to

$$w_1^i(t) = \beta \cdot A_1^i(m)$$

EQUATION 5.17

where m denotes the number of innovations available to the entrepreneur and $A_1(t) = \kappa^m$. Workers form an expectation of the wage rate in period 2 that depends on the portion of entrepreneurs that innovate successfully, which is equal to π:[10]

$$E(w_2^i(m)) = \beta \cdot E(A_2^i(m)) = \beta \cdot [\pi\kappa + (1 - \pi)] \cdot A_1(m)$$

EQUATION 5.18

A representative worker maximizes intertemporal consumption subject to the constraint that it cannot exceed intertemporal wage earnings. Assuming no training in period 2, the intertemporal budget constraint is:

$$c_1(t) + \left(\frac{1}{1+\rho}\right) c_2(t) \leq w_1(t) \cdot (1-z) \cdot h_1(t) + \left(\frac{1}{1+\rho}\right) \cdot E(w_2^i(m)) \cdot h_2(t)$$

Under risk neutrality, intertemporal utility maximization amounts to a worker choosing the optimal allocation of time between production and education and training activities (z) to maximize (expected) lifetime income. Using the budget constraint and substituting from 5.14–5.18, with the exception of 5.16, the worker's maximization problem is:

$$\max_z \beta \cdot \left\{ (1-z) + \left(\frac{1}{1+\rho}\right) [\pi\kappa + (1-\pi)](1 + \zeta z^{(1-\eta)}) \right\}$$
$$\cdot A_1(m) \cdot (1 - \delta_H) \cdot H_2(t-1)$$

The first-order condition is:

$$z = \begin{cases} \left[\frac{(1-\eta)\zeta[\pi\kappa+(1-\pi)]}{1+\rho}\right]^{1/\eta} & \text{for} \quad 0 \le \left[\frac{(1-\eta)\zeta[\pi\kappa+(1-\pi)]}{1+\rho}\right]^{1/\eta} \le 1 \\ 1 & \text{for} \quad \left[\frac{(1-\eta)\zeta[\pi\kappa+(1-\pi)]}{1+\rho}\right]^{1/\eta} > 1 \end{cases}$$

EQUATION 5.19

It is evident that the time allocated to human capital formation does not depend on the initial capital with which the young are endowed, $H_2(t-1)$; it does depend, however, crucially on whether entrepreneurs invest resources greater than $\overline{\alpha}_{RD}$ to innovate or not. This can be seen by comparing 5.19 with 5.16:

$$z = \begin{cases} z_\psi \equiv \left[\frac{(1-\eta)\zeta[\psi\kappa+(1-\psi)]}{1+\rho}\right]^{1/\eta} & \text{if} \quad \alpha_{RD} \ge \overline{\alpha}_{RD} \\ z_0 \equiv \left[\frac{(1-\eta)\zeta}{1+\rho}\right]^{1/\eta} & \text{if} \quad \alpha_{RD} < \overline{\alpha}_{RD} \end{cases}$$

EQUATION 5.20

Entrepreneurs are faced with the decision whether to invest a fraction of output in R&D (α_{RD}) in order to innovate or not. The entrepreneur's expected return in the case of investment in R&D is

$$V(R) = (1-\beta) \cdot \left\{(1-\overline{\alpha}_{RD})(1-z) + \left(\frac{1}{1+\rho}\right)[\psi\kappa + (1-\psi)][1+\zeta z^{(1-\eta)}]\right\}$$
$$\cdot A_1(m) \cdot h_1(t)$$

EQUATION 5.21

where $[\psi\kappa + (1-\psi)] \cdot A_1(m)$ is the expected technology in period 2 were the entrepreneur to invest in R&D. In the case where the investment does not take place and the entrepreneur continues to use existing technology in period 2, the expected return is:

$$V(0) = (1-\beta) \cdot \left\{(1-z) \cdot A_1(m) \cdot h_1(t) + \left(\frac{1}{1+\rho}\right)\right.$$
$$\left.\cdot(1+\zeta z^{(1-\eta)}) \cdot A_1(m) \cdot h_1(t)\right\}$$

EQUATION 5.22

The conditions in 5.20–5.22 are central to the model's conclusions because they indicate the interrelated nature of the worker's and entrepreneur's decisions and the complementarity between human capital and R&D. In 5.20 a worker's decision to invest in human capital depends on the entrepreneur's R&D decision, and from 5.21 and 5.22 the entrepreneur's decision on R&D investment depends on the worker's human capital investment decision. In turn, the complementarity between these two decisions gives rise to the possibility of multiple equilibria.

There are two possible equilibria in the model. A "high-growth investment in human capital" equilibrium where firms decide to invest in R&D leads to higher expected return for human capital. In this case $\pi = \psi$ and from 5.20, $z = z_\psi$. For investment in R&D in 5.21 to yield a higher return than the no-investment decision in 5.22 it follows that:

$$\frac{\psi(\kappa - 1)}{1 + \rho} > \frac{\overline{\alpha}_{RD}(1 - z_\psi)}{1 + \zeta z_\psi^{(1-\eta)}}$$

In "low-growth investment in human capital" equilibrium entrepreneurs do not invest in R&D, and workers do not invest as much in human capital as in the high-growth equilibrium. In this case $\pi = 0$ and $z = z_0$ and it follows that:

$$\frac{\psi(\kappa - 1)}{1 + \rho} < \frac{\overline{\alpha}_{RD}(1 - z_0)}{1 + \zeta z_0^{(1-\eta)}}$$

Given model parameters the two inequalities may be satisfied simultaneously, which gives rise to the possibility of multiple equilibria when:

$$\frac{\overline{\alpha}_{RD}(1 - z_0)}{1 + \zeta z_0^{(1-\eta)}} > \frac{\psi(\kappa - 1)}{1 + \rho} > \frac{\overline{\alpha}_{RD}(1 - z_\psi)}{1 + \zeta z_\psi^{(1-\eta)}}$$

Multiple equilibria arise in the case of intermediate values of the fixed cost of R&D investment ($\overline{\alpha}_{RD}$) and the probability and size of innovations (ψ and κ). Multiple equilibria occur because of the complementarity between human capital and R&D and the fixed cost of R&D. Profitability of R&D requires that workers make investments in human capital sufficiently large to cover this fixed cost; this constitutes a threshold externality.

Corresponding to the two equilibria there is an economic growth rate that for the high-growth equilibrium is equal to

$$\ln[\psi\kappa + (1 - \psi)] + \ln(1 - \delta_H) \int_0^1 (1 + \zeta z_\psi^{(1-\eta)}) de$$

and for the low-growth equilibrium it is equal to:

$$\ln(1 - \delta_H) \int_0^1 (1 + \zeta z_0^{(1-\eta)}) de$$

Finally, Redding points out that changes in the values of parameters, such as education productivity (ζ) and the elasticity of human capital with respect to education time $(1 - \eta)$ may result in a jump in an economy's growth rate from, for example, the low-growth human capital investment to the high-growth human capital equilibrium. Much like the Azariadis–Drazen model, this may explain why two economies with similar human capital characteristics may display different growth experiences and give rise to the possibility of a nonlinear relationship between human capital accumulation and growth.[11]

5.5   Nonlinearities in the Human Capital Growth Relationship: Summary and Conclusions

The possibility of a nonlinear impact of human capital on economic growth stems from the presence of thresholds in the levels of human and physical capital. In the context of a single economy, physical and human capital accumulation by individual agents will confer external economies to other agents in the economy, increasing their productivity and producing in some sense "increasing returns" on an aggregate basis. These spillover effects, if strong enough, will create non-concavities in the aggregate production function and will result in multiple equilibria such that two different levels of the capital stock may have the same marginal product. If the aggregate production function is no longer concave, different initial conditions may lead to different long-run steady states. Nonlinearities, especially those that are created by the presence of threshold externalities in the production of human capital, can lead to multiple steady-state growth paths, including possible low-growth or low-development "traps" where low investment in human capital (education) discourages additional human capital accumulation (acquisition of additional skills) and hence results in a low-growth equilibrium state.

Galor (2005) recognizes that the growth process is characterized by different stages of development, a fact that leads to the nonlinearities observed in the growth experiences of different countries. In his view, these nonlinearities capture the differential timing of the take-off from stagnation to growth across economies. In this case nonlinearities are consistent with differences in the transition to a high-growth steady state that eventually characterizes all economies, an interpretation that differs from multiple steady-state equilibria.

Regardless of source, the possibility of nonlinearities in the growth process is, by itself, an important research strategy. From an empirical point of view, there is strong evidence for the presence of nonlinear effects in the human capital–growth relationship. Examining the empirical evidence on this relationship will be the object of investigation in the third part of this book. We will discuss ways to uncover possible nonlinear patterns from the available data without resorting to strong parametric assumptions about the nature of the underlying relationship.

Notes

1. The idea of increasing returns producing multiple equilibria has been explored in the context of noncompetitive market environments by Murphy, Shleifer, and Vishny (1989), in connection with coordination failures.

2. Equation 5.1 is similar to the condition for the rate of human capital accumulation in the Lucas model as specified in 4.9.

3. Durlauf and Johnson introduce thresholds for both physical and human capital in their specification. We confine our analysis to human capital thresholds because this formulation is closest in spirit to the Azariadis and Drazen analysis.

4. The logistic diffusion model can be solved by defining a variable $X_i(t) = 1/A_i(t)$. In this case equation 5.8 can be written as:

$$\dot{X}_i(t) = \frac{\Phi(H_i)}{A_l(t)} - [\Psi(H_i) + \Phi(H_i)]X_i(t)$$

This is in the form of equation 4.29 and the same procedure can be used determine $X_i(t)$, from which $A_i(t)$ can be obtained by the appropriate substitution.

5. In deriving 5.9 it should be noted that when $[\Phi(H_i) + \Psi(H_i) - \Psi(H_l)] = 0$ then $A_i(t) = A_i(0)\, e^{[\Phi(H_i) + \Psi(H_i)]t}$.

6. The solution to the Bernoulli equation is found by dividing 5.10 by $B(t)^{b+1}$ and defining a new variable $X_i(t) = B(t)^{-b}$ so that $\dot{X}(t) = -bB(t)^{-(b+1)}\dot{B}(t)$. Therefore, 5.10 can be written as:

$$\dot{X}(t) = \Phi(H_i) - [\Phi(H_i) + b\Psi(H_i) - b\Psi(H_l)]X(t)$$

This is in the form of 4.29 and can be solved for $X(t)$ using the previous methodology; the solution for $B(t)$ is found by appropriate substitution.

7. On the debate whether it is the level or the growth of human capital that determines the rate of growth (see the discussion in Section 4.6), Redding's model falls into the latter category.

8. The mass of workers and entrepreneurs are both normalized to equal unity.

9. The formulation in 5.15 has many similarities to elements of the Lucas and Rebelo formulations reviewed in Section 4.3.

10. There is a continuum of enterpreneurs of mass 1 and each innovates with Poisson probability π.

11. It is clear that the "high" equilibrium is superior to the "low" in terms of the rate of growth. Redding argues that a temporary subsidy to R&D may induce an economy to select the "high" equilibrium. The same equilibrium can be achieved via a subsidy to education and training. In this model the two policies (a subsidy to R&D investment or to education) are substitutable in terms of getting an economy out of the low-equilibrium trap, highlighting once more the complementarity between the two forms of investment.

III   *The Empirics of Human Capital and Economic Growth*

6 Empirical Studies on Human Capital and Economic Growth

6.1 Introduction

This chapter will survey empirical studies on the link between human capital and economic growth. In order to render this survey manageable and to provide a bridge to the empirical work in the remainder of this book, it will concentrate mainly on studies that use statistical data from a cross section of countries and employ econometric estimation techniques. Thus, it will not consider the many studies that focus solely on one or a handful of countries and/or studies that use calibration or simulation methods. The empirical literature on the human capital-growth nexus is differentiated by the specification of the estimating equation, the way human capital is defined, the time frame considered, and the countries included in the sample. The scheme for classifying empirical studies adopted in this chapter is mainly for convenience. In practice the various empirical approaches share several common features and there is overlap between them.

Both intuition and various theories of endogenous growth discussed in Chapters 3 and 4 point, a priori, toward a positive effect of human capital on economic growth. Empirical evidence on this issue has been mixed. To provide a flavor for the various approaches discussed in this chapter we note that early contributions proved quite successful in establishing a robust link between enrollment rates (the proportion of adults enrolled in secondary education) and growth of GDP per worker (for example, the influential work of Mankiw, Romer, and Weil discussed in Section 3.2.3). Subsequent studies have questioned this result by broadening the definition of human capital (to include education at different levels) as well as alternative measures of human capital. They find that human capital explains a much smaller proportion of the variation in income per capita than claimed earlier. The early studies tended to emphasize the use of enrollment rates (flows) for primary or secondary education. More recent studies have used stock measures, that is, mean years of schooling of a country's adult population. Some researchers have differentiated measures of human capital, not only by level of education (primary/secondary/tertiary), but also by sex. Studies that treat human capital as a direct input to the production function have shown that human capital accumulation exerts an insignificant or sometimes even negative effect on growth (Benhabib and Spiegel 1994; Pritchett 2001). These studies, however, have been criticized for their use of a log–log specification. The time dimension over which the growth rate is calculated has also come under scrutiny. Studies range from those utilizing pure cross-section data to those with panel data of varying frequencies. As the frequency over which growth rates are calculated increases (5-year changes vs. 10 or 20 years) the statistical evidence on human capital accumulation and growth tends to weaken: when the temporal dimension of human capital variables is incorporated into growth regressions, outcomes of either statistical insignificance or negative sign have surfaced. In sum, in his survey of the growth literature, Temple (1999) contrasts the success of micro-level studies that have established a positive effect of schooling on wages with the failures of studies at the macro level to do so.

In the following sections we provide a general framework to assess empirically the human capital-growth link and pay particular attention to empirical tests derived from some of the theoretical propositions of the models discussed in earlier chapters. We discuss briefly the estimates obtained from the parametric framework that characterize the linear approach. These results will provide the benchmark against which we will measure the nonlinear specifications presented in later chapters. On the whole, the empirical studies reviewed in Sections 6.2–6.5 use linear estimation techniques. Following up on the theoretical models discussed in Chapter 5 and the nonlinear approach that we will discuss in greater detail in subsequent chapters, in Section 6.6 we review threshold effects from an empirical perspective. These effects act as the main engine for the presence of nonlinearities both from a theoretical and empirical standpoint, even though they describe fairly simple forms of nonlinear behavior. Most attempts to tackle nonlinear behavior empirically are based on methods that are closely related to threshold effects and their smoother generalizations. Section 6.6 serves by way of introduction to the investigation of nonlinearities in Chapters 8 and 9.

6.2   A General Empirical Framework for Estimating the Contribution of Human Capital to Economic Growth

Most of the empirical literature on growth and human capital takes as a starting point the dual question of, first, whether the quantity of education (the empirical measure most closely associated with the concept of human capital) has a positive impact on the rate of economic growth and, second, the magnitude of any such effect. One of the most popular ways of modeling empirically the macroeconomic contribution of human capital emphasizes the process of convergence to the steady state. In its general form (e.g., Barro 1991), it claims that the deviation of the rate of growth from its steady-state level depends on the distance between the initial and steady-state level of output per worker or

$$(1/v)(\ln y_{i,\tau+v} - \ln y_{i,\tau}) = g_A - a_1(\ln y_{i,\tau} - \ln y_i^*) + \epsilon_{i,\tau} \qquad \text{EQUATION } \mathbf{6.1}$$

where $(\ln y_{i,\tau+v} - \ln y_{i,\tau})$ is the growth of output per worker of country i between period τ and $\tau + v$, g_A is the steady-state growth rate, $y_{i,\tau}$ is initial and y_i^* is steady-state level of output per worker, a_1 is a measure of the rate of convergence, and $\epsilon_{i,\tau}$ is a random error term that obeys standard assumptions. The steady-state level of output per worker, y_i^*, depends on the level of human capital per worker (h_i) and a vector of variables (Z_i) that capture differences in the economic, institutional, and political environments across countries. With this in mind, the estimable form of the cross-country growth-regression approach becomes:

$$(1/v)(\ln y_{i,\tau+v} - \ln y_{i,\tau}) = g_A - a_1(\ln y_{i,\tau}) + a_2 h_{i,\tau} + a_3 Z_{i,\tau} + \epsilon_{i,\tau} \qquad \text{EQUATION } \mathbf{6.2}$$

Our interest is in the estimate of a_2.

Topel (1999) and Krueger and Lindahl (2001) point out that interpreting the estimate of a_2 is not straightforward. It is consistent with various hypotheses about the role of human capital in the process of economic growth. As Barro (1991) points out, human capital is a direct determinant of the steady-state level of output per worker. Therefore, given the current (initial) level of output per worker, a higher level of human capital also raises the distance from steady state and convergence would thus imply higher growth, or $a_2 > 0$. But a positive value for a_2 is also consistent (observationally equivalent) with the notion that human capital facilitates technological progress through innovation and imitation (see Section 4.4). According to this interpretation a_2 should be positive irrespective of a country's distance from the steady state; indeed a_2 ought to be positive even if a country finds itself at the steady state. While both of these interpretations hypothesize $a_2 > 0$, it may also be the case that $a_2 < 0$. This may come about if low values of schooling indicate greater growth opportunities for a country through "catching up," as Topel suggests, or may reflect a decrease in the return to schooling over time, as argued by Krueger and Lindahl (see discussion later in this section).

An alternative approach is the classical growth accounting methodology according to which the contribution of inputs to output growth is measured as a weighted (by output shares) average of input growth and the growth of TFP is computed as a residual from the growth of output. In its basic form, growth accounting assumes a Cobb–Douglas production function, $Y(t) = A(t)K(t)^\alpha H(t)^\gamma$. The stock of human capital $H(t)$ is the product of human capital per worker and the number of workers, $H(t) = L(t) \cdot h(t)$. Log-differencing this production function, the growth accounting framework implies:

$$(\ln Y_{\tau+\upsilon} - \ln Y_\tau) = (\ln A_{\tau+\upsilon} - \ln A_\tau) + \alpha(\ln K_{\tau+\upsilon} - \ln K_\tau)$$

$$+ \gamma(\ln L_{\tau+\upsilon} - \ln L_\tau) + \gamma(\ln h_{\tau+\upsilon} - \ln h_\tau) \qquad \text{EQUATION } \mathbf{6.3}$$

With data on the growth of output and the growth of inputs as well as the shares of physical (α) and human capital (γ) in aggregate output, the growth of TFP or $(\ln A_{\tau+\upsilon} - \ln A_\tau)$ is obtained as a residual.

A simplified version of the growth accounting methodology assumes constant returns to scale so that $\alpha + \gamma = 1$. In this case the intensive form of the growth accounting framework implies

$$(\ln y_{\tau+\upsilon} - \ln y_\tau) = (\ln A_{\tau+\upsilon} - \ln A_\tau) + \alpha(\ln k_{\tau+\upsilon} - \ln k_\tau)$$

$$+ (1-\alpha)(\ln h_{\tau+\upsilon} - \ln h_\tau) \qquad \text{EQUATION } \mathbf{6.4}$$

where, as before, lowercase letters denote quantities per worker. The contribution of inputs is calculated as their weighted growth rates and, because the weights sum to one, it requires only an estimate of the share of physical capital. Topel (1999, p. 2958) criticizes the growth accounting approach on three grounds: (1) it is not informative about the role of human capital in driving the process of economic growth (it is an accounting identity); (2) it does not investigate how the working of the labor market generates human capital accumulation; and (3) the human capital input may be poorly measured and mean years of schooling may not reflect the quality of human capital accumulated. The third is a general criticism of the empirical literature on human capital and growth and we return to it in Section 6.5.2.

The growth accounting methodology requires measures of output, inputs, and a numerical value for the share of various inputs to calculate arithmetically the growth of TFP. An alternative approach is to estimate empirically input shares rather than to assume a value for them. According to this approach, the two estimable models corresponding to the general and intensive forms in 6.3 and 6.4, respectively, are

$$(\ln Y_{i,\tau+\upsilon} - \ln Y_{i,\tau}) = (\ln A_{i,\tau+\upsilon} - \ln A_{i,\tau}) + a_1(\ln K_{i,\tau+\upsilon} - \ln K_{i,\tau})$$

$$+ a_2(\ln L_{i,\tau+\upsilon} - \ln L_{i,\tau}) + a_3(\ln h_{i,\tau+\upsilon} - \ln h_{i,\tau})$$

$$+ (\ln \epsilon_{i,\tau+\upsilon} - \ln \epsilon_{i,\tau}) \qquad \text{EQUATION } \mathbf{6.5}$$

$$(\ln y_{i,\tau+\upsilon} - \ln y_{i,\tau}) = (\ln A_{i,\tau+\upsilon} - \ln A_{i,\tau}) + b_1(\ln k_{i,\tau+\upsilon} - \ln k_{i,\tau})$$

$$+ b_2(\ln h_{i,\tau+\upsilon} - \ln h_{i,\tau}) + (\ln \epsilon_{i,\tau+\upsilon} - \ln \epsilon_{i,\tau}) \qquad \text{EQUATION } \mathbf{6.6}$$

where the subscript i indicates country and a_1, a_2, a_3, b_1, and b_2 are parameters to be estimated. With data on the growth of inputs and output, estimation of 6.5 or 6.6 provides estimates of input shares. The intensive form can be estimated in the unrestricted form of 6.6 or by imposing the restriction $b_1 + b_2 = 1$.

In the growth accounting approach, human capital per worker (h) is most commonly measured by the mean years of schooling of a country's working age population (either above 15 or 25 years of age). Some authors have argued that, rather than identifying human capital per worker with the number of years of schooling, human capital should be represented by an exponential function of mean years of schooling. This is more appropriate because it corresponds more closely to estimates of the return to schooling from micro studies. These studies estimate the return to an additional year of schooling in terms of its contribution to raising individual wages and the framework is known as *Mincerian regressions* (see the discussion in connection with equation 6.12). The logarithm of an individual's wages is regressed on years of education and other control characteristics (such as experience) and the estimated coefficient for years of schooling represents the return to an additional year. If we interpret human capital per worker as an aggregate form of earnings from human capital accumulation, according to this line of reasoning human capital becomes an exponential function of mean years of schooling, or $h = \exp^{f(EDUC)}$, where $EDUC$ measures mean years of schooling of a country's adult population and $f(\cdot)$ is a general function. In parallel with the micro treatment of education and wages that assumes $f\{\cdot\}$ to be a linear function, human capital per worker can be written in log–linear form as

$$\ln h_{i,\tau} = \beta_i + \beta_1 EDUC_{i,\tau} \hspace{4cm} \text{EQUATION } \mathbf{6.7}$$

where β_i is the level of human capital workers in country i are endowed with (not cumulated through schooling) and β_1 is the return to schooling. According to 6.7, an additional year of education increases human capital by the same percentage (β_1) irrespective of the country's level of schooling.[1]

Combining the formulation of human capital in 6.7 with the general production function $Y(t) = A(t)K(t)^\alpha H(t)^\gamma$, this approach to growth accounting yields an estimable model in general form

$$(\ln Y_{i,\tau+\upsilon} - \ln Y_{i,\tau}) = (\ln A_{i,\tau+\upsilon} - \ln A_{i,\tau}) + a_1(\ln K_{i,\tau+\upsilon} - \ln K_{i,\tau})$$

$$+ a_2(\ln L_{i,\tau+\upsilon} - \ln L_{i,\tau}) + a_3(EDUC_{i,\tau+\upsilon} - EDUC_{i,\tau})$$

$$+ (\ln \epsilon_{i,\tau+\upsilon} - \ln \epsilon_{i,\tau}) \hspace{3cm} \text{EQUATION } \mathbf{6.8}$$

or, assuming constant returns, in intensive form:[2]

$$(\ln y_{i,\tau+\upsilon} - \ln y_{i,\tau}) = (\ln A_{i,\tau+\upsilon} - \ln A_{i,\tau}) + b_1(\ln k_{i,\tau+\upsilon} - \ln k_{i,\tau})$$

$$+b_2(EDUC_{i,\tau+\upsilon} - EDUC_{i,\tau}) + (\ln \epsilon_{i,\tau+\upsilon} - \ln \epsilon_{i,\tau}) \qquad \text{EQUATION } \textbf{6.9}$$

The estimated coefficient of schooling (b_2) can be compared to the micro-oriented estimates of the return to schooling (β_1 in 6.7) if it is divided by the share of the human capital stock in aggregate output (γ).

An alternative way of assessing empirically the role of human capital, also within the general confines of the growth accounting methodology, is as an input to technological progress rather than as a direct input into aggregate production. According to this approach, aggregate production depends on inputs of labor (number of workers) and physical capital described by the production function $Y(t) = A(t)K(t)^\alpha L(t)^\beta$. Technological progress is a function of human capital per worker or $\dot{A}(t)/A(t) = f\{h(t)\}$. In this case the estimable model is:

$$(\ln Y_{i,\tau+\upsilon} - \ln Y_{i,\tau}) = f\{h_i(\tau)\} + \alpha(\ln K_{i,\tau+\upsilon} - \ln K_{i,\tau})$$

$$+\beta(\ln L_{i,\tau+\upsilon} - \ln L_{i,\tau}) + (\ln \epsilon_{i,\tau+\upsilon} - \ln \epsilon_{i,\tau}) \qquad \text{EQUATION } \textbf{6.10}$$

Alternatively, assuming constant returns to scale in physical capital and labor, the intensive form of the model is

$$(\ln y_{i,\tau+\upsilon} - \ln y_{i,\tau}) = f\{h_i(\tau)\} + \alpha(\ln k_{i,\tau+\upsilon} - \ln k_{i,\tau})$$

$$+(\ln \epsilon_{i,\tau+\upsilon} - \ln \epsilon_{i,\tau}) \qquad \text{EQUATION } \textbf{6.11}$$

For estimation purposes, $f(\cdot)$ is frequently assumed to be linear in h (see discussion in Section 6.4).

Topel (1999) and Krueger and Lindahl (2001) argued that measurement error in mean years of schooling exacerbates estimation bias in growth accounting models. Topel (1999) showed that any serial correlation in schooling will increase the noise-to-signal ratio conveyed when the change in schooling is the explanatory variable in regressions as formulated in 6.8 or 6.9 (as long as serial correlation in the true measure of schooling exceeds the serial correlation of the error term in measuring schooling). Any bias from measurement error in schooling is magnified by the use of differenced data in growth accounting regressions. He suggests that a trade-off exists between growth data at higher frequency (for example, 5- as opposed to 20-year growth rates) that increase sample size but exacerbate bias from measurement error.

In order to demonstrate this point, Topel estimated 6.9 with growth rates computed over 5-, 10-, 15-, and 20-year intervals. His estimation procedure invoked one of the properties of the endogenous growth models described in Chapter 4: along the balanced growth path the capital–output ratio is constant. With this in mind, the growth accounting formulation implies that output per worker depends only on human capital per worker, the technology parameter, and the constant (across countries) capital–output ratio.[3] Combining this insight with the formulation of human capital in 6.7, one need not consider the capital–labor ratio as an explanatory variable when estimating 6.9; the only explanatory variable is mean years of schooling.

Topel estimated such a version of 6.9, first, without country-fixed effects. He found that the coefficient of (change in) schooling increased in magnitude as the frequency of observations decreased from 5 to 20 years. While his first version of 6.9 included only the change in level of schooling as explanatory variable, in alternative specifications he included the level of schooling and initial output per worker (to check convergence) as additional explanatory variables. The schooling level coefficient was significant and its magnitude implied an increased growth rate of 0.4 percent per additional year of education (the same regardless of frequency of data). In subsequent models he introduced an interaction term between changes in schooling and initial output per worker, suggesting a nonlinear impact of schooling on growth that depends on the level of development. For 5-year growth rates he found evidence that the impact of human capital was higher at lower levels of development and dampens as countries become richer; as the frequency of observations decreased so did the dampening effect and became insignificant at 20-year growth intervals. Topel's results remained robust when country-fixed effects were added (with only 5- and 10-year growth rates to allow for sufficient observations). As indicated earlier, such effects could account for unobservable effects (experience, etc.). The largest effect for schooling (in magnitude) was obtained with 10-year data where an additional year of education increased growth by approximately 9 percent. Topel produced a range of estimates of the growth effect of an additional year of schooling and concluded that the low end of his range of estimates was consistent with micro estimates of the return to education, and the higher end of his range was consistent with the presence of positive externalities to schooling.

Krueger and Lindahl (2001) derive what they term the *macro-growth equation* for human capital from the micro-oriented Mincerian regressions. These regressions relate an individual's years of education to wages according to[4]

$$\ln w_{ji,\tau} = \beta_{0i,\tau} + \beta_{1i,\tau} EDUC_{ji,\tau} + \epsilon_{ji,\tau} \qquad \text{EQUATION } \mathbf{6.12}$$

where $w_{ji,\tau}$ is individual's j wage rate in country i in time period τ and $EDUC_{ji,\tau}$ is the individual's years of schooling. Aggregating across individuals yields

$$\ln \check{Y}_{i,\tau} = \beta_{0i,\tau} + \beta_{1i,\tau} EDUC_{i,\tau} + \epsilon_{i,\tau} \qquad \text{EQUATION } \mathbf{6.13}$$

where $\check{Y}_{i,\tau}$ represents the geometric mean wage of country i in time period τ and $EDUC_{i,\tau}$ is mean years of schooling of country i in time period τ. The aggregate wage equation in 6.13 can be thought of as the macro counterpart to the Mincerian wage regression model in 6.12, or the *Macro-Mincer* equation as it has been termed. Time differencing 6.13 yields:

$$(\ln \check{Y}_{i,\tau+\upsilon} - \ln \check{Y}_{i,\tau}) = (\beta_{0i,\tau+\upsilon} - \beta_{0i,\tau}) + \beta_{1i,\tau+\upsilon} EDUC_{i,\tau+\upsilon}$$

$$-\beta_{1i,\tau} EDUC_{i,\tau} + (\epsilon_{i,\tau+\upsilon} - \epsilon_{i,\tau}) \qquad \text{EQUATION } \mathbf{6.14}$$

There are two possibilities concerning the return of an additional year of schooling. First, the rate of return is constant over time ($\beta_{1i,\tau+\upsilon} = \beta_{1i,\tau} = \beta_{1i}$) in which case the Macro-Mincer equation becomes:

$$(\ln \check{Y}_{i,\tau+\upsilon} - \ln \check{Y}_{i,\tau}) = (\beta_{0i,\tau+\upsilon} - \beta_{0i,\tau}) + \beta_{1i}(EDUC_{i,\tau+\upsilon} - EDUC_{i,\tau})$$

$$+(\epsilon_{i,\tau+\upsilon} - \epsilon_{i,\tau})$$

In this formulation the return to an additional year of schooling is allowed to vary between countries ($\beta_{1,i}$). If it is assumed constant, this formulation resembles the growth accounting specification in 6.9. The second possibility is that the return to an additional year of schooling varies over time.

In this case the Macro-Mincer equation can be written as

$$(\ln \check{Y}_{i,\tau+\upsilon} - \ln \check{Y}_{i,\tau})$$

$$= (\beta_{0i,\tau+\upsilon} - \beta_{0i,\tau}) + \beta_{1i,\tau+\upsilon}(EDUC_{i,\tau+\upsilon} - EDUC_{i,\tau})$$

$$+ (\beta_{1i,\tau+\upsilon} - \beta_{1i,\tau})EDUC_{i,\tau} + (\epsilon_{i,\tau+\upsilon} - \epsilon_{i,\tau}) \qquad \text{EQUATION } \mathbf{6.15}$$

where $(\beta_{1i,\tau+\upsilon} - \beta_{1i,\tau})$ is the change over time in the return to an additional year of schooling. It should be noted that in formulation 6.15, both the initial *level* and the *change* in mean years of schooling appear as explanatory variables. If the return to schooling decreases over time $(\beta_{1i,\tau+\upsilon} - \beta_{1i,\tau} < 0)$, then the estimate of the coefficient on the initial level of schooling should be negative.

Krueger and Lindahl compared and contrasted the cross-country growth regression approach in 6.2 with the Macro-Mincer equation in 6.15. First, it is evident that the dependent variable in the two approaches is different. As they point out, the difference between the two would not be important if income follows a log–normal distribution with constant variance over time and the share of labor in income were also constant over time.[5] In this case the macro growth regressions are consistent with the micro framework. Second, and more importantly from an estimation perspective, the growth regression approach includes only the initial level of schooling but excludes the change in schooling, a variable highlighted by the Macro-Mincer equation. Krueger and Lindahl argued, as did Topel, that measurement error in human capital (years of schooling) implies that data on changes in schooling contain little signal questioning the findings from growth accounting regressions (e.g., 6.5 or 6.6) that include only changes in schooling (see the discussion of Benhabib and Spiegel in Section 6.4). Inclusion of both the initial level and change in schooling, as formulated by a Macro-Mincer equation, implies that measurement error would not lead to "spurious association between the level of schooling and growth, conditional on the change in schooling" (p. 1102).[6]

In empirical estimation Krueger and Lindahl first repeated the standard growth accounting estimation of 6.5 (with human capital measured by mean years of schooling). They found the same result as other researchers (e.g., Benhabib and Spiegel 1994): the estimate of α_3 was insignificant. They, however, criticized the log–log functional form of this specification and, along with Topel, proposed a log–linear specification (6.8 or 6.9) that is more in line with a Mincerian wage equation. They estimated this specification with cross-section data including the change in schooling and the initial level of schooling as well as initial output per capita as explanatory variables. Their results showed that both the level and change in schooling were positive and significant determinants of economic growth.[7]

Subsequently, Krueger and Lindahl estimated models with panel data over varying time intervals (5-, 10-, and 20-year changes). The dependent variable was the growth of GDP per capita (as in 6.9) and explanatory variables were the change in schooling, the initial level of schooling, initial output per worker and, in some specifications, an interaction term between initial output and change in schooling. The specifications did not control for physical capital accumulation (to avoid possible endogeneity between physical capital accumulation and growth). They reached the same conclusions as Topel: the frequency over which growth rates are measured was important and that the estimated coefficient on change in schooling increased in magnitude (and became statistically significant) with lower frequency data. They attributed this to the higher ratio of noise to signal in high (five-year) frequency data and also the possibility of reverse causation between economic growth and education (see Bils and Klenow 2000).

Krueger and Lindahl also estimated the model in 6.9 with cross-section data controlling for physical capital accumulation and with both the initial level and change in schooling as explanatory variables. Several specifications were estimated according to whether initial GDP per capita was included or excluded and whether initial physical capital per worker was included or excluded. In some specifications the share of capital was restricted to one-third ($b_1 = 0.35$ in 6.9). The estimated coefficient for growth in the physical capital–worker ratio was positive and highly significant (but about twice in magnitude than the conventional assumption of one-third). Moreover, both the change in schooling and the initial level of schooling were positively (and significantly) associated with economic growth. The estimated coefficient for the change in schooling was similar to estimates from Mincerian wage regressions; this was especially the case when the constraint $b_1 = 0.35$ was imposed. The model was also estimated with instrumental variables (using an alternative data series for schooling as the instrument) to allow for endogeneity between schooling and growth: the estimated coefficients for the level and change in schooling were insignificant in this case.

Finally, Krueger and Lindahl (2001) scrutinized two assumptions of the macro-growth literature: (1) the impact of schooling on growth is the same across countries; and (2) the linearity between schooling and growth. They suggested that the impact of schooling on growth differs across countries because of differences in labor market institutions and differences in the quality of education that make for a different speed with which new technologies are absorbed across countries (see discussion in Sections 6.3 and 6.4). They estimated a growth specification with per capita growth (over 5- and 10-year periods) as the dependent variable and the initial level of schooling as explanatory variable with a different slope coefficient for schooling for each country. The hypothesis of equality of schooling coefficients across countries was rejected. The average slope coefficient for (total) mean years of schooling was negative (but statistically insignificant). In addition they used male secondary and higher years of schooling in place of total years of schooling. When the slope coefficient was restricted to be equal across countries the estimated coefficient on schooling was positive and significant; when the slope coefficient was left unrestricted the average slope coefficient was negative and significant. They summed up their results as follows: "education has a heterogenous effect on economic growth across countries" (p. 1129).

Concerning the linearity assumption, they divided countries into three groups based on their initial level of education and concluded that (p. 1130) *"education was statistically significantly and positively associated with subsequent growth only for the countries with the lowest level of education"* (italics in original). For the other two groups of countries, schooling was either unrelated or negatively related with growth. They also estimated a quadratic specification between schooling and growth and found an inverted-U relationship between them (with a peak at 7.5 years of schooling). They concluded that "Both of these extensions to the standard growth specification suggest that the constrained linear specification estimated in the literature should be viewed with caution" (p. 1127). In Chapters 8 and 9 we take a close look at the linearity and equality-of-coefficients assumptions through the application of nonparametric estimation techniques to the human capital-growth relationship.

6.3   Cross-Country Growth Regressions and Human Capital

The cross-country growth regression approach centers on explaining economic growth as a function of the initial level of output per worker and variables that determine an economy's steady-state level of output per worker (e.g., Barro 1997; Barro and Sala-i-Martin 2004). Steady-state level of output per worker depends on country characteristics over which economic policy may or may not have an influence. For the purposes of this book, one important characteristic is a country's level of human capital. Most empirical specifications do not rely on deriving a formal expression for the steady-state level of output per worker but take as a starting point the general specification in 6.2 (e.g., Barro 2001). The Mankiw, Romer, and Weil (1992) framework, however, showed the steady-state level of output per worker depends on investment in physical capital, human capital, and the rate of population growth (see Section 3.2.3).

Barro (2001) estimated specification 6.2 with panel data and measured growth rates at 10-year intervals for the 1965–1995 period. He found that mean years of schooling at the secondary and higher level for males was a significant determinant of growth, but female secondary and higher schooling and male schooling at the primary level were insignificant determinants. Female schooling at the primary level was an insignificant determinant when fertility was held constant. Conversely, when fertility was excluded from the model, the impact of female primary schooling was positive and significant, leading him to conclude that the impact of primary female education on growth is mainly by way of reducing fertility. Barro and Sala-i-Martin (2004) found that mean years of schooling at the primary level for both males and females was insignificant as a growth determinant. On the other hand, the estimate for upper-level (secondary plus tertiary) mean years of schooling for males was positive and significant and that for upper-level schooling for females was negative but insignificant.

The Mankiw, Romer, and Weil (MRW) framework provides two estimable equations for the steady-state level of output per worker (described by 3.21 and 3.22) and two equations for the rate of growth (3.25 and 3.27). Estimation of 3.21 or 3.22 and 3.26 or 3.27 depends on whether the available data on human capital correspond more closely to investment and the rate of accumulation (s_H) or the (steady-state) stock of human capital ($\widetilde{h}^*$). The early literature used data on rates of enrollment that corresponded more closely to the rate of accumulation; subsequent contributions have used estimates of the number of years of schooling of the working-age population, a measure that corresponds more closely to the stock of human capital. In order to render the different models estimable, MRW assumed that variation in initial technology levels across countries ($A_i(0)$) arises from random country-specific shocks and, therefore, the expected technology level is equal across countries. In this case $A_i(0) = \exp^{c_A + \epsilon_i}$, where c_A is the constant (across countries) technology level and ϵ_i is a country-specific random shock. The technology level of country i at time t, $A_i(t)$, is therefore described by $A_i(t) = A_i(0) \exp^{g_A t} = \exp^{c_A + \epsilon_i} \exp^{g_A t}$, so that $\ln A_i(t) = c_A + g_A t + \epsilon_i$.

MRW estimated the determinants of the steady-state level of output per worker with cross-section data for 1985 with three alternative samples that included progressively fewer observations by excluding countries with poor data quality and non-OECD economies. The determinants of the steady state included the ratio of investment to GDP (a measure of s_K), growth of the labor force (g_L), and the secondary enrollment rate adjusted for the proportion of the population that is of secondary school age (s_H).[8] They claim their measure of human capital proxies the rate of investment (s_H) and thus they estimated specification 3.21. Initially, however, they estimated specification 3.9 that ignores human capital. The results were unsatisfactory insofar as the estimate, as the share of physical capital was twice the expected value of one-third. On the other hand, estimation of the human-capital augmented model in 3.21 yielded a value for the share of physical capital much closer to the expected value (one-third) and also a value for the share of human capital that was close to one-third.

In addition to estimating the determinants of the steady-state level of output per worker, MRW also estimated the transition dynamics to the steady state as formulated in 3.26. Their data were cross section and the growth rate was calculated as the average between 1960 and 1985. They found the secondary enrollment ratio was a positive and significant determinant of growth and the estimated speed of convergence was 0.014, 0.018, and 0.020 (for the three alternative samples), values consistent with the predictions from the augmented Solow–Swan model.[9] The implied share of physical capital was in the range 0.38–0.48 and the implied share of human capital was 0.23.

Bernanke and Gürkaynak (2001) reestimated the MRW framework in 3.21 with a different version of the Penn World Tables and extended the estimation period from 1985 to 1990 and 1995. Their results were less supportive of the augmented Solow–Swan model than MRW claimed. The restrictions on coefficient estimates implied by 3.21 were rejected (MRW could not reject them) and the estimated share of capital was lower than expected (one-fourth for the complete sample and less than 0.1 for the OECD sample).

In addition to reestimating the MRW framework with additional data, Bernanke and Gürkaynak considered MRW within a more general framework of models that admit a balanced growth path (reviewed in Chapters 3 and 4). They highlighted one important implication of these models: if the determinants of the steady-state level of per capita output do in fact describe variation in output per worker across countries, the hypothesis that additional variables (such as saving rates) are not significant determinants of the rate of economic growth should not be rejected. They argued that this implication of balanced-growth models was less evident for developed countries for which the Solow–Swan (and MRW) prediction that growth is solely determined by (exogenous) technical change and uncorrelated with other variables (such as saving rates or human capital) seemed to hold. This, however, was not the case for developing countries where growth rates were strongly correlated with savings rates and the rate of human capital formation. It should be noted that Bernanke and Gürkaynak examine economies that are in steady state (balanced growth path), whereas MRW allow for economies to be in transition to the steady state. In other words, if one looks at transitional dynamics alone, the critique of MRW by Bernanke and Gürkaynak is not relevant.

Empirically, the Bernanke and Gürkaynak implication for the MRW model amounts to testing *together* the determinants of the steady-state level of income along with the determinants of the balanced growth path.

In the MRW model, actual output equals balanced-growth-path output and all countries share the same production function. Therefore, the long-run growth rate is constant across countries and the empirical model consists of estimating together the steady-state level of income in 3.21 (repeated below for convenience with the addition of an error term—see previous discussion) and a constant steady-state growth rate model:

$$\ln y_{i,\tau+\upsilon} = c_A + g_A(\tau+\upsilon) + \left(\frac{\alpha}{1-a-\beta}\right)\ln s_{K,i} + \left(\frac{\beta}{1-a-\beta}\right)\ln s_{H,i}$$

$$-\left(\frac{\alpha+\beta}{1-a-\beta}\right)\ln(g_A + g_{L,i} + \delta_K) + \epsilon_i^1 \qquad \text{EQUATION \textbf{6.16}}$$

$$(1/\upsilon)(\ln y_{i,\tau+\upsilon} - \ln y_{i,\tau}) = g_A + \epsilon_i^2 \qquad \text{EQUATION \textbf{6.17}}$$

As in MRW, $s_{K,i}$ and $s_{H,i}$ are rates of investment in physical and human capital for country i, $g_{L,i}$ is the rate of growth of the labor force, g_A is the long-run (steady-state) growth rate (assumed constant across countries), and ϵ_i^1 and ϵ_i^2 are composite error terms. The hypothesis of interest is that additional variables such as s_K, s_H, and g_L do not enter 6.17 significantly. Bernanke and Gürkaynak estimated equations 6.16 and 6.17 jointly with seemingly unrelated regression (SUR) and found the exclusion restriction (i.e., the restriction that the estimated coefficients for s_K, s_H, and g_L in 6.17 are jointly equal to zero) can be rejected. They interpreted this evidence as rejection of the prediction of the Solow–Swan model that the long-run growth rate is exogenous.

Subsequently, Bernanke and Gürkaynak tested various alternative models of economic growth using the same methodology. As mentioned in Section 3.3, the assumption of an exogenous saving rate in the Solow–Swan model may not be warranted and saving may very well be endogenous. The CKR model derives the saving ratio from optimizing behavior of the representative consumer. In this case the implication of the Solow–Swan model in 6.17 is no longer valid and differences in growth rates must be allowed. Therefore, for the CKR model without human capital, the following two-equation specification was estimated:

$$\ln y_{i,\tau+\upsilon} = c_A + g_A(\tau+\upsilon) + \left(\frac{\alpha}{1-a}\right)\ln s_{K,i}$$

$$-\left(\frac{\alpha}{1-a}\right)\ln(g_{A,i} + g_{L,i} + \delta_K) + \epsilon_i^1 \qquad \text{EQUATION \textbf{6.18}}$$

$$s_{K,i} = \frac{\alpha(g_{A,i} + g_{L,i} + \delta_K)}{\rho + \sigma g_{A,i} + \delta_K} + \epsilon_i^2 \qquad \text{EQUATION } \textbf{6.19}$$

Equation 6.18 shows that, in contrast to MRW, the determinants of the steady-state level of output per worker include country-specific growth rates, $g_{A,i}$, computed as $g_{A,i} = (1/\upsilon)(\ln y_{i,\tau+\upsilon} - \ln y_{i,\tau})$. Equation 6.19 specifies the determinants of the saving rate in the CKR model.[10] They estimated 6.18 and 6.19 jointly with nonlinear SUR imposing the restriction $\alpha = 0.35$. This is because the error term in 6.18 is correlated with the regressors and only the constant term can be estimated. Estimates of the risk aversion parameter σ (an estimate of the link between the growth rate and saving rate) proved disappointing insofar as it was negative for the complete sample, and positive (but insignificant) and much lower than conventional values for the other two samples. Estimates of the rate of time preference ρ were reasonable in magnitude and significant for all samples. They concluded that there is weak support for the CKR framework where the saving rate is endogenous to growth rates.

Bernanke and Gürkaynak also tested the implications of the Lucas–Uzawa model reviewed in Section 4.3 and the AK model of Section 3.4 For the Lucas–Uzawa model, growth along the balanced path is $\zeta.z$ and thus 6.17 is replaced by:[11]

$$(1/\upsilon)(\ln y_{i,\tau+\upsilon} - \ln y_{i,\tau}) = \zeta z_i + \epsilon_i^2 \qquad \text{EQUATION } \textbf{6.20}$$

Their estimation considered two alternative scenarios. First, they assumed that saving for physical and human capital accumulation is exogenous, so 6.18 and 6.20 were estimated jointly; the variable z_i (the amount of time devoted to building of human capital) was measured by s_{Hi}. Alternatively, they assumed endogenous determination of saving for physical and human capital accumulation. In this case saving for physical capital accumulation purposes is given by 6.19. The optimal proportion of time devoted to human capital accumulation (human capital saving rate) was derived in Section 4.3 and (with $\gamma = 0$) it is given by:

$$s_{H,i} = \frac{(\zeta - \rho + g_{L,i})}{\sigma \zeta} + \epsilon_i^3 \qquad \text{EQUATION } \textbf{6.21}$$

Therefore, with endogenous saving rates, they estimated jointly, 6.18–6.21, with the exception of 6.20, where once again they replaced $g_{A,i}$ by $(1/\upsilon)(\ln y_{i,\tau+\upsilon} - \ln y_{i,\tau})$. As with the CKR model, they set $\alpha = 0.35$. With exogenous saving rates, the estimates of the constant term in 6.18

and ζ in 6.20 were reasonable in value and statistically significant. This was also true when saving rates were treated endogenously. In this case, however, the estimated values for σ and ρ were either inadmissible (σ was estimated to be negative) or implausible. They concluded that "the representative-agent model does not seem to do very well in explaining cross-country variations in saving" (p. 34).

Finally, Bernanke and Gürkaynak considered the AK model with exogenously determined saving and with the production function given by 3.37 and the steady-state growth rate by 3.38. Assuming that $A_i = c_A^1(1 + error)$ and $\ln c_A^1 = c_A^2$, so that $\ln A_i \approx c_A^2 + error$ (where c_A^1 and c_A^2 are constants), the two equations corresponding to 3.37 and 3.38 and estimated jointly were:

$$\ln(y_{i,\tau+\upsilon}/k_{i,\tau+\upsilon}) = c_A^2 + \epsilon_i^1$$

$$(1/\upsilon)(\ln y_{i,\tau+\upsilon} - \ln y_{i,\tau}) = s_{K,i}A_i - (g_{L,i} + \delta_K) + \epsilon_i^2$$

$$= c_A^1 s_{K,i} - (g_{L,i} + \delta_K) + \epsilon_i^3$$

They tested the restriction that $\ln c_A^1 = c_A^2$ and computed forecasts of the steady-state growth rate for each country obtained as $s_{K,i}A_i - (g_{L,i} + \delta_K)$, where A_i, in this case, was the output–capital ratio for 1995. Their results provided mixed support for the AK model: on the one hand, the cross-equality restriction was rejected in all cases but, on the other, the correlation coefficient between the forecasted and actual growth rates was 0.67 (for the broadest sample), confirming that the saving rate "is important for explaining the *growth* as well as the *level* of per capita output" (p. 37).

The MRW model has been used extensively in empirical research. In comparison to MRW who estimated specification 3.26, Islam (1995) reestimated MRW with specification 3.27 because his measure of human capital (mean years of schooling in the total population over age 25) corresponded to a stock measure. His data on mean years of schooling came from the Barro–Lee database, the most frequently used database on mean years of schooling (see Chapter 7 for a discussion of human capital databases). He divided the period 1960–1985 into five-year overlapping subperiods and estimated the model both in cross-section and panel form using a variant of Chamberlain's Π-matrix method.[12] The cross-section results were similar to MRW: the estimate for the stock of human capital was positive and significant (for the complete sample; it was insignificant for the other two samples). The estimated share of physical capital (α) was higher than MRW while the human capital share was similar (for the complete sample; it was lower for the other two samples). The panel results, however, revealed some important differences: (1) the estimate for mean years of schooling was negative and (for the complete sample) significant; (2) the implied value of the convergence speed was much higher than MRW; and (3) the estimate of α was lower than the cross-section results (but still higher than MRW) and was roughly the same irrespective of whether the estimated model included the human capital stock or not. Islam concluded that the extension of the MRW to consider the time dimension of human capital proved unsuccessful and "whenever researchers have attempted to incorporate the temporal dimension of human capital variables into growth regressions, outcomes of either statistical insignificance or negative sign have surfaced" (p. 1153).

Additional tests of the MRW specification with panel data and General Method of Moments (GMM) estimation methods have yielded conflicting results. Caselli, Esquivel, and Lefort (1996) found negative estimates for human capital (measured by the secondary enrollment ratio) and a share of physical capital in total output that was much higher than conventional values. Dowrick and Rogers (2002) found a negative (and significant) coefficient for the secondary enrollment rate and a physical capital share of about 0.7. Dowrick and Rogers proposed estimating an alternative model to MRW that is a variant of the growth accounting methodology (see following section). Their estimated model included the growth rate of physical capital per worker and human capital per worker (measured by mean years of schooling at the secondary level) and the level of initial per capita income as explanatory variables. In this case initial income captures the technological gap, not distance from the steady state as in MRW. The estimated model also included an interaction term between the level of human capital and distance from the technology leader (country with highest per capital income) as explanatory variable. They found a much lower output share of physical capital (about 0.2), a positive but very small share of human capital (0.01), and a positive and significant coefficient for the interaction term.

Dinopoulos and Thompson (1999) criticized the MRW model on two grounds. First, the use of secondary enrollment ratios by MRW as the measure of human capital was inappropriate because it ignores other forms of human capital accumulation and overestimates the international variation in human capital. In its place they proposed two alternatives: (1) their own index that takes account of variations in ability among the population and is based on a model of optimal household decision making (regarding time devoted to education) that incorporates diminishing returns to formal education; and (2) the Hanushek and Kimko (2000) index that takes into account variations in human capital quality (reviewed in Section 6.5.2). They argued that both the MRW secondary enrollment rate and their two alternative measures are best viewed as proxies for the (steady-state) stock of human capital and, thus, estimated specification 3.22 for the determinants of the steady-state level of output per worker. With the MRW enrollment measure as a proxy for $\tilde{h}^*$, they reported that, in contrast to MRW, the restriction implied by 3.22 was rejected. Results for their two alternative measures of $\tilde{h}^*$ yielded unreasonably large values for shares: α was close to 0.5 and β was 0.73 and 1.62 (corresponding to the two measures).

Their second criticism of MRW concerns the assumption that the (expected) technology level is equal across countries. Dinopoulos and Thompson claim this is unwarranted and refer to various theoretical R&D-based (Schumpeterian) models of endogenous growth that suggest technology levels vary systematically across countries according to a number of variables, one of which is human capital. They retain the MRW formulation for the initial technology that is given by $A_i(0) = \exp^{c_A + \epsilon_i}$ but propose the technology level in period t be given by $A_i(t) = A_i(0) \exp^{g_A t} \tilde{h}_i(t)^{c_A^e} = \exp^{c_A + \epsilon_i} \exp^{g_A t} \tilde{h}_i(t)^{c_A^e}$, where c_A^e is the technology elasticity of human capital. In this case, rather than 3.22, the estimable model is:

$$\ln y_{i,\tau+\upsilon} = c_A + g_A(\tau+\upsilon) + \left(\frac{\alpha}{1-a}\right)\ln s_K + \left(\frac{\beta + (1-\alpha)c_A^e}{1-a}\right)\ln \tilde{h}^*$$

$$- \left(\frac{\alpha}{1-a}\right)\ln(g_A + g_L + \delta_K) + \epsilon_i$$

The MRW specification assumes $c_A^e = 0$. Dinopoulos and Thompson estimated this model with nonlinear least squares under the restriction that

$\alpha + \beta = 0.6$.[13] They found strong rejection for the hypothesis $c_A^e = 0$ when the model was estimated with each of their two alternative measures of the stock of human capital. They concluded that their evidence casts serious doubt on one of the assumptions of MRW, namely the equality of expected technology levels across countries.

6.4   Cross-Country Growth Accounting and Human Capital

As explained in Section 6.2, the growth accounting methodology divides the growth of output into the weighted growth of inputs and a residual. This has been a convenient starting point for empirical research on human capital and growth. Benhabib and Spiegel (1994) estimated a general production function in three inputs (physical and human capital and labor) in log–difference form (see specification 6.5). Their measure of human capital stock was mean years of schooling of the working age population.[14] Their cross-section results showed that the estimate of change in (the log) mean years of schooling was an insignificant determinant of the growth of output. This result was invariant to alternatives that considered different sources of data for human capital, the inclusion of additional explanatory variables, or different country samples. This led them to propose that the role of human capital is not as a direct input to production but as a determinant of TFP growth as shown in 4.32.

Combining 4.32 with a general two-input production function of the form $Y(t) = A(t)K(t)^\alpha L(t)^\beta$ led Benhabib and Spiegel to specification 4.34. To estimate 4.34, they assumed that the innovation and catch-up effect, $\Psi(H_i)$ and $\Phi(H_i)$, respectively, are linear functions of the level of human capital.[15] Specifically, they assumed that $\Psi(H_i) = c_{exog} + c_{innov}H_i$ and $\Phi(H_i) = c_{imit}H_i$, where c_{innov} and c_{imit} are the coefficients of proportionality and c_{exog} is a constant. In addition, they proxied a country's level of aggregate productivity, $A(t)$, by its income per capita and the leading technology country was the country with the highest income level. They estimated the specification

$$(\ln Y_{\tau+\upsilon} - \ln Y_\tau) = c_{exog} + (c_{innov} - c_{imit})H_\tau + c_{imit}H_\tau(y_\tau^{max}/y_\tau)$$

$$+ \alpha(\ln K_{\tau+\upsilon} - \ln K_\tau) + \beta(\ln L_{\tau+\upsilon} - \ln L_\tau) + \varepsilon_\tau \quad \text{EQUATION } \mathbf{6.22}$$

where y_τ^{max} represents the highest level of income per capita, H_τ is a country's mean level of schooling, and ε_τ is a composite error term. They estimated 6.22 with cross-section data for 78 countries. The point estimate for the catch-up effect (c_{imit}) was positive and significant while that for innovation (c_{innov}) was negative but insignificant. Subsequently, they divided their sample into three groups of 26 countries according to their income level. The results for the poorest third mirrored those for the full sample: for these economies the catch-up effect was significant. For the middle-income group neither effect was significant while for the richest third the estimate for the catch-up effect was insignificant and that for the innovation coefficient was positive and significant (at the 0.10 level).

In a follow-up study, Benhabib and Spiegel (2005) replaced the restrictive specification for TFP growth in 4.32 with the more general model of technology diffusion in 5.8. As explained in Section 5.3.2, the resulting empirical specification for the growth of TFP can be written as (see 5.12)[16]

$$(\ln A_{\tau+\upsilon} - \ln A_\tau) = constant + \left(c_{innov} + \frac{c_{imit}}{b}\right) \ln H_\tau$$

$$-\frac{c_{imit}}{b} \ln H_\tau \left(\frac{A_\tau}{A_\tau^l}\right)^b + \varepsilon_\tau \qquad \text{EQUATION } \textbf{6.23}$$

where c_{innov} and c_{imit} measure, as in the earlier model, the endogenous and catch-up effects, b is the diffusion parameter, and A_τ^l is the technology (TFP) level of the leading country (United States, in their sample). The model in 6.23 nests the exponential diffusion process of their earlier paper when $b = -1$, and the logistic diffusion process in 5.8 when $b = 1$.

To estimate 6.23 Benhabib and Spiegel calculated the TFP level for 85 countries in 1960 (A_τ) and 1995 ($A_{\tau+\upsilon}$) as a residual from a constant returns-to-scale Cobb–Douglas production function in two inputs, physical capital and labor, with the share of capital set equal to one-third. Values for output, capital, and the labor force were drawn from the Penn World Tables. The nonlinear model in 6.23 was estimated with maximum likelihood, with and without a constant term. The human capital stock was measured by mean years of total schooling and data were from the Barro–Lee database. The point estimate of b was 2.3 and 3.2 (for the two specifications with and without constant, respectively), and was significantly greater than zero but not significantly different from one (in both cases). The estimate of c_{imit}/b (the coefficient on the catch-up effect) was negative (as expected) and significant. The point estimate for c_{innov} was negative (contrary to expectations) and not significantly different from zero for the specification with the constant term, but positive when the constant term was excluded. Benhabib and Spiegel showed (see 5.13) that a critical level of human capital can be calculated, below which a nation's TFP growth will diverge from the leader. Using the positive estimate of c_{innov} and mean years of total schooling of the United States as the leader's human capital stock, they calculated the critical level of human capital stock as 1.78 years of schooling in 1960 and 1.95 in 1995. Of the 85 countries in the sample, 27 had human capital below the critical level in 1960. Of the 27 countries below the critical level in 1960, 22 experienced slower productivity growth than the United States in subsequent years. In 1995 four countries had human capital below the critical level: all four had productivity levels below 15 percent of the U.S. level in 1995. Benhabib and Spiegel concluded that their results favor the logistic specification over the exponential and that their parameter estimates are consistent with the theoretical implications of the model.

Pritchett (2001) estimated the same general specification as Benhabib and Spiegel assuming constant returns to scale, that is, equation 6.6. Data on output per worker were from the Penn World Tables. The "capital" stock was generated using the perpetual inventory method with initial estimates of the capital–output ratio from two alternative sources.[17] He assumed the level of human capital per worker was not identically equivalent to mean years of schooling, as other researchers have postulated, but is equal to the discounted value (over a worker's working life) of the wage premium that an educated worker receives over the wage rate of a worker without any years of education. Under certain assumptions it follows that[18]

$$(\ln h_{\tau+\upsilon} - \ln h_{\tau}) = \ln(\exp^{0.1 \times EDUC_{\tau+\upsilon}} - 1) - \ln(\exp^{0.1 \times EDUC_{\tau}} - 1)$$

EQUATION **6.24**

where, as before, $EDUC$ is mean years of schooling of the (working age) population. Data on years of schooling were from two sources: Barro and Lee (1996, 2001) and Nehru, Swanson, and Dubey (1995).

The least squares estimate of the human capital elasticity (b_2 in 6.6) was negative (-0.05) and insignificant. This result was robust to changes in sample size (outliers were eliminated from estimation), data (data on mean years of schooling from two alternative databases were used and also estimates of output per person and output per labor force-aged person were used in place of output per worker), and estimation method (weighted least squares or instrumental variables were used with the Nehru, Swanson, and Dubey measure of mean years of schooling as an instrument for the Barro–Lee measure). Pritchett also attempted to account for differences in schooling quality by introducing a measure of standardized test scores that was available for a subsample (25) of countries. The quality measure was introduced as an additional variable and was also interacted with mean years of schooling. In this case, although the estimate of b_2 was positive (but insignificant), when the total effect of mean years of schooling was evaluated at the mean test score it was still negative (-0.46). Finally, Pritchett suggested three explanations for the contradictory evidence between micro studies (the Mincerian regressions mentioned earlier that demonstrate a consistent and positive effect of schooling on wages) and his macro evidence: (1) education may be directed at unproductive activities that generate private reward but have zero or negative social contribution; (2) slow growth in the demand for educated labor has resulted in excess supply of educational capital and lower returns to schooling; and (3) education systems have not translated increased years of schooling into enhanced productive skills.

Topel (1999) criticized the findings of both Pritchett and Benhabib and Spiegel because their log–log specification is based on the implicit assumption that one year of education has a different effect on human capital per worker that depends on the number of years of schooling: an additional year of schooling increases human capital per worker proportionately more in countries with lower levels of schooling than those with higher levels of schooling.[19] When Topel used the Pritchett formulation of human capital, the effect of education on growth was insignificant. Topel criticized the log–log formulation as being "rejected by the data, and is inconsistent with widely accepted evidence on the form of human capital earnings functions" (p. 2972).

Temple (2001) estimated the growth accounting specification in 6.5 with human capital per worker identified by mean years of schooling and two alternative estimation methods: least squares and least trimmed squares (LTS). The latter minimizes the sum of squares over a fraction of observations that is determined endogenously by the estimator and the model is estimated over the range of observations that fit best. Thus, a comparison of LTS and least squares estimates would provide an indication of the importance of influential (outlier) observations. Using the Benhabib/Spiegel data, he replicated their results with least squares. On the other hand, application of LTS to the same data provided estimates substantially different from least squares.

This finding led Temple to question the implications of the growth accounting specification. He also questioned the implicit assumption that an additional year of schooling yields higher returns at low levels of schooling than at higher levels. He explored two alternative specifications for the role of schooling in generating increases in human capital. First, he considered the formulation in 6.7 that parallels the micro treatment of schooling. In this case the estimable model is 6.8 and the estimate of a_3 can be thought of as the "macro" return to schooling (that parallels the "micro" return from Mincer-type regressions). His least squares estimate of a_3 was 0.015 and insignificant. The second specification for human capital was a nonlinear function of mean years of schooling or

$$\ln h_{i,\tau} = c_i + c_1 \ln(EDUC_{i,\tau}) + c_2(1/EDUC_{i,\tau})$$

where c_1 and c_2 are parameters to be estimated. Instead of 6.8, the estimable specification in this case is:

$$(\ln Y_{\tau+\upsilon} - \ln Y_{\tau}) = (\ln A_{\tau+\upsilon} - \ln A_{\tau}) + \alpha(\ln K_{\tau+\upsilon} - \ln K_{\tau})$$

$$+ \beta(\ln L_{\tau+\upsilon} - \ln L_{\tau}) + c_1(\ln EDUC_{\tau+\upsilon} - \ln EDUC_{\tau})$$

$$+ c_2\{(1/EDUC_{\tau+\upsilon}) - (1/EDUC_{\tau})\} + (\ln \epsilon_{\tau+\upsilon} - \ln \epsilon_{\tau}) \qquad \text{EQUATION } \mathbf{6.25}$$

His least squares estimates of c_1 and c_2 were jointly significant (0.20 level) and they were not very different from the LTS estimates. Five observations with the highest residuals from the LTS estimation were identified as potential outliers and the model in 6.25 was reestimated by re-weighted least squares (RWLS). The RWLS estimates of c_1 and c_2 were jointly significant at the 0.10 level but the magnitude of the effect of schooling on growth was economically small.

Temple (2001) went on to reestimate the growth accounting specification in intensive form with the Pritchett (2001) data set. As far as the formulation for human capital, he made the same two assumptions: 6.7 and $\ln h_{i,\tau} = c_i + c_1 \ln(EDUC_{i,\tau}) + c_2(1/EDUC_{i,\tau})$. The formulation in 6.7 yielded the growth specification in 6.9. The least squares estimate of the schooling coefficient was positive (0.08) and significant but the LTS estimate was considerably different (0.02) and "certainly lower than the typical range of private returns to schooling, which would tend to imply a coefficient in the range 0.05 to 0.15" (p. 912). As for the second human capital specification, it yielded the intensive form of 6.25:

$$(\ln y_{\tau+\upsilon} - \ln y_\tau) = (\ln A_{\tau+\upsilon} - \ln A_\tau) + \alpha(\ln k_{\tau+\upsilon} - \ln k_\tau)$$

$$+ c_1(\ln EDUC_{\tau+\upsilon} - \ln EDUC_\tau)$$

$$+ c_2\{(1/EDUC_{\tau+\upsilon}) - (1/EDUC_\tau)\} + (\ln \epsilon_{\tau+\upsilon} - \ln \epsilon_\tau)$$

In this case the least squares estimates of c_1 and c_2 were imprecise and different from the LTS estimates. Once again, LTS was used to identify potential outliers. The RWLS estimates of c_1 and c_2 were jointly significant (0.01 level) and were fairly similar to those from the estimation of 6.25 that were obtained with a slightly different data set (from Benhabib/Spiegel) and sample of countries. On the negative side the estimates showed that the marginal effect of schooling was comparable to private rates of return at very low levels of schooling (0–3 years), but at higher levels of schooling the rate of return was lower than 0.05.

Papageorgiou (2003) combined the Benhabib and Spiegel formulation of productivity growth in 4.32 with the Romer model (discussed in Section 4.5) that distinguishes between human capital as an input in final production and human capital that is used to facilitate the growth of TFP. The result was three alternative empirical specifications. The first did not distinguish between different types of human capital and assumed that the total human capital stock plays a dual role: both as an input in the aggregate production function and as an input in TFP growth according to 4.32. Empirically this is equivalent to estimating 6.22 with the addition of the growth of human capital ($\ln H_{\tau+v} - \ln H_\tau$) as an explanatory variable. The other two specifications distinguish between two types of human capital: that used in final goods production (H_Y) and that used in TFP growth (H_A). The first formulation assumes a general form for the aggregate production, $Y(t) = A\{H_A(t)\}K(t)^\alpha L(t)^\beta H_Y(t)^\gamma$, and combines it with the growth of TFP formulation in 4.32 where now H_A is used in place of the total human capital stock H. Empirically this amounts to estimating 6.22 with the addition of the growth of human capital used in production as an explanatory variable (i.e., $\ln H_{Y,\tau+v} - \ln H_{Y,\tau}$), and with the total human capital stock (H_τ) in the first two terms of 6.22 replaced by $H_{A,\tau}$. The second formulation imposes more structure on the aggregate production function, that is, $Y(t) = A(t)^{\beta+\gamma} K(t)^{1-\beta-\gamma} L(t)^\beta H_Y(t)^\gamma$.[20] This production function is combined with the TFP growth formulation in 4.32, with H_A once again in place of the total human capital stock. Empirically it results in the same specification as the more general formulation of the production function but with different constraints implied on the estimated parameters and different estimates of the innovation and catch-up coefficients (c_{innov} and c_{imit}).

Papageorgiou estimated five specifications in total: the three described above along with the general growth accounting specification in 6.8 and the Benhabib/Spiegel specification in 6.22. Each specification was estimated with cross-section data for 80 countries during 1960–1987. Human capital used directly in production (H_Y) was measured by mean years of schooling at the primary level while human capital that is used to promote TFP growth (H_A) was identified with mean years of schooling at the post-primary level (secondary plus tertiary). The aggregate human capital stock (H) was the sum of the two. His preferred specification was the model that extends the Benhabib/Spiegel specification to allow the total stock of human capital to enter both as a direct input to production and TFP growth. Following Benhabib and Spiegel (1994), Papageorgiou divided the sample into three income groups and found that, for the richest third, human capital contributed to technology creation through both channels (innovation and imitation) but was insignificant as a direct input into production. For the poorest third, human capital contributed significantly to production as a direct input and also as a facilitator of imitation but had no significant role in promoting innovation.

The distinction between different forms of human capital is one of the central themes in Vandenbussche, Aghion, and Meghir (2006), who argue that the contribution of human capital to TFP growth depends, not only on the level (amount) of human capital, but also on its composition between skilled and unskilled labor. If the composition of human capital is held constant, an increase in the level (amount) of human capital increases TFP growth. But the composition of human capital has a differential effect on growth and its effect depends on a country's distance from the technology frontier (as measured by the TFP level of the United States). Specifically, the impact of skilled human capital on TFP growth increases the closer a country is to the technological frontier. Conversely, the impact of unskilled human capital on TFP growth decreases the closer a country is to the technology frontier. They tested the main implications of their theoretical model with data from OECD countries. The reason for considering a relatively homogeneous group such as the OECD was, according to them, that human capital imparts a heterogenous effect on growth even for a homogenous group when one considers differences between skilled and unskilled labor. For estimation purposes they identified unskilled labor with primary and secondary educational attainment and skilled labor with tertiary attainment.

The empirical specification derived from their theoretical model was

$$(\ln A_{i,\tau+\upsilon} - \ln A_{i,\tau}) = a_{0i} + a_1 \ln(A_{i,\tau}/A_\tau^l) + a_2 TERT_{i,\tau}$$

$$+ a_3 \ln(A_{i,\tau}/A_\tau^l) \times (TERT_{i,\tau}) + \varepsilon_{i,\tau} \qquad \text{EQUATION } \mathbf{6.26}$$

where $A_{i,\tau}$ is the TFP level of country i at time τ, A_τ^l is the TFP level of the technology leader (United States), $TERT_{i,\tau}$ is the share of the population with a tertiary education level, a_{0i} are country-fixed effects, and $a_1 - a_3$ are parameters to be estimated. They estimated 6.26 with panel data for 19 OECD economies measured at five-year intervals over the period 1960–1995. The level of TFP was calculated by subtracting the product of capital per adult and the capital share (assumed to be equal to 0.3 for all countries) from output per adult. The share of population with tertiary education was drawn from two alternative sources: Barro and Lee (2001) and De la Fuente and Doménech (2006). The most satisfactory results were obtained when the 19 countries were divided into seven groups and dummy variables were included for each group and time period. The estimates of α_1, α_2, and α_3 were $-0.32, 0.33$, and 1.27, respectively (all were significant). Vandenbussche, Aghion, and Meghir interpreted their results as signifying that the impact of tertiary education on TFP growth is greater for economies that are closer to the frontier. For all countries with a productivity level above 74 percent of the leader, the effect of tertiary education on TFP growth was positive. Conversely, their results can be interpreted as implying that, for countries with higher levels of tertiary education, the impact of distance from the leader on TFP growth was lower. In fact, for countries with a share of population with tertiary education above 0.25 (4 of the 19 countries in 2000), the effect of distance from frontier on TFP growth was positive. Investigating further the issue of the composition of human capital, they considered two alternative measures of human capital: the number of years of tertiary education of the average adult in the population (a proxy for the stock of skilled labor) and the number of years of primary/secondary education (a proxy for unskilled labor). They reestimated the model in 6.26 and reported that only skilled human capital exerted a significant growth-enhancing effect and that skilled human capital had a greater growth-enhancing effect in countries that were less distant from the frontier.

6.5   Human Capital and Economic Growth: Additional Considerations

6.5.1   Male vs. Female Human Capital and Economic Growth

Several studies have investigated whether the impact of human capital on growth differs by sex. The most common method is to introduce two separate explanatory variables for human capital (male and female) and to test for a significantly differential effect on growth. All contributions in this area, however, maintain the linearity assumption between different types of human capital and growth.

A series of papers (e.g., Barro and Lee 1994; Barro 1997, 2001; Barro and Sala-i-Martin 2004) finds a significantly different growth effect for male and female education at the post-primary level measured by mean years of secondary plus tertiary schooling. More importantly, the general conclusion from these studies is that the impact of post-primary male education on growth is positive and significant whereas that for female education is negative and significant. One possible explanation for these findings, according to Barro (2001), is that "many countries follow discriminatory practices that prevent the efficient exploitation of well-educated females in the formal labor market" (p. 15). When it comes to education at the primary level, the results are ambiguous. Male schooling at the primary level is generally an insignificant determinant of growth; on the other hand, a significant contribution for female education at the primary level depends on whether fertility is held constant or not.

These findings have generated some controversy. Certainly, a number of studies have scrutinized their conclusions. Using panel data (with growth rates averaged over five-year periods), Caselli, Esquivel, and Lefort (1996) reproduced the Barro results with least squares estimation methods. However, when they estimated the model with GMM they found contradictory results: the estimate for male schooling (measured by mean years of schooling at the secondary level) was negative and significant while that for female secondary schooling was positive and significant. They argued that female education encompasses two effects: a positive effect on growth through reduced fertility (as also argued by Barro) and a negative human capital effect. In the case of female schooling, the positive fertility effect dominates while male educational capital has only a negative human capital effect. Forbes (2000) confirmed the Caselli, Esquivel, and Lefort results also with panel data (averaged over five-year intervals) and GMM estimation techniques. She found that the coefficient on female education (mean years of schooling at the secondary level) was positive and significant while that for male education was insignificant. Krueger and Lindahl (2001) estimated a growth equation in the form of 6.15 where both the initial level and growth of mean years of schooling were included as explanatory variables. They found significant differences by sex for the effect of initial level of primary schooling (it is positive for females and negative for males) and initial level of secondary schooling (negative for female education and positive for male). A similar pattern was reported for the change in primary and secondary schooling.

Knowles, Lorgelly, and Owen (2002) consider two alternative formulations of the MRW specification for the transition to the steady state in 3.27. The first assumes that male human capital (h^M) and female human capital (h^F) have differential output elasticities (β^M and β^F, respectively) so that the production function in 3.18 can be written as

$\tilde{y}(t) = \tilde{k}(t)^\alpha \tilde{h}^M(t)^{\beta^M} \tilde{h}^F(t)^{\beta^F}$. In this case the transition to the steady state should be modified as follows:

$$\left[\ln y_{\tau+\upsilon} - \ln y_\tau\right] = \left[g_A \upsilon + (1 - e^{-\lambda\upsilon})\ln A_\tau \frac{1 - \alpha - \beta}{1 - \alpha}\right]$$

$$+ (1 - e^{-\lambda\upsilon})\left\{\frac{\alpha}{(1 - \alpha)}\ln s_K - \ln(g_A + g_L + \delta_K)\right\} + (1 - e^{-\lambda\upsilon})$$

$$\left\{\frac{\beta^M}{(1 - \alpha)}\ln \tilde{h}^{M*} + \frac{\beta^F}{(1 - \alpha)}\ln \tilde{h}^{F*}\right\} - (1 - e^{-\lambda\upsilon})y_\tau \qquad \text{EQUATION } \mathbf{6.27}$$

The second formulation follows on a suggestion by Hill and King (1995) and rewrites 6.27 in terms of the "educational gap" (the difference between male and female educational capital) and female educational capital as[21]

$$\left[\ln y_{\tau+\upsilon} - \ln y_\tau\right] = \left[g_A \upsilon + (1 - e^{-\lambda\upsilon})\ln A_\tau \frac{1 - \alpha - \beta}{1 - \alpha}\right]$$

$$+ (1 - e^{-\lambda\upsilon})\left\{\frac{\alpha}{(1 - \alpha)}\ln s_K - \ln(g_A + g_L + \delta_K)\right\}$$

$$+ (1 - e^{-\lambda\upsilon})\left\{\frac{\beta^F + \beta^M}{(1 - \alpha)}\ln \tilde{h}^{F*} + \frac{\beta^M}{(1 - \alpha)}[\ln \tilde{h}^{M*} - \ln \tilde{h}^{F*}]\right\}$$

$$- (1 - e^{-\lambda\upsilon})y_\tau \qquad \text{EQUATION } \mathbf{6.28}$$

where $(\ln \tilde{h}^{M*} - \ln \tilde{h}^{F*})$ represents the educational gap. Klasen (2002) also considered the educational gap in his formulations of the growth model. In addition to the level of the educational gap and female educational capital in 6.28, he included the growth in the gap and growth of female education.[22] The results from Knowles, Lorgelly, and Owen and Klasen generally support the proposition that differences in educational capital by sex and the educational gap are important determinants of growth. The estimated coefficient for the educational gap from these studies indicates that reducing the difference between male and female mean years of schooling would boost growth. Klasen suggests that the gender educational gap (the level and growth in the gap together) helps account for up to 0.95 percentage points in the average rate of growth between East Asia and other groups of developing countries.

6.5.2 Quality of Human Capital and Economic Growth

In this book the concept of human capital has so far been operationalized through various measures of the *quantity* of formal education. Our empirical estimation in Chapters 7 and 9 will also use the quantity of education as the measure of human capital because we aim to achieve as wide a coverage of countries and time periods as possible. The choice of quantity as a measure of human capital is purely for practical reasons associated with data availability across a wide range of countries and time. One of the most important issues relating to human capital (in the form of educational attainment) is that there are large and significant differences in the quality of educational systems across the globe. This is perhaps the area of empirical growth research where the production of reliable and timely statistics covering a wide range of countries and years is most needed. While in our empirical investigation of Chapters 7 and 9 we do not consider quality differences, in this section we discuss a number of studies that have investigated empirically the impact of quality differences in educational systems on economic growth. Inevitably, these studies are based on restricted samples due to the relative unavailability of data on human capital quality.

In practice, there are two possibilities for arriving at a measure of the quality of human capital: school inputs (e.g., teacher salaries, expenditures on schools, and pupil–teacher ratios) and scores on internationally standardized tests of cognitive skills (science, mathematics, and reading). Researchers have tended to focus on test scores as a more comprehensive measure of the quality of human capital insofar as they capture improvements that arise, not only from formal education, but also outside of formal schooling. Lee and Barro (2001) discussed the nature of test score data as an indicator of the quality of human capital and focused on the determinants of differences in test scores across countries. They divided the determinants into two categories: family factors (income and quantity of schooling) and school inputs (pupil–teacher ratio, average teacher salary, educational expenditure per pupil, and length of school year). They found that both categories were significant determinants of test scores: family factors, as measured by income and education of parents, and resources (inputs) into education, as measured by the pupil–teacher ratio. Two other measures of resources (teacher salary and length of school year) were not as significant determinants of test scores while the estimate for educational expenditures per pupil was insignificant. They also found that parental income and length of the school year have differential effects on the three test scores (science, mathematics, and reading).[23]

Barro (2001) used data on three test scores (science, math, and reading) as explanatory variables in panel growth regressions (averaged over 10 years). The data were rather sparse with at most 43 countries included in a specific period (and in most cases fewer than 43). Moreover, as Barro acknowledges, another drawback of these data is that "later values of test scores are allowed to influence earlier values of economic growth" (p. 15). The three test scores were included as separate (and also in combination) determinants of growth along with a measure of the quantity of education (male post-secondary schooling). Science scores had a positive and significant effect on growth and, in terms of magnitude, its effect was more important than educational quantity. Mathematics scores were also a significant determinant of growth and the magnitude of this effect was larger than science scores. Finally, reading scores were an insignificant determinant. Given that scores on all three tests were available for only a handful of countries, Barro created an overall score indicator by combining science scores with reading scores and using the latter to fill in missing observations (thus increasing sample size to 43 countries). The effect of the combined test score on growth was positive and significant while the quantity of education was no longer a significant determinant of growth.

Hanushek and Kimko (2000) provide an extensive discussion of how scores from cognitive skill tests can be used to measure the quality of human capital and its effects on economic growth. They used data from six voluntary international tests of mathematics and science over the period 1964–1991.[24] The tests were organized by two organizations: the International Association for the Evaluation of Educational Assessment (IEA) and the International Assessment of Educational Progress (IAEP). Because scores from various tests taken at different times and over different subgroups are not comparable, they transformed the raw data using two different methods.[25] Their data on quality of human capital were a cross section because they averaged scores over all tests taken by each country over 1964–1991 (weighted by the inverse of the country-specific standard error) to obtain a single measure of quality for each of

31 countries. A single measure for each country is appropriate when the quality of schooling systems changes slowly over time (as they claim is the case) but precludes panel tests of the relationship between quality of human capital and growth to exploit the time dimension.

Hanushek and Kimko estimated various cross-section growth regressions where the dependent variable was growth of income per capita over 1960–1990. Their basic formulation included initial income, population growth, and the quantity of human capital (measured by the average number of total years of schooling from the Barro–Lee database) as explanatory variables. To this basic specification they added their indicator of human capital quality and reported positive and significant estimates for the quality measure and roughly a doubling of the adjusted coefficient of determination (from about 0.35 to 0.7) when it was included. The coefficient on human capital quality was not only statistically significant, but also economically important: a one standard deviation increase in the quality of human capital would raise the average annual growth rate by 1.4 percentage points while a similar increase in the quantity of human capital would increase growth by 0.25 percentage points.[26] Finally, they pointed out that when measures of quality of human capital were included in the growth regressions, estimates of the quantity of human capital were no longer significant.

Hanushek and Kimko were also concerned whether their cross-country regressions identified a causal effect between quality of human capital and growth. They investigated three related questions. The first concerns reverse causality, that is, whether higher quality of schooling increases growth which makes available a greater amount of resources that, along with other inputs, can be used to boost human capital quality. To test for this they estimated a model for the determinants of schooling quality where test scores were the dependent variable, and various measures of schooling inputs and resource availability were the explanatory variables (much like the Lee and Barro (2001) regressions). In this case each test score (math or science) and each test year comprise different observations, allowing them to increase the country-test-cohort observations to approximately 70. The explanatory variables were similar to Lee and Barro: pupil–teacher ratio in primary school; public expenditures per student; the share of expenditures on education in GDP; and the annual rate of growth of population. They found the various input measures did not exert a significant impact on test scores under various specifications of the human capital quality production function. This led them to conclude that the reverse causation (growth $\implies$ resource availability $\implies$ quality) was unlikely to be important. They made use of their estimates of the quality production function to project values for human capital quality for countries that had data on inputs but did not participate in international tests. This filling in enabled them to increase the sample of countries from 31 to nearly 80. With the additional data they reestimated the growth regressions and found once again that the quality of human capital was a significant determinant of growth: an increase in quality by one standard deviation was associated with an increase in average annual growth of 0.32 percentage points.

The second question related to whether an unknown omitted factor (e.g., labor market openness or investment in health) may lead to higher growth and higher quality of human capital at the same time and may account for the correlation between them. To investigate this Hanushek and Kimko looked at the earnings of immigrants to the United States and related them to their index of quality of human capital corresponding to the immigrant's home country. For immigrants who received their education in their home countries, quality was positively and significantly related to earnings. For those who received their education in the United States only or a combination of the United States and home country, the quality index was not significantly related to earnings. They interpreted these results as "providing consistent evidence that our measures of labor-force quality are related to individual productivity and signal a causal influence in the growth relationship" (p. 1197). Their third concern was whether the superior performance of the Asian economies accounted for their results. They omitted progressively larger subsamples of Asian economies from their growth regressions and reported that the impact of human capital quality on growth was robust to the exclusion of these countries.

The Hanushek and Kimko study has been updated and extended by Bosworth and Collins (2003) and Hanushek and Woessmann (2007). Bosworth and Collins made use of the Hanushek and Kimko methodology for projecting the quality of human capital for countries that did not have test scores by estimating a relationship (for countries with data) between test scores and country educational characteristics. Hanushek/Kimko estimated this relationship for 30 countries whereas Bosworth/Collins were able to estimate it for 34 countries (with additional data from Chile, China, Mozambique, and Nigeria). They used the estimated relationship and data on covariates (inputs into education) from the World Development Indicators to generate projections of human capital quality for 84 countries. Subsequently, they used their indicator of human capital quality to estimate the cross-country determinants of growth in real GDP per worker for the 84-country sample over 1960–2000.[27] The base specification included the growth of physical capital per worker and both the initial level and growth in the quantity of human capital per worker (total mean years of schooling) as explanatory variables. They estimated two variants, one that constrained the physical capital coefficient to equal 0.35 and the other that included a set of conditioning variables. The estimated coefficients on the quantity of human capital (level and growth) were positive and significant except when the conditioning variables were included (they became insignificant). The regression of interest added the indicator of human quality as explanatory variable. Unlike the findings of Hanushek and Kimko, the inclusion did not increase $\overline{R}^2$. The estimated coefficient on educational quality was positive and significant in the specification that excluded the conditioning variables, but lost its significance when the conditioning variables were included. Bosworth and Collins attributed this finding to the inclusion of a measure of the quality of government institutions among the conditioning variables and concluded that it is impossible to distinguish empirically the effects of educational quality from the more general effects of quality of institutions.

Hanushek and Woessmann (2007) expanded the set of international cognitive skill tests considered by Hanushek and Kimko (2000) to include several tests made available during the 1990s. The two additions to the test score data were the Trends in International Mathematics and Science Study (TIMSS) of the IEA and the Programme for International Student Assessment (PISA) administered by the OECD. With these additional tests, the number of countries with direct measures of educational quality increased to 50. They repeated the cross-section growth regressions in Hanushek and Kim with growth measured over 1960–2000 and found that the inclusion of educational quality (in a model where initial per capita income and initial quantity of schooling were the only other explanatory variables) triples the explanatory power of the model ($\overline{R}^2$ increases from 0.25 to 0.73). The estimate of quality was positive and significant, signifying that a one-standard-deviation increase in test scores would raise the long-run growth rate by two percentage points. The addition of other explanatory variables (regional dummy variables and two indicators of institutional quality, trade openness, and security of property rights) did little to change the significance of educational quality (though the magnitude of the estimates was reduced). The sample of 50 countries was subsequently divided into two groups according to membership in the OECD (member vs. nonmember) and income level (low- vs. high-income countries). The estimated coefficient for educational quality was positive and significant for both OECD and non-OECD groups and human capital quality appears to matter more for poorer countries. Several robustness tests (e.g., alternative definitions of quality and exclusion of East Asian economies) confirmed their basic conclusion.

In addition to the mean score on tests, Hanushek and Woessmann also looked at the distribution of scores by defining two variables that measure the proportion of students that meet a threshold level of achievement. The first was a score of 400 or above on the transformed international scale (meant to capture basic literacy) and the other 600 or above (to capture high achievement). The estimates for the two threshold levels were highly significant indicating that both basic and high achievement are important determinants of growth, with the magnitude of the second effect substantially higher than the first. The estimates for math and science tests separately were also positive and significant when introduced either separately or jointly. Finally, Hanushek and Woessmann investigated the hypothesis that the effect of the quality of human capital on growth depends on the nature of a country's institutions. To that effect they introduced an interaction term between educational quality and each of the two indicators of institutional quality. The estimates for test scores, openness, and the interaction between these two were all positive and highly significant.[28] They concluded that the quality of human capital and the quality of institutions have an independent effect on growth and that each reinforces the impact of the other.

6.5.3   Human Capital and the International Diffusion
of Research and Development

There exists a substantial literature concerned with whether research and development (R&D) carried out in relatively advanced economies benefits not only the countries conducting R&D, but also other nations, known as the *international diffusion of R&D*. One of the issues tackled by the international diffusion literature is the mechanism by which R&D diffuses across international borders.[29] Several studies have shown empirically that human capital (measured by the quantity of schooling) is an important factor that facilitates the international diffusion of R&D. In some ways this literature parallels and complements the literature on human capital and technological diffusion pioneered by Nelson and Phelps and Benhabib and Spiegel and reviewed in Sections 4.4 and 6.4. One important difference, however, is that the central question addressed by this literature is whether R&D spills across international frontiers and has beneficial effects on the growth of productivity of non-R&D-performing countries. The role of human capital in this process is a secondary issue. This section provides a brief summary of the role of human capital in this literature.

The central issue is whether a measure of a country's "foreign" R&D (R&D carried out by its economic partners with potential spillover benefits) has a positive effect on the growth of domestic TFP. A country's foreign R&D is computed as a weighted average of resources devoted to R&D by the main industrial countries. The weights used to compute this measure are meant to capture links between the domestic economy and the foreign countries conducting R&D. These weights have been a matter of considerable debate. Some authors have used bilateral trade shares (either aggregate trade or trade in specific categories such as capital goods), others have used bilateral foreign direct investment (FDI) shares, while others have used the bilateral geographic distance. In addition to foreign R&D, this literature has introduced human capital (measured by schooling achievement) as an independent determinant of TFP growth and also interacted it with the measure of foreign R&D. The interaction term is meant to test the role of human capital as a facilitator of the diffusion of R&D globally. For example, Coe, Helpman, and Hoffmaister

(1997) have estimated the following specification

$$(\ln A_{i,\tau+\upsilon} - \ln A_{i,\tau}) = \delta_i + \delta_\tau + \delta_1(\ln FRD_{i,\tau+\upsilon} - \ln FRD_{i,\tau})$$

$$+ \delta_2(h_{i,\tau+\upsilon} - h_{i,\tau}) + \delta_3(MCAP_{i,\tau+\upsilon} - MCAP_{i,\tau})$$

$$+ \delta_4\{(\ln FRD_{i,\tau+\upsilon} \times MCAP_{i,\tau+\upsilon}) - (\ln FRD_{i,\tau} \times MCAP_{i,\tau})\}$$

$$+ \delta_5\{(\ln FRD_{i,\tau+\upsilon} \times h_{i,\tau+\upsilon}) - (\ln FRD_{i,\tau} \times h_{i,\tau})\} + \epsilon_{i,\tau}$$

where FRD_i measures the foreign R&D of country i, $MCAP_i$ is the ratio of imports of machinery and equipment from industrial countries to GDP for country i, δ_i and δ_τ represent country- and time-fixed effects, respectively, and $\delta_1-\delta_5$ are parameters to be estimated. The measure of foreign R&D of country i was constructed according to $FRD_i = \sum_{j=1}^{j=22} w_{ij}RD_j$, where RD_j is the stock of R&D of each of 22 industrial countries ($j = 1, \ldots, 22$), and the weight (w_{ij}) is the bilateral machinery and equipment import share of country i from country j with $\sum_{j=1}^{j=22} w_{ij} = 1$. The measure of human capital ($h_{i,\tau}$) used by Coe, Helpman, and Hoffmaister was the secondary enrollment ratio. It is noteworthy that in this specification the change in human capital appears as the determinant of TFP growth.

They estimated this formulation for 77 developing countries with panel data over the period 1971–1990 (with growth rates computed at five-year intervals). The growth of TFP was obtained as a residual from a constant returns-to-scale Cobb–Douglas production function with two inputs (physical capital and labor); the share of physical capital in GDP (α) was set at 0.4. They estimated a number of alternative specifications (e.g., with/without interaction effects and with/without country/time effects). The estimated effect for foreign R&D (δ_1) was generally positive and significant and the impact of secondary enrollment (δ_2) was also positive and significant when its interaction effect was omitted. When the interaction term was included, estimates for the coefficients δ_2 and δ_5 were of opposite sign and generally insignificant. Nonetheless, the total effect of schooling (the elasticity of TFP with respect to schooling) was positive and significant.[30] The general conclusion of this study was that the impact of education (as measured by the secondary enrollment ratio) on TFP was positive and significant. No clear-cut conclusion, however, could be drawn concerning the role of human capital in facilitating the diffusion of foreign R&D (the interaction term was generally insignificant).

Savvides and Zachariadis (2005) considered a specification similar to Coe, Helpman, and Hoffmaister with some important modifications: (1) In line with the literature on technology diffusion and human capital reviewed in previous chapters, the level of human capital was assumed to be a determinant of TFP growth; (2) They criticized the use of foreign R&D *stocks* by Coe, Helpman, and Hoffmaister to construct the measure of FRD as being in line with first-generation growth models that are subject to scale effects. Instead, they considered R&D intensity (the ratio of foreign R&D spending to GDP), a variable that is more in line with second-generation growth models; and (3) They did not consider aggregate TFP but TFP in the manufacturing sector alone for a number of developing countries because this is the sector most likely to benefit from foreign R&D spillovers. Specifically, they estimated the following

$$(\ln A_{i,\tau+\upsilon} - \ln A_{i,\tau})$$

$$= \delta_i + \delta_\tau + \delta_1 \sum_{k=1}^{k^T} FRD_{i,\tau-k} + \delta_2 \sum_{k=1}^{k^T} h_{i,\tau-k} + \delta_3 \sum_{k=1}^{k^T} MCAP_{i,\tau-k}$$

$$+ \delta_4 \sum_{k=1}^{k^T} FDI_{i,\tau-k} + \delta_5 \sum_{k=1}^{k^T} (FRD_{i,\tau-k} \times h_{i,\tau-k})$$

$$+ \delta_6 \sum_{k=1}^{k^T} (FDI_{i,\tau-k} \times h_{i,\tau-k}) + \delta_7 \sum_{k=1}^{k^T} (MCAP_{i,\tau-k} \times h_{i,\tau-k}) + \epsilon_{i,\tau}$$

where FDI_i is the ratio of country i's foreign direct investment to its GDP and $k = 1, \ldots, k^T$ is the number of lags included in order to test the time framework over which the various determinants of TFP growth operate.[31] Interaction effects were included between human capital and the three channels through which foreign technology may diffuse to the domestic manufacturing sector. Thus, in addition to facilitating the diffusion of foreign R&D, they considered other aspects of human capital as a facilitator of foreign technology diffusion (foreign direct investment and imports of capital goods).

Savvides and Zachariadis estimated this specification with data from 32 developing countries over the period 1965–1992. As in specification 6.5, the growth of TFP was constructed as a residual from the estimation of a two-input (physical capital and labor) production function for the manufacturing sector of each of the 32 countries (the human capital term was omitted from 6.5). Unlike equation 6.5, however, they assumed and estimated a different capital and labor elasticity for each country. Data on value added and the number of workers employed in the manufacturing sector came from the Industrial Statistics Database of the United Nations Industrial Development Organization (UNIDO), while estimates of the capital stock in the manufacturing sector came from Larson, Butzer, Mandlak, and Crego (2000). To correspond with the Coe, Helpman, and Hoffmaister estimation, Savvides and Zachariadis also used the secondary enrollment ratio as their measure of human capital. They constructed *FRD* as a weighted average of the R&D intensities of the G-5 economies (France, Germany, Japan, United Kingdom, and United States) with weights measured by shares of imports of capital goods from the G-5.

Savvides and Zachariadis estimated a number of alternative specifications (e.g., including/excluding various interaction effects). When none of the interaction terms were included, the estimated coefficient for the secondary enrollment ratio was positive and significant. When the interaction effect between foreign R&D and secondary education was included, the estimate of δ_5 was positive and significant providing support for the hypothesis that education facilitates the diffusion of foreign R&D; the total effect of education on TFP growth in this case was insignificant.[32] When the interaction term with *FDI* was included the estimate of δ_6 was positive (and marginally insignificant), indicating a role for human capital in the absorption of foreign investment. In this case the total effect of education was positive and significant. The estimate of δ_7 (the interaction of schooling and imports of technology goods) was negative and significant. They investigated this counterintuitive result by decomposing total imports of technology goods into two categories (imports of machinery and imports of transportation equipment) and tested the impact of these two separately. The interaction term with transportation imports was negative and significant and that for machinery imports was insignificant. The total effect for transportation imports was, however, positive and significant while that for machinery imports was insignificant. They conjectured that in developing economies transportation equipment may be utilized more easily than machinery imports because the former most likely require lower overall levels of skill.

The general conclusion is that human capital may play an important role in countries that do little, if any, R&D by facilitating the absorption of foreign technologies created in countries located close to the technology frontier. The transfer of technology from frontier countries takes several forms (transmission of ideas and imports of goods that embody foreign technology or foreign direct investment) and human capital may be an important link in the successful diffusion of these technologies globally.

6.6   Threshold Effects and Nonlinearities

The empirical literature discussed in the previous sections is based on linear econometric specifications derived from models that are intrinsically linear. One of the principal objectives of this book is the investigation of the human capital-growth nexus from a nonlinear perspective. This section offers an introduction to empirical modeling of nonlinearities and serves as a bridge to the material covered in subsequent chapters. This section acts as a transition from linear to nonlinear models and is based on the notion of threshold effects.

A threshold represents a gateway from one description of the world into another which may be quite different. More precisely, a threshold effect describes a process by which the magnitude of the response variable changes significantly as an observable triggering stimulus exceeds some critical value. The type of nonlinearity that is associated with threshold effects focuses on regime switching that is induced by observable factors such as, in our case, human capital accumulation or initial endowments or some other model characteristic. This puts the threshold effect literature on a different footing from other types of nonlinearity-inducing mechanisms such as Markov-Switching, for example, where an unobservable state determines regime switches. Threshold effects offer a simple methodology for capturing economically meaningful nonlinear behavior and are also relatively easy to estimate because they rely on variants of least squares methods (or, as discussed in Chapter 8, local least squares methods).

Most of the theoretical models that deal with the relationship between human capital and growth assume that this relationship is linear: increasing the level (or growth) of human capital should yield a higher rate of economic growth irrespective of the level of human capital. This assumption is not borne by the empirical evidence, as outlined in Kalaitzidakis et al. (2001). As discussed in considerable detail in Chapter 5 several authors, including Azariadis and Drazen (1990), observe that there are persistent differences between groups of countries whereby some low-income economies are caught in a low-growth environment and lag behind countries similar in terms of endowments. In Chapter 5 we discussed several theoretical contributions that seek an explanation in the existence of technological externalities with a "threshold" property that allow economies with similar structures to exhibit different growth experiences. Once human capital attains a certain threshold level, then aggregate production possibilities may expand a lot more rapidly. Economies that have not attained this threshold level may stagnate in a persistent state of low development.

From a modeling point of view, threshold effects yield a specific type of nonlinearity that is quite restrictive. The process induced by thresholds can be described by piecewise linear segments. Thresholds in this case act as "knots" that connect the different segments together. In other words, a threshold effect is an "all-or-nothing" effect as values below and above the threshold result in different regimes. Alternatively, such regime change could occur gradually and not as abruptly by means of a smooth transition. The amount of smoothing allowed at the knots that connect the linear segments will result in a different type of nonlinear effect. Assuming that smoothing is arbitrary, there is a large class of such smooth transition nonlinear effects that includes threshold effects as a special case. In fact, in Chapters 8 and 9 we discuss such models. In general, threshold effects of the simple all-or-nothing variety or the smooth generalizations have proven to be powerful devises that introduce nonlinearity in growth theory.

In the context of the nonlinear empirical growth literature, among the first studies were Durlauf and Johnson (1995), Quah (1996), Easterly and Levine (1997), and Liu and Stengos (1999). One of the conclusions of these studies was a nonlinear relationship between initial GDP and economic growth. Durlauf and Johnson (1995) used the regression-tree methodology, a methodology that allows for multiple thresholds and divides countries into four subgroups according to their initial level of per capita income and literacy rate. They found substantial differences in their estimated coefficient for the secondary enrollment ratio in growth regressions: it was insignificant for two of the subsamples and positive for the other two. Liu and Stengos (1999) confirmed the results of Durlauf and Johnson (1995) with a semiparametric partially additive model that allows for two nonlinear components: one for the initial level of GDP and the other for the secondary enrollment rate. The presence of non-linearities was mainly due to grouping of countries according to their level of initial income, whereas the effect of human capital (as measured by the secondary enrollment rate) was, in essence, linear. Kalaitzidakis et al. (2001) generalized this approach to allow for more than two non-linear components and included different measures of human capital in the estimated function. While Durlauf and Johnson focused on identifying homogenous subgroups of countries under the implicit assumption that the effect of human capital on economic growth was the same for all countries within a subgroup, Kalaitzidakis et al. allowed the effect of human capital to differ both across each country and also each time period. Moreover, while Durlauf and Johnson and Liu and Stengos used only the secondary enrollment ratio, Kalaitzidakis et al. employed a variety of measures of human capital. In Chapter 9 this approach will be studied in greater detail.

Notes

1. Topel points out that, if it is assumed that wages are distributed as log normal, (log) human capital per worker is a function of both mean years of schooling and the variance of human capital within each country. Equation 6.7 assumes that the variance of human capital within each country is relatively stable (so can be subsumed in country-specific terms, β_i). Also differences in experience (usually measured by life expectancy and age of the workforce) that could enter as arguments of $f(\cdot)$ are also assumed constant within countries and, therefore, usually ignored in empirical work. When Topel included the average age and life expectancy as explanatory variables in his estimation of the determinants of output per worker, he found neither of these variables to be significant. He attributed this to the little variation in the average age of the economically active population across countries.

2. In this book we use $a_1, a_2, \dots$ and $b_1, b_2, \dots$ to denote parameters to be estimated empirically. We use the same symbols to denote parameters in different models. This is done for convenience to minimize the use of different symbols. Their economic interpretation, however, differs between empirical specifications and they are not comparable between models (e.g., a_1, a_2, and a_3 are used in both 6.5 and 6.8 but their interpretation is different).

3. For the constant returns to scale production function $Y(t) = A(t)K(t)^{\alpha} H(t)^{1-\alpha}$, output per worker along the balanced growth path is given by $y(t) = (K/Y)^{\alpha/(1-\alpha)} \cdot h(t) \cdot A(t)$.

4. Mincerian regressions have a long history in empirical work as a method of gauging the private return to education, i.e., the return that accrues to an individual from acquiring more education. Experience and other determinants of wage rates are generally included in regression models such as 6.12. Some authors, including Topel, assume these characteristics are constant and, therefore, subsumed in the constant term, as is done in 6.12. Psacharopoulos (1994), Psacharopoulos and Patrinos (2002), and Bils and Klenow (2000) provide a summary of estimates of the return to education from Mincerian regressions for a variety of countries.

5. A Cobb–Douglas production function with constant exponents over time (a production function used frequently in empirical work and encountered in this section) would satisfy these requirements.

6. Gemmell (1996) included both the change and the initial level of mean years of schooling as determinants of per capita growth between 1960 and 1985. He considered both primary and secondary schooling for his complete sample. The estimates for both the level and change in primary schooling were positive and significant. Secondary schooling estimates, however, had no significant effect on growth either in level or change form. Estimates for three separate subsamples showed that both the level and change in schooling had a significant effect for the different subsamples: primary schooling for the poorest-country sample, secondary schooling for the intermediate sample, and tertiary schooling for the Organization for Economic Cooperation and Development (OECD) countries.

7. Acceptance of the Topel and Krueger and Lindahl proposition that both the change in schooling and the initial level of schooling should be included as explanatory variables has implications for hypotheses testing. For instance, consider the specification in 6.6 with the addition of the initial level of schooling:

$$(\ln y_{i,\tau+\upsilon} - \ln y_{i,\tau}) = (\ln A_{i,\tau+\upsilon} - \ln A_{i,\tau}) + b_1(\ln k_{i,\tau+\upsilon} - \ln k_{i,\tau})$$

$$+ b_2(\ln h_{i,\tau+\upsilon} - \ln h_{i,\tau}) + b_3(\ln h_{i,\tau})$$

$$+ (\ln \epsilon_{i,\tau+\upsilon} - \ln \epsilon_{i,\tau})$$

This specification can be rewritten in terms of the current and lagged level of schooling as

$$(\ln y_{i,\tau+\upsilon} - \ln y_{i,\tau}) = (\ln A_{i,\tau+\upsilon} - \ln A_{i,\tau}) + b_1(\ln k_{i,\tau+\upsilon} - \ln k_{i,\tau})$$
$$+ b_2(\ln h_{i,\tau+\upsilon}) + b_4(\ln h_{i,\tau})$$
$$+ (\ln \epsilon_{i,\tau+\upsilon} - \ln \epsilon_{i,\tau})$$

where $b_4 = b_3 - b_2$. In this case the hypothesis of interest (that the initial schooling level has a positive impact on growth holding the change of schooling constant or $b_3 > 0$) amounts to testing $b_2 + b_4 > 0$.

8. The data for output per worker and the investment ratio were from the Penn World Tables and those for schooling from United Nations databases.

9. From 3.25 the speed of convergence, λ, is equal to $(1 - \alpha - \beta)(g_A + g_L + \delta_K)$. A reasonable value for $g_A + \delta_K$ is 0.05 and for the growth of the labor force is 0.01. With the income share of physical capital and human capital approximately one-third ($\alpha \approx 1/3$, $\beta \approx 1/3$), it follows that $\lambda \approx 0.02$.

10. To derive the saving ratio for physical capital accumulation in the CKR model, we note that the rate of accumulation for this model is $\dot{\tilde{k}} = f(\tilde{k}) - (g_A + g_L + \delta_K)\tilde{k} - \tilde{c}$ (see Section 3.3). For the Cobb–Douglas production function, it is true that $\tilde{k}/f(\tilde{k}) = \alpha/f'(\tilde{k})$. In the steady state both the rate of capital accumulation, $\dot{\tilde{k}}$, and growth rate of consumption, $\dot{\tilde{c}}/\tilde{c}$, in 3.36 are zero. Using these two and the definition of saving as $1 - (\tilde{c}/\tilde{y}) = 1 - (\tilde{c}/f(\tilde{k}))$, the saving ratio for the CKR model is $\alpha(g_A + g_L + \delta_K)/(\rho + \sigma g_A + \delta_K)$ and is shown in 6.19.

11. They work with the Lucas–Uzawa model that omits the contemporaneous spillover effect; in the methodology of Section 4.3, $\gamma = 0$.

12. This is a minimum distance method proposed by Chamberlain (1982), where the reduced form Π-matrix contains all the relevant information and restrictions implied by the panel data model.

13. The restriction is necessary because with only two independent coefficients estimable, it is impossible to recover estimates of the three parameters of interest, α, β, and c_A^e. They suggest that the restriction is plausible given the results of MRW.

14. As explained in Section 6.2 in connection with equations 6.3 and 6.5, when the stock of human capital is identified with mean years of schooling (h in our notation or human capital per worker) it is implicitly assumed that the stock of human capital equals the product of the labor force and human capital per worker or $H = h \cdot L$. The distinction between human capital stock and human capital per worker does not arise if one considers constant returns to scale and the intensive form is estimated (as in specifications 6.4 or 6.6).

15. As indicated in the previous note, Benhabib and Spiegel measured the stock of human capital by mean years of schooling in the working age population (or h in our notation). Rather than changing notation and in order to render the discussion here comparable to both Section 4.4 and the original, we retain their notation whereby H represents mean years of schooling.

16. Benhabib and Spiegel made the simplifying assumption that the endogenous and catch-up functions are constant across time and linear in form so that $\Phi(H) = c_{imit} \cdot H$, $\Psi(H) = c_{innov} \cdot H$, and $\Psi(H^l) = c_{innov} \cdot H^l$ where H^l is the leader's human capital stock.

17. Pritchett refers to the calculated series for K as Cumulated Depreciated Investment Effort because, as he claims, it does not approximate the capital concept in the production function when the government is the main contributor of investment resources.

18. The Pritchett formulation is derived from $\ln h(t) = \ln\left(\sum_{t=0}^{T}(\delta_w)^t\right) + \ln w_0(t) + \ln(\exp^{r_E \times EDUC} - 1)$ where δ_w is the discount factor over which a worker's wages are discounted over her or his working life (T), w_0 is the wage rate of a worker with no years of schooling, and r_E is the increase in wages from an additional year of schooling (assumed equal to 0.1 by Pritchett). The formulation in 6.24 is derived from the discrete form of the rate of change of the stock of human capital per worker that is approximately $d\ln h(t)/dt \approx d\{\ln(\exp^{r_E \times EDUC} - 1)\}/dt$. This derivative assumes that both the discount rate (δ_w) and the wage rate of unskilled labor (w_0) are constant over time.

19. According to the Pritchett formulation (see previous note), $d\ln h(t)/dEDUC = r_E/(\exp^{r_E \times EDUC} - 1) \longrightarrow \infty$ as $EDUC \longrightarrow 0$. As the number of years of schooling decreases, the additional effect of one year of education on human capital goes to infinity.

20. In order to arrive at this production function, we note from Section 4.5 that the Romer production function includes three inputs (labor, human capital used in final goods production, and intermediate inputs) and is of the form $Y = H_Y^\gamma \cdot L^\beta \cdot \int_0^A x_i^{1-\beta-\gamma} di = H_Y^\gamma \cdot L^\beta A x^{1-\beta-\gamma}$ in symmetric equilibrium. The capital stock is equal to total production of intermediate goods $(K = x \cdot A)$ and the resulting production function can be written as $Y = A^{\beta+\gamma} K^{1-\beta-\gamma} L^\beta H_Y^\gamma$.

21. Equation 6.28 can also be written in terms of male educational capital, $\widetilde{h}^{M*}$, and the educational gap (with appropriate changes to coefficient signs). Knowles, Lorgelly, and Owen estimated and contrasted the two versions of 6.28.

22. Klasen also estimated several other specification where the dependent variables were the investment share of GDP, the growth of population, and the growth

of the labor force. Knowles, Lorgelly, and Owen focused mainly on the determinants of the steady-state level of income per capita rather than the growth rate. In keeping with the theme of this book we focus on the formulations for the growth of per capita income.

23. In addition to test scores, they considered two other indicators of schooling quality encapsulated by educational success: the repetition rate (the percentage of repeaters in the total number of students enrolled at a given level) and the dropout rate (percentage of children who start primary school but do not attain the final grade of primary school). While they found similar results for the determinants of these two indicators of quality, they did not use them in regressions explaining economic growth.

24. Unlike Lee and Barro, Hanushek and Kimko did not use data from reading tests because of their concern about language differences across countries and the validity of putting reading scores on a unidimensional scale along with science and mathematics scores. Moreover, they claim that math and science scores approximate more closely the R&D-promoting facet of human capital.

25. One transformation converts each series to a mean of 50. The second takes advantage of the availability of a consistent set of scores over time for the United States, and the mean for each series was formulated to follow the mean pattern of the U.S. scores. The two transformations provided two alternative measures of human capital quality for each country.

26. In the remainder of their paper (and especially the conclusion) they acknowledged that the magnitude of the effect of quality on growth (greater than one percentage point) is implausibly large, a result they were unable to explain.

27. Two countries, Hong Kong and Swaziland, were included in the sample for the baseline human capital production function but were excluded from the growth regressions. To generate projections for human capital quality, Bosworth/Collins estimated two specifications (and thus two measures of quality): (1) the Hanushek and Kimko regression specification; and (2) they added an index of institutional quality as an additional predictor of human capital quality.

28. Estimates with protection against expropriation as the indicator of institutional quality also yielded a positive but insignificant coefficient for the interaction effect.

29. It is not our intention to review this literature here. Rather, our focus is on the role human capital plays in the transmission mechanism. Keller (2004) provides a thorough review of the issues and a concise discussion of various studies in this area.

30. The elasticity was evaluated at the mean level of foreign R&D and is given by $\delta_2 + \delta_5 \times \ln \overline{FRD}_i$, where $\overline{FRD}_i$ is the mean level of foreign R&D of country i.

31. Including lags was important because they considered annual rates of growth of TFP.

32. The total effect was evaluated at the mean value of FRD in a manner similar to that described in the previous note.

7 Human Capital and Economic Growth: Linear Specifications

7.1 Introduction

The purpose of this chapter is to provide a systematic empirical investigation of the human capital economic-growth nexus from a linear perspective. The specifications estimated in this chapter adopt the two main linear approaches described in previous chapters: the transition to the steady-state approach formalized by Mankiw, Romer, and Weil (1992) and the growth accounting methodology. Chapter 9 will examine the human capital–growth relationship from a nonlinear perspective using both these approaches.

In Section 7.2 we recap the theoretical and parametric framework that characterizes the growth regression approach of Mankiw, Romer, and Weil (MRW). In this section we also estimate the MRW specification with panel data and growth rates that are averaged across five-year periods. We focus on various measures of human capital that use the stock definition, that is, mean years of schooling. In Section 7.3 we use the growth accounting framework to derive an empirical specification for the determinants of total factor productivity growth and estimate it with panel data. The empirical results from the estimation of the linear framework that characterizes both these approaches provides the benchmark against which we will measure and evaluate the nonlinear specification of these two approaches. We will specify and estimate with the same data sets the nonlinear counterparts to both approaches in Chapter 9.

7.2   Cross-Country Growth Regressions and Measures of Human Capital

As indicated in Chapter 6, one of the most popular empirical approaches to evaluating the impact of human capital on economic growth is the MRW model that was outlined in Section 3.2.3. MRW estimated the specification in 3.26 with cross-section data and with the secondary enrollment rate (adjusted for the proportion of the population that is of secondary school age) as a measure of human capital (s_H). Islam (1995) repeated the estimation with mean years of schooling as the measure of human capital stock and with panel data. Barro and Sala-i-Martin (2004) also used panel data and estimated a general growth regression equation of the form 6.1 with various definitions of human capital. In general, as the frequency over which growth rates are calculated increases (5-year changes vs. 10 or 20 years) there is less evidence of a positive effect of human capital accumulation on growth. Kalaitzidakis et al. (2001) adopted the MRW framework to investigate the human capital-growth relationship with both parametric and nonparametric techniques. Our first objective in this chapter is to use the MRW framework and follow the methodology in Kalaitzidakis et al. to test the effect of human capital on economic growth with panel data and parametric techniques.

We employ a balanced cross-country panel data set that covers nine nonoverlapping five-year periods: 1960–64, 1965–69,..., 1990–94, 1995–98, and 1999–2003. The balanced panel is constructed by deleting countries for which data are missing for some of the subperiods. There are 639 observations from 71 countries at various stages of development. Table 7.1a shows the list of countries. We use a balanced panel because it typically comprises a more homogeneous group of countries than an unbalanced one. Balanced data include only countries for which there are no missing values for the entire period under investigation, and the group of included countries is more homogeneous since missing values are typically associated with developing countries (especially those at the lowest end of the income range) for which the quality of data is an additional issue of concern.

TABLE **7.1a** Countries in the Data Set

Country Code	Country Name	Country Code	Country Name
DZA	Algeria	KEN	Kenya
ARG	Argentina	KOR	Korea, Rep.
AUS	Australia	LSO	Lesotho
AUT	Austria	MWI	Malawi
BGD	Bangladesh	MYS	Malaysia
BRB	Barbados	MUS	Mauritius
BEL	Belgium	MEX	Mexico
BOL	Bolivia	NPL	Nepal
BWA	Botswana	NLD	Netherlands
BRA	Brazil	NZL	New Zealand
CMR	Cameroon	NIC	Nicaragua
CAN	Canada	NER	Niger
CHL	Chile	NOR	Norway
COL	Colombia	PAK	Pakistan
CRI	Costa Rica	PAN	Panama
DNK	Denmark	PNG	Papua New Guinea
DOM	Dominican Republic	PRY	Paraguay
ECU	Ecuador	PER	Peru
SLV	El Salvador	PHL	Philippines
FJI	Fiji	PRT	Portugal
FIN	Finland	SEN	Senegal
FRA	France	ZAF	South Africa
GHA	Ghana	ESP	Spain
GRC	Greece	LKA	Sri Lanka
GTM	Guatemala	SWE	Sweden
GUY	Guyana	CHE	Switzerland
HND	Honduras	SYR	Syrian Arab Republic
HKG	Hong Kong, China	THA	Thailand
ISL	Iceland	TGO	Togo
IND	India	TTO	Trinidad and Tobago
IDN	Indonesia	GBR	United Kingdom
IRL	Ireland	USA	United States
ISR	Israel	URY	Uruguay
ITA	Italy	ZMB	Zambia
JAM	Jamaica	ZWE	Zimbabwe
JPN	Japan		

We use mean years of schooling as our measure of human capital. Although we recognize that this is an imperfect proxy, we use it because data across a wide variety of countries and time are only available on two measures: mean years of schooling and rates of school enrollment. The latter, a flow measure, is not the preferred choice of empirical growth practitioners who tend to prefer the former, a stock measure. We acknowledge that mean years of schooling is only a quantitative measure of education and there are vast differences in quality between school systems across countries. However, as discussed in Chapter 6, qualitative measures of human capital are not widely available and when they exist, they do so for a small group of relatively developed countries.

Data on mean years of formal education are from the Barro and Lee (2001) database. The Barro–Lee data on human capital is one of the most widely used data sets in empirical growth research. This data set uses census estimates of mean years of schooling from multilateral agencies and is available quinquennially. There are substantial gaps in census data availability that are filled in by interpolation using data on enrollment rates. This data set, however, has a number of shortcomings. As well as not accounting for differences in quality across educational systems, it measures only formal education, ignoring the informal education sector. In many countries this is a substantial source of human capital accumulation in the form of on-the-job training, skill acquisition, and other types of knowledge that enhance the productivity of labor. However, as Barro and Lee point out, on the whole it provides a "reasonable proxy for the stock of schooling capital for a broad group of countries" (p. 542). The latest version of the data set improves on earlier versions in a number of ways, notably reducing measurement error. It also enables disaggregation of human capital into several subcategories, such as differences in human capital by sex and by level of education.

In addition to Barro and Lee there are several other data sets that provide estimates of mean years of schooling for various countries. These include Nehru, Swanson, and Dubey (1995), De la Fuente and Doménech (2006), and Cohen and Soto (2007).[1] It is not our intention to compare their relative merits (for a brief discussion see Bosworth and Collins (2003)). We note, however, that De la Fuente and Doménech data cover only OECD economies while the data in Nehru, Swanson, and Dubey end in 1987, factors that render both data sets inadequate for our empirical purposes. The Cohen–Soto data set covers 95 countries and data on educational attainment are available at the beginning of each decade for the 1960–2000 period. It is based on national census data rather than data from multilateral agencies, as is Barro–Lee. It covers a sufficiently wide range of countries and time periods and is thus an alternative to

Barro–Lee for our empirical investigation. We have chosen to use the Barro–Lee data set because it is the one most frequently used by previous researchers (including us in previous work) and so the results presented in this book can be compared in a consistent fashion (at least in terms of source of data for human capital) with previous work. An interesting exercise, however, would be to use data from the Cohen–Soto database and the empirical methods described in this book to compare the results obtained with those reported here.

Our first measure of human capital is total mean years of schooling of a country's entire population ages 15 and over (symbolized by *SCT*). This is an aggregate measure of human capital that is intended to provide an overall indication of the level of education of a country's adult population (workforce) and is the most frequently used measure of human capital in empirical research. In addition to this aggregate measure, we also consider differences by sex as measured by mean years of schooling in the male population (*SCM*) and female population (*SCF*) ages 15 and over. We also consider differences by level of education: mean years of schooling at the primary level (*SCP*) and at the post-primary level (secondary and tertiary combined, *SCH*). We combine educational achievement at the secondary and tertiary level into one measure (post-primary education) for a number of reasons: (1) a number of countries have very low or zero values for educational achievement at the tertiary level; (2) to limit the number of measures of human capital; and (3) some of the theoretical mechanisms that link human capital of different educational levels to economic growth, discussed in Chapters 4 and 5, draw a distinction between basic education (primary) and education that enables the creation and diffusion of ideas (post-primary). Finally, we consider differences both by sex and level of education: the educational attainment of males and females at the primary level (*SCPM* and *SCPF*, respectively) and at the post-primary level (*SCHM* and *SCHF*, respectively).

Following MRW, we estimate the unrestricted version of 3.27 and rewrite it as

$$(1/\upsilon)(\ln y_{i,\tau+\upsilon} - \ln y_{i,\tau}) = a_0 + a_1 D_\tau + a_2 D_j + a_3 \ln s_{Ki,\tau} + a_4 \ln(g_{Li,\tau}$$

$$+ g_A + \delta_K) + a_5 \ln y_{i,\tau} + a_6 \ln EDUC_{i,\tau} + \varepsilon_{i,\tau} \qquad \text{EQUATION } \textbf{7.1}$$

where τ refers to the beginning year (e.g., 1960, 1965, ..., 1995, 1999), υ is the number of years over which the growth rate is calculated, and D_τ and D_j are dummy variables for each subperiod and for the countries in Latin America (LA) and sub-Saharan Africa (SSA), respectively. The need for dummy variables to identify the time period is clear from the derivation of equations 3.26 and 3.27. Geographic dummy variables have been included by many previous researchers to account for idiosyncratic economic conditions in these two regions (e.g., high degrees of income inequality in Latin America or high ethno-linguistic fractionalization in Africa).

We measure saving for purposes of physical capital accumulation (s_K) by the share of investment in GDP. The other explanatory variables are the growth of the labor force (g_L) and initial level of income per capita ($y_{i,\tau}$). Finally, $EDUC$ refers to the various measures of mean years of schooling that were described previously in this section. Our data (other than mean years of schooling) come from two sources. The growth of GDP per capita and the growth of the labor force are from the World Development Indicators database of the World Bank. Initial GDP at the beginning of each period and investment as share of GDP are from the Summers–Heston Penn World Tables, version 6.1 (PWT 6.1).

Estimation results from the linear parametric regressions are presented in Table 7.2. Several alternative versions of equation 7.1 are estimated using various measures of educational attainment. The results in Table 7.2 show that the estimate of the dummy variable for SSA is negative and significant and that for LA negative and marginally insignificant. Other researchers have also reported negative (significant) estimates for the SSA dummy variable and the "negative Africa dummy" is a subject of considerable research. Estimates of the dummy variables for the different subperiods are positive and mostly significant for the pre-1975 period (the reference subperiod is 2000–2003). The dummy for 1980–84 is negative and significant, reflecting a period of global recession. Post-1985 dummy variables are generally insignificant except for the 1995–98 time period indicating the pickup in world growth in the latter half of the 1990s. The estimate for investment in physical capital is positive and strongly significant and that for initial GDP negative and also significant. Finally, the estimate for the growth of the labor force is insignificant. These results are generally in line with findings in the existing literature that also adopts a parametric specification as in equation 7.1.

As far as the variable of interest in this book, the impact of human capital on growth depends on the measure of human capital. Regression specification (1) confirms that an increase in total mean years of schooling will have a positive effect on growth, although the effect is not statistically significant. In specification (2) we differentiate between total years of education by sex and find that formal education for males has a positive effect on growth, but female education has the opposite effect; both estimates are statistically significant. We return to this result in Chapter 9 where we will offer a contrasting view with estimates obtained from the semiparametric model. When education is differentiated by level (primary vs. post-primary), specification (3) shows that primary education has a significant and positive effect on growth, whereas post-primary education has a negative and significant effect. Again we will return to this point when discussing semiparametric estimates in Chapter 9. Specification (4) reveals that, in our sample, it is male education at the primary level that contributes positively (and significantly) to growth, not post-primary male education. On the other hand, specification (5) shows that the result for female formal education is reversed: post-primary female education has a negative and significant effect on growth but primary female education has no effect on growth.

Several general conclusions emerge from Table 7.2. First, coefficient estimates for the share of investment are of the anticipated sign, highly significant, and robust to alternative measures of human capital. Estimates for initial level of per capita income are negative and significant and consistent with conditional β-convergence. Estimates for the growth of the labor force are consistently insignificant. Finally, and more importantly, the estimates for human capital are sensitive to the choice of measure. Most of the estimates are significant, though the estimate for total years of schooling is positive and insignificant. Some measures of female human capital (SCF and $SCHF$) show a negative and significant effect while some measures of male human capital (SCM and $SCPM$) show a significant positive effect. In sum, the parametric results confirm the inability of previous studies to reach a consensus regarding the role of human capital in economic growth as they identify fairly conflicting gender and level effects.

In Chapter 9 all these results will be compared and contrasted with those obtained from nonparametric estimation of the nonlinear version of 7.1.

7.3   Cross-Country Growth Accounting and Measures of Human Capital

In this section we estimate the growth accounting approach to human capital and growth. We investigate the contribution of human capital to the growth of total factor productivity from a different perspective to that considered in Section 7.2. The previous section was based on the MRW approach that stipulates a specific production function, which is combined with equations for the accumulation of the reproducible factors to arrive at equations for the steady state of per capita income and the transition process to the steady state. As outlined in previous chapters, another strand of the literature follows an approach based on: (1) the estimation of a production function that includes human capital as either a direct input or as a determinant of total factor productivity (e.g., Benhabib and Spiegel 1994; Edwards 1998; Pritchett 2001); or (2) the assignment of specific values to the coefficients of the production function (the shares of inputs) to compute the residual which is then evaluated, along with the factors of production (including human capital), for their contribution to differences in the level or growth of per capita GDP (e.g., Benhabib and Spiegel 2005; Hall and Jones 1999; Klenow and Rodríguez-Clare 1997). The majority of studies in this area, however, are based on very restrictive assumptions: a Cobb–Douglas production function with Hicks-neutral technology.

In this section we follow Mamuneas, Savvides, and Stengos (2006) and assume a general production function that describes the technology of country i at time t and expressed in general form as

$$Y = f(K, E, H, t)$$

EQUATION 7.2

where Y represents aggregate output, K the aggregate physical capital stock, E the effective or human capital-augmented labor (defined shortly), H the average human capital (in this case identified by mean years of schooling per person of working age), and t is a technology index (measured by a time trend). Total differentiation of 7.2 with respect to time and division by Y yields

$$\widehat{Y} = \widehat{A} + \varepsilon_K \widehat{K} + \varepsilon_E \widehat{E} + \varepsilon_H \widehat{H} \qquad \text{\small EQUATION \textbf{7.3}}$$

where $(\hat{\ })$ denotes a growth rate, $\widehat{A} = (\partial f / \partial t)/Y$ is the exogenous rate of technological change, and $\varepsilon_Q = \partial \ln Y / \partial \ln Q$ ($Q = K, E, H$) denotes output elasticity. As will be explained shortly, the last term in 7.3 measures the externality effect of human capital accumulation. Assuming a perfectly competitive theory of distribution, the output elasticities of effective labor and capital should be equal to the observed income shares of labor, s_L, and capital, s_K. The income share of labor can be defined in two ways: the income share of effective labor (E) or the income share of "traditional" or workforce labor (L). These two are equal since the value of labor (the numerator of the income share) is the same independently of the definition of the labor input as L or E (the corresponding price and quantity indices, however, will differ). Equation 7.3, however, is not useful for empirical purposes because the growth rate of effective labor, $\widehat{E}$, is not directly observable.

In order to arrive at an estimable formulation, we assume that the effective labor input is expressed as

$$E = g(L, H) \qquad \text{\small EQUATION \textbf{7.4}}$$

where $g(\cdot)$ is a general function. This general function has two arguments: the "raw" abilities of workers to contribute to total production and the level of human capital that enhances those "raw" abilities and thus contributes to making "raw" labor more productive. Therefore, we can decompose $\widehat{E}$ as

$$\widehat{E} = \eta_L \widehat{L} + \eta_H \widehat{H} \qquad \text{\small EQUATION \textbf{7.5}}$$

where η_L and η_H are effective labor elasticities with respect to labor and average human capital, respectively. Substituting 7.5 in 7.3 we have:

$$\widehat{Y} = \widehat{A} + \varepsilon_K \widehat{K} + \varepsilon_E \eta_L \widehat{L} + (\varepsilon_E \eta_H + \varepsilon_H)\widehat{H} \qquad \text{\small EQUATION \textbf{7.6}}$$

In contrast to 7.3, the last term in parentheses in 7.6 measures the total effect of human capital. It is made up of two components: a direct effect of human capital as contributor to aggregate growth, or $\varepsilon_E \eta_H \widehat{H}$, and the externality effect (described by the Lucas model of Section 4.3), or $\varepsilon_H \widehat{H}$. The output elasticity of "raw" labor is $\varepsilon_E \eta_L$. Direct estimation of 7.6 corresponds to the well-known growth accounting methodology discussed in Section 6.2 and equation 6.5.

We can define the growth of total factor productivity (TFP) of country i in year t as

$$\widehat{TFP}_{it} = \widehat{Y}_{it} - s_L \widehat{L}_{it} - s_K \widehat{K}_{it} \qquad \text{EQUATION } \textbf{7.7}$$

where s_L and s_K are shares of labor and capital income, respectively. We note that the cost shares of effective and "traditional" labor are the same independently of how labor is defined. Hence, $s_E \equiv s_L$, and in what follows we will use these interchangeably.

Factor shares generally vary across countries and across time. Mamuneas, Savvides, and Stengos (2006) calculated the growth of TFP in 7.7 by obtaining direct values of the share of capital and labor from the national account statistics of a limited number of countries for which the required data were available. Gollin (2002) also computed the capital and labor share of income from national account statistics of various countries and found the former lies in the range 0.20 to 0.35 and was not correlated with country income levels or growth rates. Because we want to employ as wide a range of countries and time periods, in this book we follow the practice of several researchers (e.g., Benhabib and Spiegel 2005; Hall and Jones 1999) and we let s_L and s_K be fixed both across time and countries, setting s_L to equal two-thirds and s_K one-third. Therefore, given values for the growth of aggregate output labor and physical capital, we can use 7.7 to obtain values for the growth of TFP. It is important to note that the measure of TFP in 7.7 contains the component of output growth that cannot be explained by the growth of "traditional" inputs (K and L).

Subscripting equation 7.6 by country and year (it), taking a discrete approximation of the continuous growth rates, and adding 7.7 to it we have

$$\widehat{TFP}_{it} = \widehat{A}_{it} + \left[(\varepsilon_K - s_K) \widehat{K}_{it} + (\varepsilon_E \eta_L - s_E) \widehat{L}_{it} \right]$$

$$+ (\varepsilon_E \eta_H + \varepsilon_H) \widehat{H}_{it} \qquad \text{EQUATION } \textbf{7.8}$$

where we have made use of the equality between s_L and s_E. The first term ($\widehat{A}_{it}$) is the exogenous rate of technological change and the final term in parentheses is the total contribution of human capital. As indicated earlier, the latter is made up of two components: the direct or private effect and the indirect or externality effect. The second term in brackets is the scale effect. Having fixed s_L and s_K to sum to unity across countries and time, we implicitly assume constant returns to scale.[2] Perfectly competitive market conditions imply that output elasticities are equal to shares and the term in brackets will be equal to zero if $\eta_L = 1$.[3] In what follows, we assume this term is equal to zero.

Of central importance to our estimation is the final term in 7.8 that captures the contribution of human capital to aggregate production. In this chapter we assume it is linear ($\varepsilon_E \eta_H + \varepsilon_H = \theta$) and we model it as $\theta \widehat{H}_{it}$. By contrast, in Chapter 9 we will allow this effect to be modeled as a general unknown function $\theta(\cdot)\widehat{H}_{it}$ that, nonetheless, depends on several observable characteristics. Assuming that human capital influences TFP growth in a linear fashion, equation 7.8 can be written as:

$$\widehat{TFP}_{it} = \widehat{A}_{it} + \theta \widehat{H}_{it} \qquad \text{EQUATION } \textbf{7.9}$$

In estimating empirically equation 7.9, we model $\widehat{A}_{it}$ (the exogenous rate of growth of technological change) as a function of geographic- and time-specific dummy variables. We introduce the same two geographic-specific dummy variables as in Section 7.2, one for SSA, or D^A, and the other for LA, or D^{LA}, that capture idiosyncratic features of exogenous technological change that is common to countries in these regions.[4] Time-specific dummy variables, or D_t, capture the procyclical behavior of TFP growth. Equation 7.9 can therefore be written in estimable form as

$$\widehat{TFP}_{it} = a_0 + a_{LA} D_{it}^{LA} + a_A D_{it}^A + \sum_{t=1}^{T-1} a_t D_t + \theta \widehat{H}_{it} + u_{it}$$

$$= X_{it} \beta + \theta \widehat{H}_{it} + u_{it} \qquad \text{EQUATION } \textbf{7.10}$$

where $X_{it} = (D_{it}^A, D_{it}^{LA}, D_t)$ and the error term satisfies $E(u_{it} \mid X_{it}, \widehat{H}_{it}) = 0$.

We estimate specification 7.10 with a balanced panel data set over the period 1965–95. We construct six nonoverlapping five-year periods over which we compute growth rates: 1965–69, 1970–74, ..., 1990–95. In terms of country coverage, this data set is similar, but not identical, to

TABLE **7.1b** List of Countries in TFP Index Construction

Algeria	Finland	Korea	Singapore
Argentina	France	Malawi	Spain
Australia	Germany	Malaysia	Sri Lanka
Austria	Ghana	Mali	Sudan
Bangladesh	Greece	Mauritius	Sweden
Belgium	Guatemala	Mexico	Switzerland
Bolivia	Haiti	Mozambique	Tanzania
Brazil	Honduras	Netherlands	Thailand
Cameroon	Iceland	New Zealand	Tunisia
Canada	India	Norway	Turkey
Chile	Indonesia	Pakistan	Uganda
China	Iran	Panama	United Kingdom
Colombia	Ireland	Paraguay	United States
Costa Rice	Israel	Peru	Uruguay
Cyprus	Italy	Philippines	Venezuela
Denmark	Jamaica	Portugal	Zaire
Ecuador	Japan	Rwanda	Zambia
Egypt	Jordan	Senegal	Zimbabwe
El Salvador	Kenya	Sierra Leone	

the one used in Section 7.2. The list of countries is in Table 7.1b. Data on real aggregate output (Y) and the real physical capital stock (K) come from Nehru and Dhareshwar (1993). Their data end in 1985 and we have updated and extended them to 1995 with additional data from the World Development Indicators (WDI). The extension for real output is straightforward because the data are available in WDI. To extend the data on the physical capital stock, we obtained data on real investment from WDI and used the perpetual inventory method. Data on the number of workers (L) are from the Summers–Heston (PWT 6.1) database. Finally, we use the various measures of mean years of schooling described in Section 7.2 as alternative indicators of human capital per worker.

We examine several hypotheses regarding the role of human capital in promoting TFP growth within the growth accounting framework. The results are in Table 7.3. The estimates for geographic region (Latin America and sub-Saharan Africa) are negative and significant and verify that these regions have lagged behind others in terms of productivity growth. The estimates of the time-specific dummy variables are negative and significant for all subperiods. Thus, we note a secular decline in productivity growth globally in comparison to the reference period 1965–69.

TABLE **7.2** Least Squares Estimation of Equation 7.1 (Dependent Variable: *rate of growth*; absolute *t*-statistics in parenthesis)

	(1) SCT	(2) SCM & SCF	(3) SCP & SCH	(4) SCPM & SCPF	(5) SCHM & SCHF
a_0	0.0469	0.0638	0.0288	0.0644	0.0512
	(1.9352)	(2.3313)	(1.1199)	(2.1560)	(1.9825)
D_{1960}	0.0174	0.0167	0.0138	0.0170	0.0151
	(4.5904)	(4.4206)	(3.6883)	(4.5383)	(4.0539)
D_{1965}	0.0135	0.0127	0.0103	0.0129	0.0121
	(3.8669)	(3.5937)	(2.7724)	(3.7538)	(3.4395)
D_{1970}	0.0188	0.0186	0.0164	0.0187	0.0175
	(4.8686)	(4.9857)	(4.3988)	(5.0347)	(4.6580)
D_{1975}	0.0051	0.0050	0.0033	0.0052	0.0040
	(1.2542)	(1.2426)	(0.8200)	(1.2980)	(0.9948)
D_{1980}	−0.0110	−0.0111	−0.0121	−0.0110	−0.0118
	(3.1396)	(3.1600)	(3.4478)	(3.1485)	(3.3616)
D_{1985}	0.0033	0.0032	0.0024	0.0032	0.0028
	(0.9189)	(0.8907)	(0.6665)	(0.8975)	(0.7862)
D_{1990}	0.0013	0.0012	0.0009	0.0011	0.0010
	(0.3556)	(0.3246)	(0.2534)	(0.3115)	(0.2773)
D_{1995}	0.0081	0.0080	0.0080	0.0081	0.0079
	(2.5334)	(2.4938)	(2.4876)	(2.5129)	(2.4573)
D_{Africa}	−0.0067	−0.0106	−0.0081	−0.0099	−0.0071
	(3.1147)	(4.0288)	(3.6066)	(3.5645)	(3.2814)
$D_{Lat. Am.}$	−0.0053	−0.0070	−0.0071	−0.0068	−0.0066
	(1.2780)	(1.7361)	(1.7183)	(1.6371)	(1.5906)
$\log s_k$	0.0150	0.0145	0.0145	0.0142	0.0159
	(4.8430)	(4.8207)	(4.7762)	(4.7147)	(5.3304)
$\log(gL + gA + \delta)$	−0.0091	−0.0083	−0.0089	−0.0080	−0.0077
	(1.0010)	(0.8984)	(0.9951)	(0.8482)	(0.8518)
$\log y\tau$	−0.0036	−0.0041	−0.0017	−0.0045	−0.0027
	(1.9272)	(2.2086)	(0.8464)	(2.4571)	(1.4031)
$\log$ (SCT)	0.0024				
	(0.8911)				
$\log$ (SCM)		0.0102			
		(2.4161)			
$\log$ (SCF)		−0.0120			
		(1.9487)			
$\log$ (SCH)			0.0068		
			(2.3574)		
$\log$ (SCH)			−0.0047		
			(1.9800)		
$\log$ (SCPM)				0.0098	
				(1.6848)	
$\log$ (SCPF)				−0.0105	
				(1.3013)	
$\log$ (SCHM)					0.0015
					(0.9897)
$\log$ (SCHF)					−0.0020
					(7.7594)
R^2	0.2453	0.2548	0.2542	0.2524	0.2532
NPFF[1]	4.15	4.24	4.31	4.42	3.55

NPFF[1] is a test of a linear null hypothesis (equation 7.1) against the semiparametric alternative. The test is distributed as a standard normal variate.

TABLE 7.3 Least Squares Estimation of Equation 7.10 (Dependent Variable: *TFP growth*; absolute *t*-statistics in parenthesis)

	SCT	SCM	SCF	SCP	SCH	SCPM	SCPF	SCHM	SCHF
a_4	0.0216	0.0215	0.0222	0.0215	0.0223	0.0217	0.0220	0.0231	0.0221
	(7.0757)	(7.0309)	(7.2709)	(7.1751)	(7.3447)	(7.2819)	(7.2884)	(7.7504)	(7.2689)
D_{1975}	−0.0114	−0.0114	−0.0113	−0.0114	−0.0121	−0.0114	−0.0114	−0.0124	−0.0121
	(2.9701)	(2.9663)	(2.9644)	(2.9662)	(3.1789)	(2.9694)	(2.9711)	(3.2557)	(3.1827)
D_{1980}	−0.0077	−0.0077	−0.0076	−0.0077	−0.0082	−0.0077	−0.0077	−0.0084	−0.0082
	(2.0255)	(2.0247)	(1.9893)	(2.0249)	(2.1539)	(2.0241)	(2.0156)	(2.2083)	(2.2166)
D_{1985}	−0.0213	−0.0213	−0.0214	−0.0213	−0.0219	−0.0213	−0.0214	−0.0223	−0.0218
	(5.6483)	(5.6401)	(5.6622)	(5.6452)	(5.7988)	(5.6495)	(5.6582)	(5.9061)	(5.78037)
D_{1990}	−0.0097	−0.0097	−0.0098	−0.0097	−0.0103	−0.0098	−0.0098	−0.0108	−0.0103
	(2.5756)	(2.5580)	(2.5984)	(2.5685)	(2.7281)	(2.5794)	(2.5919)	(2.8537)	(2.7045)
D_{1995}	−0.0136	−0.00136	−0.0138	−0.0136	−0.1425	−0.0137	−0.0138	−0.0148	−0.0142
	(3.4577)	(3.4357)	(3.5073)	(3.4450)	(3.6055)	(3.4674)	(3.4909)	(3.7452)	(3.5758)
D_{Africa}	−0.0157	−0.0157	−0.0153	−0.0158	−0.0154	−0.0156	−0.0154	−0.0153	−0.0154
	(5.3274)	(5.3654)	(5.1592)	(5.2779)	(5.2933)	(5.3006)	(5.0763)	(5.2928)	(5.3094)
$D_{Lat.\,Am.}$	−0.0103	−0.0103	−0.0104	−0.0103	−0.0103	−0.0102	−0.0103	−0.0104	−0.0103
	(1.2780)	(3.8720)	(3.8988)	(3.8728)	(3.8630)	(3.8402)	(3.8779)	(3.9288)	(3.8630)
EDUC growth	0.0010	0.0018	0.0037	0.0022	−0.0006	−0.0009	−0.0026	−0.0018	−0.0017
	(0.1060)	(0.1871)	(0.5452)	(0.2095)	(0.1580)	(0.0834)	(0.3363)	(1.2155)	(0.0404)
R^2	0.1386	0.1387	0.1392	0.1387	0.1395	0.1388	0.1388	0.1424	0.1395

Importantly for this book's focus, what emerges from Table 7.3 is that the growth of human capital, regardless of how it is defined (total or differentiated by sex or level of education), is an insignificant determinant of productivity growth. This conclusion will be contrasted with the results of Chapter 9, where we will see that the inability of the linear parametric framework to identify an effect of human capital on productivity growth does not necessarily mean that such an effect does not exist.

7.4   Summary

Parametric estimates of the human capital-growth relationship are based on the assumption of a unique response coefficient for human capital. However, recent theoretical work reviewed in Chapter 5 has questioned the validity of this assumption and its justification in empirical work. As a result the growth experience of countries may be different (or similar) depending on their level of human capital or, to put it differently, the growth experience is a nonlinear function of human capital. While nonlinearities in the income convergence process have been extensively discussed in the literature (e.g., Quah 1996), relatively little has appeared with regard to human capital.

In this chapter we began our investigation of the impact of human capital on growth by assuming a linear relationship between the two. In Chapter 9 we will estimate a partially linear semiparametric regression model that allows for a nonlinear effect on both initial income and human capital on income growth. Our focus will be on the second type of nonlinearity. Before we can present our results for nonlinearities, in Chapter 8 we outline the basic nonparametric techniques that are used in Chapter 9 because these techniques are relatively less well known than their linear counterparts. The focus of Chapter 8 will be on the use of nonparametric techniques in applied growth research.

Notes

1. These data sets are available at: http://www.worldbank.org (Nehru, Swanson, and Dubey); http://www.cid.harvard.edu/ciddata/ciddata.html (Barro and Lee); http://iei.uv.es/~rdomenec/human/human.html (De la Fuente and Doménech); and http://www.iae-csic.uab.es/soto/data.htm (Cohen and Soto).

2. Mamuneas, Savvides, and Stengos (2006) allowed the contribution of capital and labor (shares) to vary across countries and time and, therefore, could test directly the constant returns-to-scale hypothesis.

3. Several of the most popular specifications of human capital described in Chapters 3 and 4 assume unitary elasticity for labor. For example, Lucas (1988) postulates that $E = L \cdot H$, while the Mincerian-type production function for human capital (e.g., Hall and Jones 1999) assumes $E = L \cdot \exp^{f(H)}$ where $f(H)$ is a general function.

4. We do not include country-specific dummy variables to avoid problems associated with multicollinearity.

8 A Primer on Nonparametric Methods and Their Application to Research in Human Capital and Economic Growth

8.1 Introduction

In this chapter we present an introduction to nonparametric methods with a view to their specific application in testing the human capital-growth relationship. A more complete and detailed exposition of these methods is provided in Härdle (1990), Härdle and Linton (1994), Li and Racine (2006), Pagan and Ullah (1999), Silverman (1986), and Stock (1989). In the Appendix we offer a summary of the more technically oriented material, such as marginal integration and the semiparametric smooth coefficient model, that we make use of in Chapter 9 to estimate the semi-parametric growth equation and the semiparametric growth accounting approach, respectively.

Popular estimation methods such as ordinary least squares (OLS) or maximum likelihood (ML) are based on certain underlying assumptions about the nature of the relationship under investigation. For example, in the growth empirics described in Chapter 7 a researcher assumes that a linear relationship holds between the variables of interest as well as a particular probability density function for the error term. The main consequence of relying on parametric assumptions is the gain in computational simplicity as well as a certain ease of interpreting the estimates. If the parametric assumptions are incorrect, however, the estimates obtained are contaminated with features that do not reflect accurately the true nature of the model that generated the data. This is why estimates from parametric methods are typically preferred when one has confidence that the underlying parametric assumptions are correct, subject to the important proviso that if this were not the case these estimates would be unreliable. In that case we would be better off using methods that do not rely on specific assumptions about the data-generating process but take an agnostic view. These methods are generally known as *nonparametric methods*. In this chapter we offer an introduction to these methods as they are applied and used in empirical growth research.

8.2   A General Overview of Nonparametric Econometric Methods

Before we embark on the discussion of the main tools of nonparametric methodology, it is instructive to present the basic idea behind them by means of a graph. Figure 8.1 presents the scatter plot of some unknown relationship that may, for example, represent the relationship between growth of income per capita (Y) and the stock of human capital (X). Each observation in the scatter plot has two coordinates that correspond to the y- and x-values. A typical parametric method such as OLS would produce an estimate of a line that goes through the scatter of data. In that case, in the absence of any information about the possible functional form of the relationship between growth and human capital, the least squares approach yields a straight line as an estimate of the underlying relationship. The straight line suggests that there is some constant rate at which an extra unit added on to human capital (say an extra year of schooling) would result in a higher (or lower) rate of growth. That would occur at low and high levels of human capital alike, an observation that is not consistent with diminishing (or increasing) returns to human capital accumulation, a desirable property featured by several growth models discussed in earlier chapters.

A nonparametric estimator works in a different way and we can visualize it as follows. Let us suppose that at each observed data point there is a circle with a given radius. The radius controls the size of the circle and, for the moment, let us assume that all circles have the same radius. In Figure 8.1 we have drawn three such circles. Each circle contains a

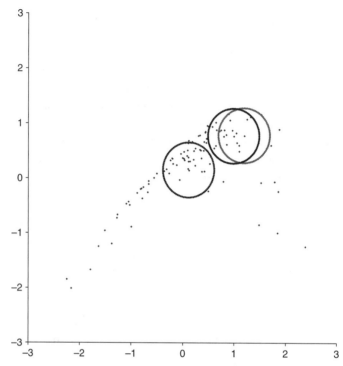

FIGURE **8.1**   A scatter plot of simulated growth data

number of data points and because there is a circle centered at each data point (for clarity of presentation we have only drawn three), the sets of points contained by each circle overlap with each other and, thus, it may be that most observations in a given circle belong to other circles as well. Each circle defines a neighborhood of points that are centered at a given point. Suppose that we are looking at the circle centered at point A with coordinates (y_A, x_A). Then the nonparametric method averages all the y-values that correspond to the data points in the circle to obtain the estimate of the regression function at the x-coordinate of A, x_A. That will give the estimate of the regression function at the x-value corresponding to the center, x_A. Since there are as many (overlapping) circles as data points, each one centered at a different point, we will obtain a different average of y-values for each x-value corresponding to the center of each circle. Therefore, the regression function is now evaluated at each x-point and that will trace a nonlinear function of the relationship between per capita growth and human capital. As we will see below, the shape of what defines the neighborhood of points (the circle in our example) is known as *kernel* and the radius that defines its size is known as *bandwidth* (also referred to as *window width* or *smoothing parameter*). The method just described is also commonly referred to as the *kernel method*.

We start the more detailed presentation of kernel methods by looking at density estimation, first, and then proceed to regression models.

8.2.1   Density Estimation

We introduce our discussion of density estimation by looking at a specific example: the distribution of average growth rates (denoted by x) over the period 1960–2003 for the same group of countries we considered in Section 7.2 and shown in Table 7.1a. One way of looking at the distribution of these growth rates is to assume a particular distribution, say normal, and use estimates of the first two moments, mean and variance, that completely characterize the normal density to graph it. The estimator of the density is

$$\widetilde{f}(x) = \frac{1}{\sqrt{2\pi\widehat{\sigma}^2}} e^{-\frac{1}{2\widehat{\sigma}^2}(x-\widehat{\mu})^2}, \qquad -\infty < x < \infty \qquad \text{EQUATION } \mathbf{8.1}$$

where $\widehat{\mu}$ and $\widehat{\sigma}^2$ are estimates of the mean and variance obtained the usual way (e.g., maximum likelihood) as $\widehat{\mu} = \frac{1}{n}\sum_{i=1}^{n} x_i$ and $\widehat{\sigma}^2 = \frac{1}{n}\sum_{i=1}^{n}(x_i - \widehat{\mu})^2$. The area under this curve defined over an interval between two particular values of the growth rate, say 0.01 and 0.02, will give us the probability that a country chosen at random among the set of countries in our sample would have a growth rate that falls in this [0.01, 0.02] interval.

Figure 8.2 presents a graph that is based on the assumption of normality of growth rates. If the normality assumption is correct, then this is all that is needed to describe the global distribution of growth rates over the period 1960–2003 and there is nothing else to add. However, if the distribution is not normal we would need a lot more information to describe the data than the first two moments, and relying on only those two will be quite misleading. If we let the "data talk" and have them

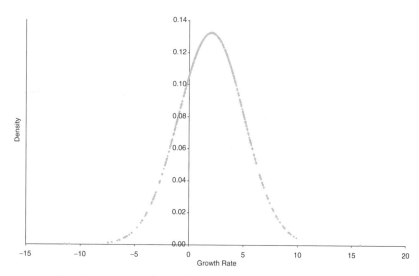

FIGURE **8.2** Density estimator of growth rates assuming normality

dictate the shape of the growth distribution, the graph we obtain will not suffer from the requirement that the correct form of the distribution be known a priori in order to make correct inferences. Knowing the correct functional form of the data distribution is nearly impossible in practice and, therefore, in parametric density specification a researcher proceeds to assume specific forms for it. These assumptions are often incorrect and lead to misleading inferences. Estimation of the density nonparametrically, on the other hand, lets the "data talk." Figures 8.3 and 8.4 present two versions of the most well-known type of nonparametric density estimator, the histogram. These two figures plot histograms of the growth rate for the same group of countries as Figure 8.2 where we assumed growth rates to be normally distributed. It is evident that there are important differences between parametric and nonparametric densities, with nonparametric density describing a distribution that is less symmetric than the normal and with more than one "spike." We are now in a position to explore a bit more carefully what constitutes a nonparametric density estimator.[1]

The simplest nonparametric estimator, the histogram, divides the range of data (growth rates) into distinct nonoverlapping intervals known as *bins*. These bins form the bases of rectangles (*bars*) whose heights

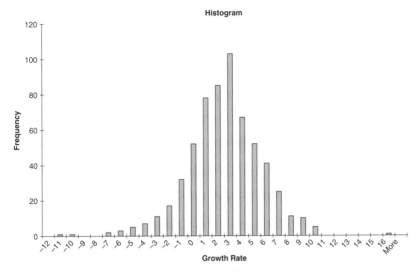

FIGURE **8.3** Histogram of growth rates with 0.5 bin length

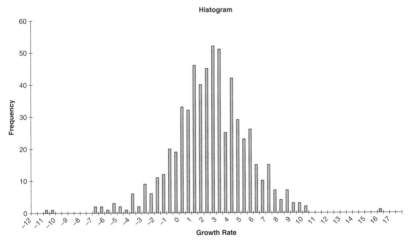

FIGURE **8.4** Histogram of growth rates with 0.25 bin length

denote the proportion of data that fall in that bin. For example the height of the bar that includes all the observations of countries with growth rates between 1.5 and 2.5 percentage points is the proportion of growth rates x_i such that $(2 - \frac{1}{2} < x_i \leq 2 + \frac{1}{2})$. We can then write the density estimator as

$$\widehat{f}(x_* = 2)$$
$$= \frac{1}{n} \left\{ \text{number of observations falling in the interval } \left(2 - \frac{1}{2}, \ 2 + \frac{1}{2}\right) \right\}$$

EQUATION **8.2**

where n is the number of observations and x_* is the point at which we estimate the density; in our example $x_* = 2$ and denotes the center of the bin.

This definition assumes that the length of the bin is one. If we let this length be any other number, say λ, then we can modify the definition to:

$$\widehat{f}(x_*) = \frac{1}{n\lambda} \left(\text{number of observations falling in the interval } \left(2 - \frac{\lambda}{2}, \ 2 + \frac{\lambda}{2}\right) \right)$$

EQUATION **8.3**

Figures 8.3 and 8.4 present the histogram for the growth data for two different choices of bin length, 0.5 and 0.25, respectively. The problem with such an estimator is that by changing arbitrarily the length of the bin we can get a different picture of the data. Wider bins correspond to smoother histograms, whereas the opposite is the case with narrower bins, as is evident from Figures 8.3 and 8.4. This is a fundamental issue that arises with all types of estimators that are based on *local smoothing* techniques; these estimators are known in the nonparametric literature as *local smoothers*. The local nature of the histogram is that it treats all observations in a given bin as a separate cluster (nonoverlapping cluster in that case) where all the members (observations) of this cluster are of "equal" weight. In other words, we have a neighborhood of points that defines the local character of the method.

A histogram is composed of these different bins. A distinguishing feature of the histogram is the nonoverlapping nature of these bins, something that depends on the choice of origin, besides the choice of length of the bin. This adds an additional degree of arbitrariness to the method, especially when the data are not spread equally (uniformly) over its range. One way of handling the dependence on the origin issue is to allow for overlapping bins. In that case observations in a bin of a given length still get equal weight within the bin as before, yet each observation now serves as the center of a bin of a particular length. Even though the choice of bin length is still very important in obtaining different views of the data, at least we are no longer faced with the issue of dependence on the origin of the data. This density estimator is expressed more formally by defining the parameter λ (mentioned previously), which gives the chosen length of the bin and the indicator function, I_i, as follows:

$$I_i = \left\{ \frac{1 \text{ if } x_i \in (x_* - \lambda/2, \ x_* + \lambda/2}{0 \text{ otherwise}} \right\}$$

The indicator function is a function that takes the value of one if the x observation lies in the range $x_* \pm (\lambda/2)$ and is zero otherwise, where x_* denotes the center of the bin. In this case the parameter λ is known as the *bandwidth* or *window width* and is extremely important in nonparametric estimation because it is responsible for the local character of the estimation method by controlling how many observations enter each bin. It is the parameter that controls how large is the neighborhood (locality) of observations that have the same weight.

Next we rescale our data by introducing an additional parameter, $\psi_i = \frac{x_i - x_*}{\lambda}$. This rescaling changes the indicator function to:

$$I_i(\psi_i) = \left\{ \frac{1 \text{ if } -1/2 \leq \psi_i \leq 1/2}{0 \text{ otherwise}} \right\}$$

In other words, ψ_i standardizes the distance between x_i and x_* in terms of the bandwidth λ. The indicator function $I(\cdot)$ is a particular weighting function where the data are given equal weight. The density estimator for the case of overlapping bins, given the choice of bandwidth, is:

$$\widehat{f}(x_*) = \frac{1}{n\lambda} \sum_{j=1}^{n} I\left(\frac{x_j - x_*}{\lambda} \right)$$

EQUATION 8.4

Again, as in the case of the simple histogram, the weights of all observations in each bin are equal. This may not be desirable, however, because observations close to the point of interest x_* (the center of the bin) where we obtain the estimate of the density get the same weight as observations at the boundaries of the bin. In its place, we can define a weighting function that gives more weight to the center (observations that are closer to x_*) and gradually less weight as we move away from it. For example, one can use the normal variate as a possible weighting function. For a given choice of bandwidth, the density estimator in this case is:

$$\widehat{f}(x_*) = \frac{1}{n\lambda} \sum_{j=1}^{n} \frac{1}{\sqrt{2\pi}} e^{-\frac{1}{2}\left(\frac{x_j - x_*}{\lambda}\right)^2}$$

There are several other possibilities of weighting functions that depend on the shape of the function and whether the support of the observations on which they are defined is a bounded or an unbounded interval. The weighting function is referred to as the *kernel function*. Other than the normal and the uniform (rectangular) kernel that we have already described, kernels encountered in the literature are the Epanechhnikov, the triangular, and so forth. The kernel function typically has the property of being itself a symmetric density function that integrates to one, although some kernel functions do not satisfy this property (see Pagan and Ullah (1999) for more details). In general, a kernel function can be written as

$$K(\psi_i) = K\left(\frac{x_i - x_*}{\lambda}\right)$$

and the general density kernel estimator can be written as:

$$\widehat{f}(x_*) = \frac{1}{n\lambda} \sum_{j=1}^{n} K\left(\frac{x_j - x_*}{\lambda}\right) \qquad \text{EQUATION } \mathbf{8.5}$$

Figure 8.5 shows the kernel estimate of the density of the growth rates using a standard normal kernel. Our choice of bandwidth corresponds to Silverman's (1986) "rule of thumb" where the bandwidth is a function that depends on the number of observations and the standard deviation of the data so as to account equally for the bias and the variance of the estimator. It is given by $cs_x n^{-1/5}$, where s_x is the standard deviation of x and c is a constant, typically used to make the product cs_x be close to one. Smaller bandwidths give more emphasis to local detail and reduce the bias of the estimator, but at the same time they include fewer observations in the local neighborhood and, as such, they result in larger variances. The opposite is true in the case of larger bandwidths, where the variance improves at the expense of more bias. It is clear that the choice of bandwidth is important as it affects the degree of smoothing (local averaging) that is allowed by the estimator. Usually an "eyeball" method gives a good enough indication of the appropriate degree of smoothing in

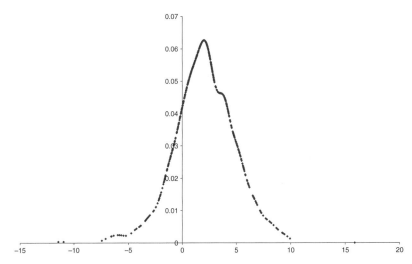

FIGURE **8.5** Kernal density estimator of growth rates

the estimated curve. In the Appendix we discuss in more detail some of the standard methods for bandwidth selection.

The kernel function does not have, relatively speaking, such an important role to play in terms of over or under smoothing and the choice of kernel does not tend to distort the picture of the true density, other than to introduce a less jagged appearance than the histogram. Furthermore, since smooth kernel functions have an infinite number of derivatives as compared with the jagged rectangular kernel which is not differentiable, they can serve better as mathematical tools that admit approximations such as Taylor expansions.

There are some problems worth noting when applying kernel density estimation. When the data are sparse (such as at the tails) there is a tendency for some distortions to appear at the tail estimates because a fixed bandwidth may not be able to include a sufficient number of observations locally. In that case if one chooses a large enough bandwidth to account for data sparsity at the tails there would be over smoothing in the rest of the density. As a solution one can use different bandwidths at different parts of the density with different data clustering. This is known as *adaptive smoothing* and its implementation is discussed by Pagan and Ullah (1999) and Li and Racine (2006). Another problem arises when the data are truncated at some point (bounded from below or above). In that case the density estimates may indicate probability mass outside the domain of the data. To avoid this problem a researcher may transform the data or, alternatively, use methods that rely on more complicated kernel functions that may not integrate to one, as explained by Pagan and Ullah (1999).

8.2.2   Estimation of Regression Functions

Nonparametric regression assumes little about the shape of the regression function beyond some degree of smoothness. An additional advantage of nonparametric regression techniques is their ability to deliver estimators and inference procedures that are less dependent on assumptions about functional form. Nonparametric techniques estimate the value of the regression function at a given point using neighboring observations. Nonparametric regressions typically involve either local averaging or some form of least squares estimation. Unfortunately, nonparametric methods also have undesirable features that are not present in parametric analysis. The two more important are the "curse of dimensionality" and the need to select a smoothing parameter.

As in the case of density estimation, nonparametric estimation of a regression function provides point-wise estimates. That is, we obtain an estimate at some point x_* using information that lies in its neighborhood by local averaging. The size of the neighborhood depends on the choice of bandwidth and the choice of the weighting scheme depends on the chosen kernel. The procedure is repeated for every point of the domain of the independent variable(s). Local averaging estimation may involve carrying out a simple arithmetic average of all the values of the dependent variable that correspond to the observations of the independent variables in the neighborhood around x_*. This is what is known as the *constant kernel method* and is equivalent to estimating a weighted least squares (WLS) regression of the values of the dependent variable in the neighborhood subsample on a constant using weights that are suggested by the choice of kernel. For example, if we were to use the rectangular (uniform) kernel, all observations in the neighborhood would be given equal weight and we would simply have a local OLS regression. Alternatively, one can estimate local WLS or OLS regressions on a constant and the other independent variables in the neighborhood around x_* with all these additional regressors in the local regression being in deviation from the focal point x_*. This is known in the literature as *local linear regression*. The method can be generalized to include powers of the independent variables or the local polynomial method (see Fan and Gijbels (1996) or the Appendix for more details). This estimation methodology is based on a Taylor series expansion of the unknown regression function around a particular point and, depending on the order of the expansion, one can allow more terms in the local regression estimation with a gain in bias reduction (the approximation would be more accurate) but at the expense of local precision. Obviously from a practical point of view, in a local neighborhood one would run out of data points quickly and as such using higher order polynomial terms in local regression would not be feasible.

We provide a more formal presentation of the method. A typical parametric regression model such as a linear regression model is a best relationship between the dependent variable, Y, and a function of the explanatory variable X, say $g(X)$, where $X_i \in R^q$ and β is a $q \times 1$ vector of parameters. It is well established that the optimal prediction function $g(X)$ is the conditional mean function of Y given X, that is, $g(X) = E[Y|X]$. Suppose we have data given by an i.i.d. sample $(Y_i, X_i), i = 1, \ldots, n$. We are interested in estimating:

$$Y_i = g(X_i) + u_i \quad (i = 1, \ldots, n)$$

EQUATION 8.6

When $E(Y|X) = X'\beta$, this is a linear regression model and one only needs to estimate the unknown parameter β in order to estimate the optimal predictor $g(X) = X'\beta$. In practice, however, the optimal functional form $g(\cdot)$ is not known and a parametric regression functional form is likely to be misspecified. Naturally, estimation results based on a misspecified parametric model will give misleading conclusions.

Nonparametric estimation methods do not make specific assumptions about functional form. Let us consider the following nonparametric regression model

$$Y_i = E[Y_i|X_i = x] + u_i \quad (i = 1, \ldots, n)$$

EQUATION 8.7

where $u_i = Y_i - E[Y_i|X_i = x]$ and $E(u_i|X_i = x) = 0$, $E[u_i^2|X_i = x] = \sigma^2(x)$. We write, as before, $E[Y_i|X_i = x] = g(x)$, and for convenience of exposition $q = 1$, that is X_i is a scalar. The functional form $g(\cdot)$ is unknown. Suppose that X_i is a discrete random variable taking values $(x_1, \ldots, x_*, \ldots, x_d)$. In the context of a very simple growth regression model and where growth rates describe five-year averages, Y_i denotes per capita growth for a country in a particular subperiod and X_i represents the given five-year period. Here, we treat each observation as being a country in a given five-year subperiod that would differ from another observation of possibly the same country for a second subperiod. In this case x_1 could represent the period 1960–64 and would take the value of one, x_2 the period 1965–69 and take the value of two, and so on. Suppose we want to find an estimate of the average per capita growth rate in a particular five-year period x_*. Let n^* be the observations that correspond to the value x_* of X. A sensible estimator of $g(x_*) = E[Y_i | X_i = x_*]$ would be

$$\widehat{g}(x) = \frac{\sum_{j=1}^{n^*} Y_j}{n^*} \qquad \text{EQUATION } \mathbf{8.8}$$

which is the simple average of the Y's (the per capita growth rates) over the specific five-year period x_*.

Using our previous notation, we denote the bandwidth by λ (which is smaller than the distance between the discrete values that X takes) and we define I_i to be the indicator function, that is, a function that takes the value of one if X lies in the range $x_* \pm (\lambda/2)$ and is zero otherwise. We can write $\sum_{j=1}^{n} I_j = n^*$, since λ is such that $I_i = 1$ only if $X_i = x_*$. Also, $\sum_{j=1}^{n} I_j Y_j = \sum_{j=1}^{n^*} Y_j$. Hence, we can rewrite the estimator of $g(x_*)$ given in equation 8.8 as:

$$\widehat{g}(x) = \frac{\sum_{j=1}^{n} Y_j I_j}{\sum_{j=1}^{n} I_j} \qquad \text{EQUATION } \mathbf{8.9}$$

We note that the difference between 8.8 and 8.9 is that in the former we use only n^* observations whereas in the latter we use all n available data. The two equations yield, of course, exactly the same estimate.

Using a more general kernel function $K(\cdot)$ that is differentiable we can obtain the general kernel estimator $\widehat{g}(x)$ as:

$$\widehat{g}(x) = \frac{\sum_{j=1}^{n} Y_j K\left(\frac{X_j - x}{\lambda}\right)}{\sum_{j=1}^{n} K\left(\frac{X_j - x}{\lambda}\right)}$$

This estimator is obtained at every point that the regressor takes values. In other words, it is computed as a weighted average of the Y's with the weights given by the corresponding X observations around any given point x. We can rewrite it as

$$\widehat{g}(x) = \sum_{j=1}^{n} r_j(x) Y_j$$

where $r_j(x) = \left[K\left(\frac{X_j - x}{\lambda}\right)\right] / \left[\sum_{j=1}^{n} K\left(\frac{X_j - x}{\lambda}\right)\right]$. Hence, $\widehat{g}(x)$ is a linear weighted average of the Y's. It is worthy of note that different weights would lead to different estimators such as splines or k-nearest neighbors.

8.2.3 Kernel Estimators

As discussed before, one way to construct the local averaging weights is to use a unimodal function centered at zero that declines in either direction at a rate controlled by a scale parameter. Natural candidates for such functions, the kernels, are probability density functions. Let K be a bounded function which integrates to one and is symmetric around zero. We write the weights $r_j(x)$ once more as:

$$r_j = \frac{\frac{1}{\lambda n}\left[K\left(\frac{X_j - x}{\lambda}\right)\right]}{\frac{1}{\lambda n} \sum_{j=1}^{n} K\left(\frac{X_j - x}{\lambda}\right)}$$

The shape of these weights (by construction they sum to one) is determined by K while their magnitude is controlled by λ, the bandwidth or smoothing parameter. As we noted above, a larger value of λ results in greater weight being put on observations that are far from x. A variety of different kernels is available; in practice the most commonly used is the standard normal, that is, $K\left(\frac{X_j - x}{\lambda}\right) = \frac{1}{\sqrt{2\pi}} \exp\left[-\left(\frac{X_j - x}{\lambda}\right)^2\right]$.

In the more general case in which we are conditioning upon two or more explanatory variables (i.e., $x = (x_1, x_2)$) the procedure followed is the same as with one explanatory variable. Analytically, the model becomes:

$$y = g(x_1, x_2) + \epsilon$$

When constructing the weights from which we approximate the regression functions, instead of one kernel estimator we have a product of two so that, in this case, K is the product of two kernels, K_1 and K_2, from the standard normal distribution, or $K = \left[K_1 \left(\frac{X_{1j} - x_1}{\lambda_1} \right) K_2 \left(\frac{X_{2j} - x_2}{\lambda_2} \right) \right]$. In this case we have to select two smoothing parameters, λ_1 and λ_2. The choice of smoothing parameter is important and several criteria and different methods have been discussed in the literature for the selection of the optimal smoothing parameter. There are two main conditions that characterize the behavior of λ. The first is that $\lambda \to 0$, which ensures that averaging takes place over a shrinking bandwidth, thus eventually eliminating bias. The second is that $\lambda n \to \infty$ (where n denotes the sample size), which ensures that the number of observations being averaged grows, which allows the variance of the estimate to decline to zero.

One choice of smoothing parameter is $\lambda = c \times st.dev(x)n^{-\frac{1}{4+p}}$, where c is a constant, $st.dev(x)$ is the standard deviation of the conditioned variable, and p is the number of variables included in x. In the case of one explanatory variable $\lambda = c \times st.dev(x)n^{-\frac{1}{5}}$ and for the bivariate case ($i = 1, 2$), $\lambda_i = c_i \times st.dev(x_i)n^{-\frac{1}{6}}$. This selection of λ is based on a "rule of thumb" proposed by Silverman (1986). Another way to select the smoothing parameter is to choose it so as to minimize the mean integrated squared error. This is the *cross validation method* and the Appendix presents a brief description of this method. From an econometric standpoint, there are three essential results for a simple kernel estimator: (1) it is consistent; (2) averaging takes place over a neighborhood which shrinks at an appropriate rate so that the resulting rate of convergence balances bias against variance; and (3) it is asymptotically normal.

Local averaging estimators have the advantage that as long as the weights are known or can be easily calculated, the estimated regression function is also easy to calculate. The disadvantage of such estimators is that it is often difficult to impose additional structure on the estimating regression function. That is because very few relationships of interest to economists are so simple. The method can be implemented in the presence of multiple explanatory variables, but our ability to accurately estimate the relationship deteriorates as the number of such variables increases. This is what is known as the *curse of dimensionality*, which poses the most serious complication for pure (local) nonparametric estimators. Every estimation method has some costs associated with it and in the case of nonparametric estimation, it is the need for very large data samples if an accurate measurement of the function is to be made. More-over, the size of the sample required increases rapidly with the number of variables involved in any relation. The curse of dimensionality can be mitigated somewhat by introducing additional structure such as a semi-parametric specification, by assuming higher order differentiability, or by imposing additive separability. Some models allow the nonlinearity to be located either in the conditional mean or the conditional vari-ance. Effectively, estimation involves a combination of parametric and nonparametric methods, leading to the estimators being described as semiparametric, the subject of the following section.

8.3   A General Semiparametric Partially Linear Model

In this section we discuss a commonly used semiparametric model, the semiparametric partially linear (PLR) model. Generally speaking, a semi-parametric model is a model part of which takes a parametric form and the remaining part is nonparametric. Equivalently we can say that, on one hand, the model has a finite dimensional parameter of interest but, on the other, the model also contains some unknown functions that can be viewed as characterized by infinite dimensional parameters.

Recently, semiparametric models have attracted much attention among statisticians and econometricians because under certain condi-tions, the finite dimensional parameter vector in a semiparametric model can be consistently estimated at the parametric $\sqrt{n}$-rate.

8.3.1   The Partially Linear Model

A semiparametric partially linear model is given by

$$Y_i = X_i\beta + g(Z_i) + u_i \quad (i = 1, \ldots, n)$$

EQUATION 8.10

where $X_i \in R^r$, β is the true but unknown parameter of dimension $r \times 1$, $Z_i \in R^q$, and the functional form $g(\cdot)$ is not specified (unknown to researchers). The data are i.i.d. with $E(u_i|x_i, z_i) = 0$. The finite-dimensional parameter β is the parametric part of the model and the unknown function $g(\cdot)$ is the nonparametric part of the model. Some con-ditions are necessary to identify the parameter β. It can be easily shown that x cannot contain a constant or, in other words, β cannot contain an intercept term. In deriving the asymptotic distribution of the semiparametric estimator of β one requires that $E\{[X - E(X|Z)][X - E(X|Z)]'\}$ be a positive definite matrix. This implies that z cannot contain a constant and none of the components of x can be a deterministic function of z because, otherwise, we will have $X - E(X|Z) \equiv 0$ for that component (see Robinson (1988) for details). Fan, Li, and Stengos (1995) generalized the model by allowing for conditionally heteroskedastic errors, where $E(u_i^2|x, z) = \sigma^2(x, z)$ of unknown form, and they obtained a $\sqrt{n}$-consistent estimator of β. Fan and Li (1999) obtained a $\sqrt{n}$-consistent estimator of β for (weakly) dependent time series data.

8.3.2   Robinson's (1988) Estimator

We consider the partially linear model in 8.10 and illustrate the steps involved in estimating β. Taking the conditional expectation of equation 8.10 (conditional on z_i), we obtain:

$$E(Y_i|z_i) = E(X_i'|z_i)\beta + g(z_i)$$

EQUATION 8.11

Subtracting equation 8.11 from equation 8.10 yields:

$$Y_i - E(Y_i|z_i) = (x_i - E(X_i'|z_i))\beta + u_i$$

EQUATION 8.12

The intuition behind this is to eliminate the unknown function $g(Z_i)$ by subtracting the second equation from the first. Although the unknown function $g(\cdot)$ does not appear in the resulting equation, we have introduced the new unknown functions $E(Y_i|Z_i)$ and $E(X_i|Z_i)$. These conditional expectation functions, however, can be estimated consistently by kernel methods. Hence, we can replace the unknown conditional expectations with their kernel estimators to obtain a feasible estimator of β. That is, we replace $Y_i - E(Y_i|Z_i)$ and $X_i - E(X_i|Z_i)$ by $Y_i - \widehat{Y}_i$ and $X_i - \widehat{X}_i$, respectively, where

$$\widehat{Y}_i \equiv \widehat{E}(Y_i|Z_i) = \frac{1}{n\lambda^q} \sum_j Y_j K\left(\frac{Z_i - Z_j}{\lambda}\right) / \widehat{f}(Z_i)$$

$$\widehat{X}_i \equiv \widehat{E}(X_i|Z_i) = \frac{1}{n\lambda^q} \sum_j X_j K\left(\frac{Z_i - Z_j}{\lambda}\right) / \widehat{f}(Z_i)$$

and

$$\widehat{f}(Z_i) = \frac{1}{n\lambda^q} \sum_j K\left(\frac{Z_i - Z_j}{\lambda}\right)$$

A feasible estimator of β can then be obtained by replacing $E(Y_i|Z_i)$ and $E(X_i|Z_i)$ by $\widehat{E}(Y_i|Z_i)$ and $\widehat{E}(Y_i|Z_i)$, respectively, in equation 8.12 and applying least squares method. There are a number of technical problems that arise in this context and they need to be tackled. One is the presence of the random denominator $\widehat{f}(Z_i)$, as well as the choice of the bandwidth λ (see the Appendix for details).

8.3.3   A Simple Differencing Estimator

An alternative way of estimating the parameter β that relies on standard OLS regression methods is due to Yatchew (1997). This method is very easy to use and does not need any of the kernel machinery that we have introduced thus far. The downside of the method is that it is not applicable if we have a high-dimensional unknown part in the model because it is limited to three regressors in the nonparametric part ($q \leq 3$). Suppose for the sake of exposition that $q = 1$, that is, we have one Z to work with in equation 8.10. The method works as follows. First, we sort the data (Y_i, X_i, Z_i) in ascending order according to Z_i, the variable that enters the nonparametric part. Second, we obtain the first differences of the ordered data and estimate a least squares regression of the differenced $Y -$ *variable* on the differenced $X -$ *variable* in order to obtain an estimate of β.

The resulting estimator $\widehat{\beta}$ from the second step was obtained using OLS and we did not have to resort to kernel estimation. The reason for this is that sorting the data brings all the neighboring Z's together and their first differences will be very small as the number of observations increases. Consequently, if the unknown function $g_i = g(Z_i)$ is continuous, then small differences in the Z's will result in small differences in the g_i's as well. Hence, when we first difference the sorted data, the unknown function g will be differenced away and can be ignored. This estimator is not as efficient as Robinson's estimator, since the OLS variance–covariance matrix of the second step estimator makes use of a moving average of the error term that is introduced inadvertently when taking differences. One can improve on the efficiency of the estimator by taking more differences but the extra noise introduced will always result in a less efficient estimator. Furthermore, as mentioned earlier, it cannot be applied if the dimension of Z is greater than three. If one wants to recover the shape of the unknown $g - function$, it can be accomplished by regressing $(Y_i - X_i\widehat{\beta})$ on Z_i using the kernel methods described earlier. The differencing estimator is very convenient for exploratory analysis of simple models, especially when we are mainly interested in the linear part of the model and suspect that the continuous variable(s) that enter(s) the unknown part of the regression function is(are) nonlinear.

8.4   Modeling Economic Growth via the Semiparametric Partially Linear Regression Model

A semiparametric PLR specification of the cross-country growth regression function is a particularly useful way of studying the contribution of human capital to economic growth from a nonlinear perspective. In specifying the human capital-economic growth relationship, we model nonlinearities arising from both initial income and human capital (discussion of this issue is postponed to Chapter 9). Using a version of the PLR model that allows for additive semiparametric components, we obtain graphical representations of the nonparametric components for both initial income and human capital. These graphs will enable us to identify nonlinearities (if any) and will be used as a guide to a more suitable parametric specification.

In this section we provide a brief description of the PLR model that allows for additive semiparametric components (or the additive semiparametric PLR model) as applied to economic growth. Following the presentation in 8.10, the semiparametric PLR specification of the linear model estimated in equation 7.1 can be rewritten as

$$y_{it} = X'_{it}\beta + g(Z_{it}) + u_{it} \qquad \text{EQUATION \textbf{8.13}}$$

where X_{it} is a variable of dimension q, β is $q \times 1$ vector of unknown parameters, Z_{it} is a continuous variable of dimension p, and $g(\cdot)$ is an unknown function. In the context of equation 7.1, y_{it} is the average growth rate of per capita income, $X_{it} = \{D_t, D_j, \ln s_{Kit}, \ln(g_{Lit} + g_A + \delta_K)\}$, and $Z_{it} = \{Z_{1it}, \ldots, Z_{pit}\}$ where Z_{1it} refers to initial income $(\ln x_{it})$

and $Z_{2it}, \ldots Z_{pit}$ refer to various measures of human capital. In some specifications of 8.13, alternative measures of human capital will be allowed to enter the estimating equation jointly. As explained earlier, Robinson (1988) provides a way of obtaining a $\sqrt{n}$-consistent estimator of the parameter vector β by concentrating out the influence of the nuisance variables, the Z's.

Such an approach, although very useful if one were interested solely in the parameter vector β, conceals the influence of the individual Z's in the regression function. For our purposes, a more useful approach is to try to uncover the shapes of the individual components of Z_{it}, (i.e., initial income and measures of human capital). In order to accomplish this we have to impose more structure on equation 8.13 by assuming an additive structure on the unknown components. This is the *additive semiparametric PLR model* and it can be written as:

$$y_{it} = \alpha + X'_{it}\beta + g_1(Z_{1it}) + \cdots + g_{pit}(Z_{pit}) + u_{it}$$

$$= \alpha + X'_{it}\beta + \sum_{s=1}^{p} g_s(Z_{sit}) + u_{it} \qquad \text{EQUATION } \textbf{8.14}$$

Linton and Nielsen (1995), Fan, Härdle, and Mammen (1998), and Fan and Li (2003) use marginal integration to estimate the components of the additive semiparametric PLR model.[2] This method has also been used by Liu and Stengos (1999) where they set $p = 2$. In our estimation of the additive semiparametric PLR model in Chapter 9, we allow p to be greater than two depending on various measures of human capital considered by the growth model estimated.

Application of marginal integration to the additive PLR model in 8.14 implies that the asymptotic distribution of $(\widehat{g}_s(Z_s) - g_s(Z_s))$ ($s = 1, \ldots, p$) is the same as if the other component $g_l(Z_l)$ for $l \neq s$ and γ were known. In other words, $\widehat{g}_s(Z_s)$ behaves in the same way as if it were a one-dimensional local nonparametric estimator and avoids the curse of dimensionality that plagues many nonparametric and semiparametric applications. In the following chapter we will provide estimates of the individual components $g_s(Z_{sit})$ ($s = 1, \ldots, p$) and their respective pointwise 95 percent confidence intervals as a diagnostic tool to establish any nonlinearities that may exist in these components and to suggest adequate parametric representations of the human capital-growth relationship.

Notes

1. There are obvious differences in the shapes of the two nonparametric density estimators (histograms) in Figures 8.3 and 8.4 and we discuss these below. For an excellent treatment of what we can only discuss briefly here, see Silverman (1986).

2. The Appendix provides a brief review of marginal integration.

9 Human Capital and Economic Growth: Nonlinear Specifications

9.1 Introduction

In this chapter we employ a general nonparametric econometric framework that allows the effect of human capital on economic growth to differ both across countries and time. The semiparametric estimation techniques described in Chapter 8 are especially useful tools that allow a researcher to investigate nonlinearities between economic growth and various facets of human capital encapsulated by alternative measures of human capital that were described in Chapter 7.

The large empirical growth literature that was summarized in Chapter 6 assumes that human capital exerts the same effect on economic growth intratemporally (across countries) and intertemporally (across time). Drawing on theories emphasizing threshold externalities (discussed in Chapter 5), several researchers have questioned this assumption. At the same time there is a substantial body of work that examines the impact of the initial level of income per capita on growth (the "convergence" hypothesis). Several studies (e.g., Durlauf and Johnson 1995; Easterly and Levine 1997; Liu and Stengos 1999; Quah 1996) have established a nonlinear relationship between initial income and economic growth. In this chapter we allow for such a nonlinear effect between initial income and growth but our focus is on the human capital-growth relationship.

Durlauf and Johnson (1995) assume that countries follow different laws of motion to the steady state. They used a regression-tree methodology that divided countries into four subgroups according to their initial level of per capita income and literacy rate. They confirmed the distinct linear laws of motion for the four subgroups and found substantial differences in the estimate for the coefficient of secondary enrollment in growth regressions: it was insignificant for two of the subsamples and positive for the other two. Liu and Stengos (1999) confirmed the Durlauf and Johnson results by estimating a semiparametric partially additive model that allowed for two nonlinear components, one in initial level of income and the other in the secondary enrollment rate. Kalaitzidakis et al. (2001) generalized this approach and allowed for more than two nonlinear components by including several different measures of human capital in the same semiparametric function. In effect, Kalaitzidakis et al. pursued an extension of Durlauf and Johnson in one significant direction. Durlauf and Johnson focused on identifying homogenous subgroups of countries and assumed that the contribution of human capital to economic growth is the same for all countries within each subgroup. Kalaitzidakis et al., on the other hand, allowed the effect of human capital to differ across each country and also across each time period. Moreover, while Durlauf and Johnson and Liu and Stengos used only the secondary enrollment ratio, they employed a variety of measures of human capital that are frequently used by researchers in applied growth studies. Ketteni, Mamuneas, and Stengos (2007a) also used this approach to consider three nonlinear components: initial income level, human capital, and investment in information technology.

In this chapter we revisit the two approaches to human capital and growth that we looked at in Chapter 7 from a linear perspective, but now from a nonlinear perspective. In Section 9.2 we reestimate the Mankiw, Romer, and Weil (1992) framework but assume that the impact of initial income and human capital on growth is nonlinear. We employ the semiparametric linear model that allows several different economic variables to enter the nonparametric component; for our purposes the nonparametric component contains initial income and various facets of human capital (measured by alternative indicators of mean years of schooling). In Section 9.3 we revisit the growth accounting framework and adopt the smooth coefficient semiparametric model that allows the effect of human capital growth on TFP growth to be nonlinear.

9.2   Nonlinear Estimation of Human Capital-Growth Regressions

9.2.1   Testing Linear vs. Nonlinear Specifications

In this section we test the relationship between human capital and growth within the MRW framework but from a nonlinear perspective, that is, the semiparametric PLR framework of Chapter 8. This framework was also used by Kalaitzidakis et al. (2001) to test the human capital-growth regression. To begin with we investigate whether the semiparametric PLR functional form in 8.13 represents an appropriate formulation for the cross-country regression equation. First we test a general linear model (the null hypothesis is 7.1) against the semiparametric formulation in 8.13 (the alternative where initial income and human capital enter nonparametrically) via a test proposed by Li and Wang (1998). This nonparametric functional form test statistic ($NPFF^1$) is distributed asymptotically as a standard normal variate (see Table 7.2). However, in small to medium samples the actual distribution of the test statistic is skewed to the left and one needs to bootstrap the statistic to obtain accurate critical values (see Li and Wang, 1998, for details). The second specification test is the semiparametric PLR formulation (the null hypothesis) against a general nonparametric model (the alternative) via a test proposed by Fan and Li (1996). Under the null hypothesis, this test statistic ($NPFF^2$) also follows the asymptotic standard normal distribution.

The last row of Table 7.2 reports the values for the $NPFF^1$ test statistic for the various growth regression specifications that were estimated. The linear model is rejected against the PLR semiparametric alternative in every case.[1] The rejection of the linear model is consistent with the possibility of nonlinearities in the way initial income and human capital impact growth. Second, we use the $NPFF^2$ test statistic with bootstrap critical values to test the null of the semiparametric PLR against a general nonparametric alternative. In this case our results showed no evidence against the null.

TABLE **9.1** Semiparametric Model: Stock Measures (Dependent Variable: *rate of growth*; *t*-statistics in parenthesis; Investment-PWI)

	(1) SCT	(2) SCM & SCF	(3) SCP & SCH	(4) SCPM & SCPF	(5) SCHM & SCHF
D_{1960}	0.0119	0.0121	0.0131	0.0127	0.0117
	(2.9052)	(2.9688)	(3.1702)	(3.1513)	(2.7821)
D_{1965}	0.0098	0.0110	0.0110	0.0112	0.0096
	(2.3968)	(2.7077)	(2.6812)	(2.8061)	(2.3135)
D_{1970}	0.0144	0.0137	0.0124	0.0135	0.0134
	(3.5503)	(3.4148)	(3.0952)	(3.4105)	(3.2832)
D_{1975}	0.0031	0.0040	0.0026	0.0049	0.0016
	(0.7722)	(1.0000)	(0.6697)	(1.2500)	(0.4069)
D_{1980}	−0.0129	−0.0131	−0.0135	−0.0127	−0.0141
	(3.3010)	(3.3852)	(3.5375)	(3.3035)	(3.6193)
D_{1985}	0.0016	0.0019	0.0007	0.0026	0.0004
	(0.4275)	(0.5103)	(0.1822)	(0.6951)	(0.1100)
D_{1990}	0.0021	0.0029	0.0018	0.0030	0.0018
	(0.5582)	(0.7623)	(0.4795)	(0.7994)	(0.4470)
D_{1995}	0.0072	0.0075	0.0072	0.0074	0.0066
	(1.8907)	(1.9978)	(1.9368)	(1.9822)	(1.7601)
D_{Africa}	−0.0112	−0.0100	−0.0104	−0.0110	−0.0085
	(4.4930)	(3.8846)	(4.2098)	(4.2532)	(3.4704)
$D_{Lat.Am.}$	−0.0029	−0.0014	−0.0003	−0.0014	0.0017
	(0.8843)	(0.4310)	(0.0973)	(0.4374)	(0.5257)
$\log s_k$	0.0173	0.0171	0.0176	0.0175	0.0187
	(7.0402)	(6.9804)	(7.1119)	(7.1108)	(7.7499)
$\log(g_L + g_A + \delta_K)$	−0.0112	−0.0139	−0.0113	−0.0141	−0.0132
	(1.2598)	(1.5832)	(1.3050)	(1.6030)	(1.5133)
R^2	0.2612	0.2750	0.2923	0.2773	0.2637

Table 9.1 shows the results from applying the semiparametric PLR model (see 8.14) to the same data that were used in Chapter 7 to estimate the MRW framework from a linear perspective. This table presents coefficient estimates for the parametric component of the model that includes geographic- and time-specific dummy variables, the investment share of income, and the growth of labor. Initial income and human capital enter the model nonlinearly and these results will be discussed in the next subsection. The semiparametric results of Table 9.1 and the parametric estimates of Table 7.2 (that correspond to the linear component of the semiparametric model) are overall qualitatively similar. The semiparametric regressions, however, provide a better fit of the data compared to their linear parametric counterparts.

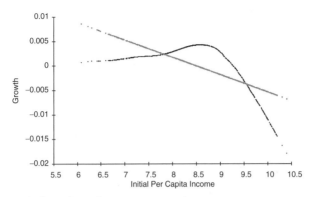

FIGURE **9.1** Total effect of initial income on growth

9.2.2 Semiparametric PLR Results

Having established the appropriateness of the semiparametric PLR formulation for the growth equation, we present estimation results for the nonlinear components. There are two nonlinear components in the additive semiparametric PLR model of 8.14: initial income and various measures of human capital. Before investigating the effects of human capital on growth, first we look at the effect of initial income. Figure 9.1 shows the growth effect of the initial level of per capita income, that is, $g_1(Z_{1it})$ in equation 8.14. The horizontal axis shows the logarithm of initial per capita income and the vertical axis $g_1(Z_{1it})$ in standardized form (taking deviations from the mean). In this, as well as all subsequent graphs, we plot both the semiparametric estimates and the linear benchmark that allows us to compare differences between these two estimates. Visual inspection of Figure 9.1 demonstrates that the relationship between per capita growth and initial income is clearly nonlinear. This is in agreement with other empirical evidence (see Durlauf and Johnson 1995; Liu and Stengos 1999; Kalaitzidakis et al. 2001; and Quah 1999) on convergence. As will be argued shortly, this nonlinear relationship can be modeled as a fourth degree polynomial in initial income. Its curvature implies that, on average, middle income countries experience the highest growth rates.

Our first measure of human capital is the overall indicator of the quantity of education discussed in Chapter 7, total mean years of schooling (*SCT*). Figure 9.2 shows the estimate of the growth effect of total years of schooling, that is, $g_2(Z_{2it})$ in equation 8.14. The horizontal axis shows the

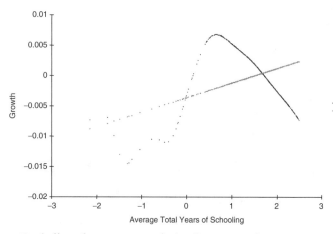

Figure **9.2** Total effect of average years of schooling on growth

logarithm of total mean years of schooling and the vertical axis $g_2(Z_{2it})$ in standardized form. We maintain this labeling of axes for all the other measures of human capital. The estimated relationship between mean years of schooling and growth of per capita GDP is an inverted "U" shape in Figure 9.2. For values of schooling less than 2.5 mean years the growth rate of income increases with years of schooling. The marginal effect of years of schooling on growth becomes negative when average education is higher than 7.5 years. Kalaitzidakis et al. (2001) found that the beneficial effects of human capital on growth are limited to economies with middle levels of human capital (between 0.9 and 4.4 years of schooling) and for countries with more than 4.4 years of schooling there was no relationship between schooling and growth. The shape of our semiparametric fit in Figure 9.2 is quite similar except the marginal effect of human capital becomes negative for countries with schooling years greater than 7.5. The negative marginal effect of human capital at higher levels of schooling may be the result of decreasing returns to human capital setting in at higher levels. The graph also suggests that the positive effects of human capital on economic growth are limited to economies with lower-middle human capital, while for economies with very low human capital the effect may be negative. For economies with either high or low human capital, the results are contrary to the common belief that higher educational attainment translates into higher wage and productivity benefits in

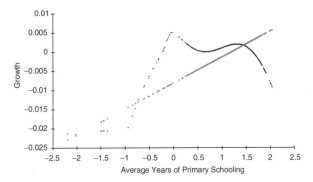

FIGURE **9.3** Total effect of average years of primary schooling on growth

the marketplace and thus faster growth. To explore further the growth effects of human capital, we decomposed total years of schooling by level of education and sex and, in what follows, we present these results.

Nelson and Phelps (1966) and Benhabib and Spiegel (1994) argue that the stock of human capital affects growth because it affects countries' ability to innovate as well as adapt and absorb new technologies, speeding up technological diffusion and productivity catch-up. Their approach suggests that secondary and tertiary education levels are more relevant for technological innovation, absorption, and diffusion than primary schooling. Therefore, we decompose total mean years of schooling by level of education to investigate the importance of primary and post-primary education for economic growth. Both mean years of primary and post-primary education are included together in estimating equation 8.14. Figures 9.3 and 9.4 present graphically the semiparametric curves for primary and post-primary mean years of schooling, respectively.[2] In Figure 9.4 post-primary education has generally a positive (but declining) marginal effect on growth. Kalaitzidakis et al. (2001) found no relationship between growth and post-primary education. For schooling at the primary level in Figure 9.3, we find that the positive effect exists only up to 2.7 years of schooling. Beyond that there seems to be no relationship between growth and primary education. This result is in accordance with intuition and theories of development that stress the beneficial effects of primary education for the low-income human capital economies.

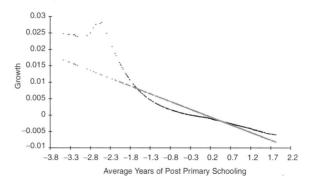

FIGURE **9.4** Total effect of average years of post primary schooling on growth

Both female and male education can affect growth directly through participation by both male and female workers in production activities. Educated females can also affect income growth indirectly through nonmarket home production activities. Higher education of females reduces fertility and infant and child mortality, increases parental education quality, and increases health and life expectancy of family members. Thus female and male education may affect growth in quite different ways. To investigate potential differences we decompose average years of schooling by sex. Figures 9.5 and 9.6 show the nonparametric estimates of mean years of schooling of the male and female population, respectively. In Figure 9.5, over the range 1.5 to 6 years of education, the effect of male schooling on growth is positive but declining. Beyond 6 years of education, the effect is positive and rising. In the case of female education, the relationship between female schooling and growth is overall positive. When female education reaches 4.5 years of schooling, the effect is still positive but starts to decline. Kalaitzidakis et al. produced similar shapes for the relationship between male and female schooling and growth with the turning point occurring earlier at about 4 years in male education and 3.2 years in female education. The negative growth effect of male education in low human capital countries could be because of what Pritchett (2001) suggests may occur in these countries whereby investment in education may be directed toward unproductive activities. Education more often serves as a means to acquiring positions of power that allow the possibility of extracting rents and this may be more prevalent for male education. The positive effect of female education on growth at low levels

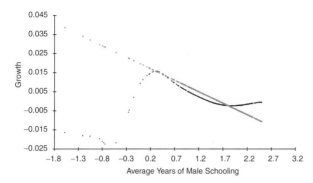

FIGURE **9.5** Total effect of average years of male schooling on growth

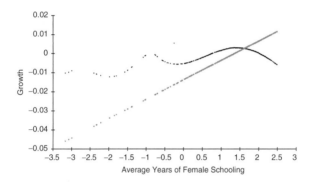

FIGURE **9.6** Total effect of average years of female schooling on growth

of education suggests that although the female labor market participation rate may be substantially lower than males in these countries, females can increase growth indirectly through their nonmarket activities, that is, there are large social gains for female participation in education, especially in developing countries. A possible explanation for the negative effect of female education on growth for high human capital countries is that higher educational levels may not be translated into higher wage employment for female workers. The existence of the gender wage gap in many countries supports this suggestion and, as argued by some of the studies reviewed in Section 6.5.1, it may act as a break on growth.

We have also explored possible differences in the level of education by sex. Figures 9.7 and 9.8 present the nonparametric fit for male and female education at primary level, respectively, and Figures 9.9 and 9.10 do the

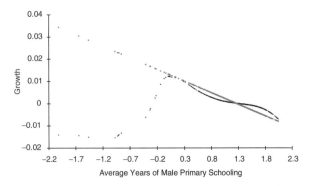

FIGURE **9.7** Total effect of average years of male primary schooling on growth

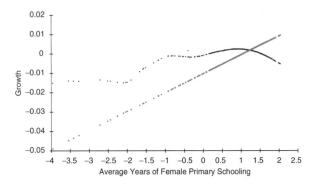

FIGURE **9.8** Total effect of average years of female primary schooling on growth

same at the post-primary level. In Figure 9.7 there is mainly a positive but declining effect of male primary education on growth, whereas for female primary schooling in Figure 9.8 the effect is also mainly positive but relatively constant (linear). Similar results are found for the effect of male post-primary education on growth, which is positive (yet declining). More interestingly, the post-primary effect of female education is positive and increasing at low levels of schooling. Our results show that the beneficial effects of education are not so clearly divided between the sexes, with female and male education at different levels contributing positively on growth, although in different ways.

We use the graphical representations of the nonparametric components in Figures 9.1–9.10 as a guide to an appropriate parametric specification for the human capital-growth regression. Figure 9.1 suggests

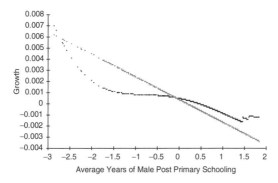

FIGURE **9.9** Total effect of average years of male post primary schooling on growth

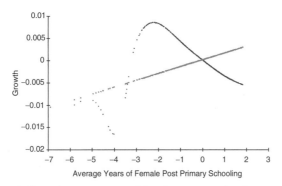

FIGURE **9.10** Total effect of average years of female primary schooling on growth

a fourth degree polynomial in initial income and Figure 9.2 a cubic polynomial in human capital as possible parametric specifications for these variables. Results from estimation of these parametric specifications are in Table 9.2. A standard likelihood ratio test rejects the estimates of the linear model in Table 7.2 (equation 7.1) in favor of the nonlinear model in Table 9.1 in all cases. The parametric results of Table 9.2 confirm the visual presentations in Figures 9.1–9.10.

Three main conclusions emerge from our results: (1) The relationship between human capital and economic growth is nonlinear; (2) For very low and very high human capital countries, we find a negative relationship between human capital and growth (as evidenced by the two portions in Figure 9.2: less than 1 year of schooling and greater than 7 years). We suggest that at very low levels of human capital lack of primary education

TABLE **9.2** Polynomial Estimation (Dependent Variable: *rate of growth*; absolute t-statistics in parenthesis)

	$h_1 = SCT$ $h_2 = SCF$	$h_1 = SCM$ $h_2 = SCH$	$h_1 = SCP$ $h_2 = SCH$	$h_1 = SCPM$ $h_2 = SCPF$	$h_1 = SCHM$ $h_2 = SCHF$
a_0	3.7965	2.5721	−2.1686	3.2479	2.6060
	(0.9964)	(0.6851)	(0.5473)	(0.8544)	(0.6724)
D_{Africa}	−0.0108	−0.0146	−0.0130	−0.0152	−0.0092
	(4.2545)	(5.2550)	(5.0957)	(5.2861)	(3.2788)
$D_{Lat.Am.}$	−0.0060	−0.0075	−0.0089	−0.0081	−0.0072
	(1.8856)	(2.3400)	(2.7708)	(2.5518)	(2.1685)
$\log s_K$	0.0154	0.0143	0.0162	0.0144	0.0166
	(6.3033)	(5.9358)	(6.7141)	(5.9226)	(6.8460)
$\log(g_L + g_A + \delta_K)$	−0.0190	−0.0170	−0.0150	−0.0137	−0.0191
	(2.1305)	(1.9217)	(1.7120)	(1.5144)	(2.1720)
$\log y_r$	−1.8192	−1.1354	1.0927	−1.4829	−1.2187
	(0.9677)	(0.6122)	(0.5597)	(0.7901)	(0.6379)
$(\log y_r)^2$	0.3230	0.1846	−0.2081	0.2522	0.2090
	(0.9360)	(0.5414)	(0.5811)	(0.7316)	(0.5963)
$(\log y_r)^3$	−0.0252	−0.0129	0.0178	−0.0188	−0.0155
	(0.8996)	(0.4679)	(0.6133)	(0.6717)	(0.5448)
$(\log y_r)^4$	0.0007	0.0003	−0.0006	0.0005	0.0004
	(0.8563)	(0.3888)	(0.6580)	(0.6081)	(0.4818)
$\log h_1$	0.0056	0.0155	0.0182	0.0057	0.0040
	(1.6441)	(1.2643)	(4.2613)	(0.5330)	(1.0125)
$(\log h_1)^2$	0.0001	−0.0414	−0.0036	−0.0285	0.0067
	(0.0368)	(4.4249)	(2.3761)	(4.2681)	(2.9413)
$(\log h_1)^3$	−0.0005	0.0138	−0.0025	0.0105	0.0006
	(0.5164)	(4.6816)	(2.4355)	(3.0689)	(1.9232)
$\log h_2$		0.0233	0.0007	0.0215	−0.0056
		(4.5746)	(0.3221)	(3.9162)	(1.4143)
$(\log h_2)^2$		0.0031	0.0041	0.0014	−0.0036
		(1.7810)	(3.1440)	(0.6294)	(1.8808)
$(\log h_2)^3$		−0.0043	0.0003	−0.0039	−0.0003
		(4.9319)	(1.4254)	(3.7298)	(1.1887)
R^2	0.2712	0.3053	0.3026	0.337	0.2904

Tests	$\chi^2_{0.05}$ (d.f.)				
y_r linear	12.84 (3)	8.96 (3)	8.89 (3)	8.01 (3)	12.87 (3)
h_1 linear	10.31 (2)	7.53 (2)	11.61 (2)	5.70 (2)	13.64 (2)
h_2 linear	−	22.47 (2)	3.43 (2)	13.84 (2)	10.44 (2)
h_1 & h_2 linear	−	27.15 (4)	13.44 (4)	21.39 (4)	14.87 (4)

Dummy variables were estimated for each five-year period but are omitted for clarity. The critical values of $\chi^2_{0.05}$ for two, three, and four degrees of freedom are 5.99, 7.82, and 9.49, respectively.

acts as a break on economic growth, and at very high levels distortions in labor markets may hinder growth; and (3) We find support for several theories that stress the beneficial growth effect of human capital at the post-primary level as the result of absorption of new technologies. This finding is the result mainly of post-primary male educational attainment.

9.3   Human Capital and Total Factor Productivity Growth: A Nonlinear Specification

In this section we extend the growth accounting framework of Chapter 7 to study the role of human capital in the growth of TFP by allowing for a nonlinear relationship between the two. Our point of departure is equation 7.9, which is now written in a more general form as:

$$\widehat{TFP}_{it} = \widehat{A}_{it} + \theta(\cdot)\widehat{H}_{it} \qquad \text{EQUATION } \mathbf{9.1}$$

Equation 9.1 resembles the growth accounting specification in 7.8 where $\theta(\cdot) = (\varepsilon_E \eta_H + \varepsilon_H)$ is now a function of the level of human capital H. In equation 7.9, the parametric specification of growth accounting, $\theta(\cdot)$ was assumed to be a constant coefficient, θ, that does not depend on H. Clearly, the proper interpretation of 7.8 would allow for a nonlinear θ-function as in 9.1. Therefore, the generalization of 7.9 in 7.10 that was used to estimate the parametric growth accounting approach should now be replaced by

$$\widehat{TFP}_{it} = a_0 + a_{LA}D_{it}^{LA} + a_A D_{it}^A + \sum_{t=1}^{T-1} a_t D_t + \theta(H_{it})\widehat{H}_{it} + u_{it}$$

$$= X_{it}\beta + \theta(H_{it})\widehat{H}_{it} + u_{it} \qquad \text{EQUATION } \mathbf{9.2}$$

where, as in Chapter 7, $X_{it} = (D_{it}^A, D_{it}^{LA}, D_t)$ and the error term satisfies $E(u_{it} \mid X_{it}, H_{it}, \widehat{H}_{it}) = 0$.

The central issue in 9.2 is the estimation of the $\theta(\cdot)$ function. Our estimation of this function is based on the smooth coefficient semiparametric model (see Fan 1992; Fan and Zhang 1999; and Li, Huang, and Fu 2002). It is a generalization of varying coefficient models and follows the local polynomial linear regression of Stone (1977) and Fan (1992) as well as the widely used Nadaraya–Watson constant kernels. In the Appendix we provide a more detailed description of the method. In what follows, we outline an intuitive presentation of the method based on a Taylor series approximation; additional details are available in Mamuneas, Savvides, and Stengos (2006). A similar generalization is in Ketteni, Mamuneas, and Stengos (2007b) where $\theta(\cdot)$ is a function of both the level of human capital and the level of investment in information technology.

The data are given as $\{Y_i, W_i\}$, $i = 1, \ldots n$, a realization from an i.i.d. random vector $\{Y, W\}$. The covariates are defined on $W \subseteq \Re^q$. We are interested in estimating nonparametrically the unknown regression function $E(Y|W = w)$, where this is a general unknown function of w. We accomplish this by introducing some potentially relevant information expressed in terms of a parametric function $m(W, \gamma)$. One can then proceed by minimizing the following local nonlinear least squares criterion function over the parameter space

$$Q_n(w, \gamma) = n^{-1} \sum_{i=1}^{n} \{Y_i - m(W_i, \gamma)\}^2 K_\lambda(W_i - w) \qquad \text{EQUATION } \mathbf{9.3}$$

where $K(.)$ is a real-valued multivariate kernel and λ is the bandwidth.

In our estimation problem, let us define $W_i = \{X_i, H_i, \widehat{H}_i\}$, where for notational simplicity we suppress the observation subscript. The regression function is given as:

$$E(Y|X = x, H = h, \widehat{H} = \widehat{h}) = x\beta + \theta(h)\widehat{h}$$

In general, $\theta(\cdot)$ is an unknown function and we approximate it by a second-order Taylor series at any given point, say h_0, as

$$\theta(h) \simeq \theta(h_0) + \theta'(h_0)(h - h_0) + (1/2)\theta''(h_0)(h - h_0)^2$$

where $\theta'(h_0)$ is the first derivative and $\theta''(h_0)$ the second derivative of $\theta(h)$ evaluated at h_0. We let $m(W, \gamma)$ be equal to

$$m(X_i, H_i, \widehat{H}_i, \gamma) = X_i\beta + \left[(\delta_1 + \delta_2(H_i - h) + \delta_3(H_i - h)^2\right]\widehat{H}_i \qquad \text{EQUATION } \mathbf{9.4}$$

where $\gamma = (\beta, \delta_1, \delta_2, \delta_3)$ and we form the objective function given in 9.3. The parameter estimates of δ_1, δ_2, and δ_3 will give us the estimates of $\theta(\cdot)$, its first derivative and its second derivative, respectively.

Results from the estimation of the nonlinear function $\theta(\cdot)$ are presented in Figure 9.11 where our measure of human capital is total mean years of

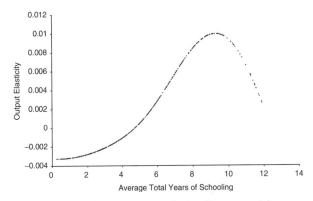

FIGURE **9.11** Marginal effect of average years of schooling on total factor productivity

schooling. This figure depicts the elasticity of TFP growth with respect to human capital growth as a function of the level of human capital. Figure 9.11 shows that the effect of total years of schooling on TFP growth is nonlinear. The elasticity with respect to human capital is increasing for a wide range of mean years of schooling and remains positive. There is a clear threshold effect of human capital on TFP growth. For less than 4.7 years of schooling, the contribution of human capital growth to TFP growth is negative but it increases with the level of human capital. For the range between 4.7 and 10.3 years, the return to education is positive and increasing. After 10.3 years of schooling, the effect is decreasing but still positive.

In order to check further our semiparametric results and compare them to the parametric results of Chapter 7, we decomposed years of schooling at the primary level by sex. Figures 9.12 and 9.13 present the elasticity graphs for male and female education at the primary level. It is worth noting that the shapes of the two graphs resemble the shape of the overall elasticity for total mean years of schooling and there appear to be no differences between the sexes. We obtained similar results for the decomposition of post-primary education by sex. The semiparametric results are in marked contrast to those from the linear approach to growth accounting that was presented in Chapter 7 where the human capital elasticities were small in magnitude and insignificant as contributors to TFP growth.

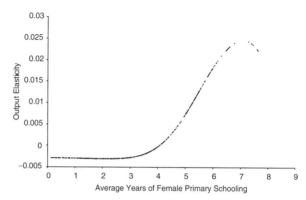

FIGURE **9.12**   Marginal effect of average years of primary female schooling on total factor productivity

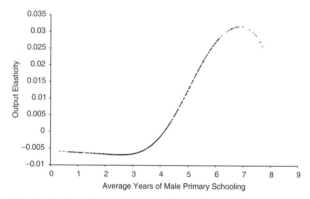

FIGURE **9.13**   Marginal effect of average years of primary male schooling on total factor productivity

9.4   Summary

The impact of human capital accumulation on economic growth remains controversial. Like many issues, conclusions reached depend on the definition of the variable, the methodology used, and the time period over which the model is estimated. In Chapters 7 and 9 we investigated the nature of the human capital-growth relationship within the standard framework of the Mankiw, Romer, and Weil (1992) cross-country growth model and the growth-accounting framework. We made use of a consistent data set and alternative definitions of human capital to compare the effects of various facets of human capital under two alternative empirical assumptions: the linear framework of Chapter 7 and the semiparametric model in Chapter 9 that treats the contribution of human capital to growth nonlinearly.

Our results are largely in agreement with previous nonlinear empirical approaches to human capital and growth. We find a nonlinear relationship between the most widely used measure of human capital (mean years of schooling) and economic growth. At low levels of human capital the effect is negative and becomes positive at middle levels. For countries with high human capital the positive effect tapers off. We explore two dimensions of educational attainment: differences by sex and level of education. We find a positive relationship between male schooling and growth at higher levels of schooling. On the other hand, female educational attainment has a negative effect on growth at high levels of schooling. We suggest this may be related to the workings of the labor markets in high human capital countries and the possibility that in these countries higher educational levels may not be translated into possibilities for higher wage employment for female workers. We also find that male post-primary education has a strong positive effect on growth. This is consistent with the argument that the growth effect of post-primary education works through the adoption of new technologies.

In general, our findings support the hypothesis that the effect of human capital on growth is nonlinear. Our evidence is consistent with theoretical arguments that there exist threshold levels of human capital and the growth experience of a country may well differ according to which side of the threshold it finds itself in. On the other hand, as Durlauf and Johnson (1995) point out, our evidence is also consistent with a model in which countries pass through distinct phases of development toward a unique steady state. Our graphical analysis provides a guide to the appropriate parametric modeling of initial income and human capital in cross-country growth regressions. The visual presentation of the semiparametric results serves a very useful dual purpose for empirical growth researchers. First, it can suggest the general shape of nonlinearities that may exist in the growth process and, second, it can provide practical guidance to a researcher on how to formulate an appropriate parametric growth model to capture empirically the determinants of economic growth.

Notes

1. In this case there is no need to obtain bootstrap critical values because these are lower than the critical values from a standard normal distribution and the null can be rejected using critical values from the standard normal.

2. In addition, initial income was included in the nonparametric component of this and all other semiparametric models estimated. The results are similar to those of Figure 9.1 and we will not present them but instead will focus our discussion on various facets of human capital.

Appendix: Nonparametric Methods

A.1   Estimating Regression Functions by Local Linear Methods

The nonparametric regression equation we consider is:

$$Y_j = g(X_j) + u_j \qquad (j = 1, \ldots, n)$$

EQUATION **A.1**

The nonparametric kernel estimator discussed in Chapter 8 is

$$\widehat{g}(x) = \frac{\sum_{j=1}^{n} Y_j K\left(\frac{X_j - x}{\lambda}\right)}{\sum_{j=1}^{n} K\left(\frac{X_j - x}{\lambda}\right)}$$

EQUATION **A.2**

which can be obtained as the solution of a in the following minimization problem:

$$\min_{a} \sum_{i=1}^{n} (Y_j - a)^2 K\left(\frac{X_j - x}{\lambda}\right)$$

EQUATION **A.3**

Let $\widehat{a} = \widehat{a}(x)$ be the solution that minimizes (A.3). It is easy to see that $\widehat{a} \equiv \widehat{g}(x)$ as given in (A.2).

Note that (A.3) uses a constant a to approximate $g(x)$ (or Y) in the neighborhood of x, because (A.2) only uses a local (X_j's close to x) average of Y_j's to estimate $g(x)$. For this reason, $\widehat{g}(x)$ given in (A.2) is called a *local constant estimator*. One can also use a *local linear estimator* to estimate $g(x)$. An advantage of a local linear method is that it also gives an estimator for $g^{(1)}(x)$, the first derivative of $g(x)$. The local linear method is based on the following minimization problem:

$$\min_{\{a,b\}} \sum_{j=1}^{n} (Y_j - a - (X_j - x)b)^2 K\left(\frac{X_j - x}{\lambda}\right) \qquad \text{EQUATION } \mathbf{A.4}$$

Let $\widehat{a} = \widehat{a}(x)$ and $\widehat{b} = \widehat{b}(x)$ be the solution of (A.4). It can be shown that $\widehat{a}(x)$ is a consistent estimator of $g(x)$ and $\widehat{b}(x)$ is a consistent estimator of $g^{(1)}(x) \equiv dg(x)/dx$. Intuitively, (A.4) is easily understood because it is just like a "local least squares" estimator. Hence, the slope estimator $\widehat{b}$ estimates the local slope $g^{(1)}(x)$. For a full exposition of the method, see Fan and Gijbels (1996).

A.2   Selection of Smoothing Parameters

A very relevant question any nonparametric method faces is the choice of smoothing parameters in the estimation of the unknown regression function $g(.)$. Here we discuss one such choice that uses only a least squares cross-validation method. One can choose λ by the least squares cross-validation method as

$$CV(\lambda) = n^{-1} \sum_{i=1}^{n} [Y_i - \widehat{g}_{-i}(X_i)]^2 \qquad \text{EQUATION } \mathbf{A.5}$$

where

$$\widehat{g}_{-i}(X_i) = (n\lambda)^{-1} \sum_{j \neq i} Y_j K\left(\frac{X_j - X_i}{\lambda}\right) \Big/ \widehat{f}_{-i}(X_i)$$

where $\widehat{g}_{-i}(X_i)$ and $\widehat{f}_{-i}(X_i)$ are the estimates of the regression function and the density by excluding observation i from the calculations. They are known as the *leave one out estimators*. The function $CV(\lambda)$ is minimized with respect to λ. It acts as a proxy to the integrated mean squared error, which is then minimized.

A.3   A Smooth Coefficient Regression Model

Let y_i denote the dependent variable, x_i a $p \times 1$ vector of independent variables, and z_i a $q \times 1$ vector of other exogenous variables that may affect the behavior of the coefficients of the x-variables. Consider the following linear model

$$y_i = \alpha(z_i) + x_i^T \beta(z_i) + \varepsilon_i = (1, x_i^T) \begin{pmatrix} \alpha(z_i) \\ \beta(z_i) \end{pmatrix} + \varepsilon_i$$

EQUATION **A.6**

$$y_i = X_i^T \delta(z_i) + \varepsilon_i$$

where $\delta(z_i) = (\alpha(z_i), \beta(z_i)^T)^T$ is a smooth but unknown function of z.

One can estimate $\delta(z)$ using a local least squares approach as

$$\widehat{\delta}(z) = \left[(n\lambda^q)^{-1} \sum_{j=1}^n X_j X_j^T K \left(\frac{z_j - z}{\lambda} \right) \right]^{-1} \left\{ (n\lambda^q)^{-1} \sum_{j=1}^n X_j y_j K \left(\frac{z_j - z}{\lambda} \right) \right\}$$

$$= [D_n(z)]^{-1} A_n(z)$$

where

$$D_n(z) = (n\lambda^q)^{-1} \sum_{j=1}^n X_j X_j^T K \left(\frac{z_j - z}{\lambda} \right),$$

$$A_n(z) = (n\lambda^q)^{-1} \sum_{j=1}^n X_j y_j K \left(\frac{z_j - z}{\lambda} \right)$$

is a kernel function and $\lambda = \lambda_n$ is the smoothing parameter for sample size n.

The intuition behind the local least squares estimator is straightforward. Let us assume that z is a scalar and $K(\cdot)$ is a uniform kernel. The expression for $\widehat{\delta}(z)$ becomes:

$$\widehat{\delta}(z) = \left[\sum_{|z_j - z| \leq \lambda} X_j X_j^T \right]^{-1} \sum_{|z_j - z| \leq \lambda} X_j y_j$$

In this case $\widehat{\delta}(z)$ is simply a least squares estimator obtained by regressing y_j on X_j using the observations of (X_j, y_j) that their corresponding z_j is close to z ($|z_j - z| \leq \lambda$). Since $\delta(z)$ is a smooth function of z, $|\delta(z_j) - \delta(z)|$ is small when $|z_j - z|$ is small. The condition that $n\lambda^q$ is large ensures that we have sufficient observations within the interval $|z_j - z| \leq \lambda$ when $\delta(z_j)$ is close to $\delta(z)$. Therefore, under the conditions that $\lambda \to 0$ and $n\lambda^q \to \infty$, one can show that the local least squares regression of y_j on X_j provides a consistent estimate of $\delta(z)$. In general it can be shown that

$$\sqrt{n\lambda^q}(\widehat{\delta}(z) - \delta(z)) \to N(0, \Omega)$$

where Ω can be consistently estimated. For more details, see Li, Huang, and Fu (2002) and Li and Racine (2006).

A.4   The Partially Linear Additively Separable Regression Model and the Use of Marginal Integration

Fan, Härdle, and Mammen (1998) applied marginal integration to the following general additive partially linear regression model

$$Y_i = \alpha + X_i^T \beta + g_1(Z_{1i}) + g_2(Z_{2i}) + \cdots + g_p(Z_{pi}) + u_i, \quad i = 1, \dots, n$$

EQUATION **A.7**

where X_i is a discrete variable of dimension q, β is a $q \times 1$ vector of parameters, α is a scalar parameter, the Z_{si}'s are univariate continuous variables, and $g_s(\cdot)$ $(s = 1, \dots, p)$ are unknown smooth functions. The observations $\{Y_i, X_i, Z_{1i}, \dots, Z_{pi}\}_{i=1}^n$ are i.i.d. One needs also the identification restriction that $E[g_s(Z_s)] = 0$ for $s = 1, \dots, p$.

Fan and Li (2003) allow X_i to be continuous as well as discrete. The important result from applying marginal integration to the extended additive regression model (A.7) is that the asymptotic distribution of $(\widehat{g}_s(z) - g_s(z))$ $(s = 1, \dots, p)$ is the same as if the other components $g_l(.)$ for $l \neq s$ and β were known. In other words, $\widehat{g}_s(z)$ behaves in the same way as if it were a one-dimensional local smoother. For details about the asymptotic properties of the estimators of the parameters α, β, and $g_s(z)$ $(s = 1, \dots, p)$, see Fan, Härdle, and Mammen (1998) and Fan and Li (2003).

The idea behind marginal integration can best be illustrated in the context of a very simple model with only two regressors. The model has the following additive structure

$$Y_i = \alpha + g_1(Z_{1i}) + g_2(Z_{2i}) + u_i, \quad i = 1, \dots, n$$

EQUATION **A.8**

where $\{Y_i, Z_{1i}, Z_{2i}\}_{i=1}^n$ are independently and identically distributed i.i.d. random variables, $E(u_i|Z_{1i}, Z_{2i}) = 0$, α is an unknown parameter, $g_1(\cdot)$

and $g_2(\cdot)$ are unknown univariate functions that obey the identifiability condition that $E(g_1(Z_1)) = 0$, and $E(g_2(Z_2)) = 0$.

As shown by Stone (1985, 1986), the additive components $g_s(\cdot)$ $(s = 1, 2)$ in (A.8) can be consistently estimated at the same rate as a fully nonparametric regression with only one regressor. In other words, the additive regression model in some sense provides a way of tackling the curse of dimensionality problem that is one of the most important weaknesses of nonparametric estimation methods. Linton and Nielsen (1995), Fan, Härdle, and Mammen (1998), and Fan and Li (2003) employ marginal integration as a way of obtaining estimates of the components of the additive regression model. Linton and Nielsen (1995) deal with a simple additive model with two components as in equation (A.8), whereas Fan, Härdle, and Mammen (1998), and Fan and Li (2003) extend the regression function to allow for a more general partially linear formulation as in equation (A.7).

Marginal integration in the context of equation (A.8) can be described as follows. Let $E(Y|Z_1 = z_1, Z_2 = z_2) = a(z_1, z_2)$. One can estimate $a(z_1, z_2)$ by a nonparametric local smoother, say $\widehat{a}(z_1, z_2)$, and then obtain an estimator of $\{g_1(z_1) + \alpha\}$ by integrating $\widehat{a}(z_1, z_2)$ over z_2, that is, $\widetilde{m}_1(z_1) = n^{-1} \sum_{j=1}^{n} \widehat{a}(z_1, Z_{2j})$. Since $E(g_1(Z_1)) = 0$, we can obtain the estimator of $g_1(z_1)$ by subtracting the sample mean of $\widetilde{m}_1(.)$ from $\widetilde{m}_1(z_1)$, that is, $\widetilde{g}_1(z_1) = \widetilde{m}_1(z_1) - n^{-1} \sum_{i=1}^{n} \widetilde{m}_1(Z_{1i})$. Similarly, we can obtain an estimator for $g_2(z_2)$.

Equation (A.8) can be extended to allow for an additive linear component. In that case we have

$$Y_i = \alpha + X_i^T \beta + g_1(Z_{1i}) + g_2(Z_{2i}) + u_i \qquad \text{EQUATION } \textbf{A.9}$$

where X_i is a variable (discrete or continuous) of dimension q, β is a $q \times 1$ vector of parameters, and α is a scalar parameter as before. We can obtain a $\sqrt{n}$-consistent estimator of β using Robinson's (1988) approach. Let us denote such an estimator by $\widehat{\beta}$. Equation (A.9) can be then written as

$$Y_i - X_i^T \widehat{\beta} = \alpha + g_1(Z_{1i}) + g_2(Z_{2i}) + u_i + X_i^T (\beta - \widehat{\beta}) \qquad \text{EQUATION } \textbf{A.10}$$

where $u_{i,} + X_i^T (\beta - \widehat{\beta})$ is the new composite error term. We can apply marginal integration to equation (A.10) in a fashion similar to equation (A.8) to obtain estimates of $g_1(z_1)$ and $g_2(z_2)$.

Glossary

$g_c = \dot{c}/c$ growth of consumption per worker

$g_h = \dot{h}/h$ growth of human capital–worker ratio

$g_k = \dot{k}/k$ growth of physical capital–worker ratio

$g_L = \dot{L}/L$ growth of the labor force

$h(t) = H(t)/L(t)$ human capital per worker

$\tilde{h}(t) = H(t)/[A(t) \cdot L(t)]$ human capital per effective unit of labor

$k(t) = K(t)/L(t)$ physical capital per worker

$\tilde{k}(t) = K(t)/[A(t) \cdot L(t)]$ physical capital per effective unit of labor

$p(x)$ inverse demand for intermediate product

q incremental capital–output ratio

r^h return to human capital

r^k return to physical capital

$s_H = S_H/Y$ saving ratio for human capital formation

$s_K = S_K/Y$ saving ratio for physical capital formation

$u(\cdot)$ instantaneous utility function

w wage rate

x input of intermediate product

$y(t) = Y(t)/L(t)$ output per worker

$\tilde{y}(t) = Y(t)/[A(t) \cdot L(t)]$ output per effective unit of labor

y^* steady-state level of output per worker

$\tilde{y}^*$ steady-state level of output per effective unit of labor

z proportion of an agent's time devoted to human capital formation and not production

$\Phi(H)$ contribution of human capital to closing the technology gap or "catch-up" effect

$\Psi(H)$ contribution of human capital to new innovations or "endogenous" effect

α, β, γ share (elasticity) of various inputs in output (specific input considered depends of model)

δ_H	depreciation rate of human capital
δ_K	depreciation rate of physical capital
ζ	efficiency of human capital accumulation
η	elasticity of human capital accumulation with respect to investment in physical accumulation
$\theta = K/H$	ratio of physical capital to human capital
κ	productivity enhancing effect of investing time in education
λ	speed of convergence to the steady state
ξ	efficiency with which firms generate new intermediate products
π	probability of innovating
ρ	rate of time preference
σ	elasticity of marginal utility
φ	technology available to each agent in transforming current to future labor supply
ψ	probability that the innovation will be successful
ω	growth rate of the theoretical level of technology

Chapters 8, 9, and Appendix

Some of the symbols used in these chapters are the same as those in Chapters 1–7 but signify different concepts. This duplication is necessary because some of the symbols (such as σ to signify elasticity of marginal utility above and variance below) are standard in the respective literatures and, more practically, we were running out of symbols. Their interpretation, however, is clear from the context within which they are used.

$E(.\vert.)$	conditional expectation
$I(.)$	indicator function

$f(.)$	probability density function (pdf)
$g(.)$	regression function
$\mathcal{K}()$	Kernel function
λ	bandwidth (depending on context that clearly distinguishes it from speed of convergence)
μ	mean of a random variable (depending on context that clearly distinguishes it from a costate variable)
σ	variance of a random variable
ψ	standardized bandwidth (depending on context that clearly distinguishes it from probability of innovation)

Bibliography

Aghion, P., and P. Howitt. 1998. *Endogenous Growth Theory*. Cambridge, MA: MIT Press.

Arrow, K. 1962. "The Economic Implications of Learning by Doing." *Review of Economic Studies* 29:155–173.

Azariadis, C., and A. Drazen. 1990. "Threshold Externalities in Economic Development." *Quarterly Journal of Economics* 105:501–526.

Barro, R. J. 1991. "Economic Growth in a Cross Section of Countries." *Quarterly Journal of Economics* 106:407–433.

———. 1997. *The Determinants of Economic Growth: A Cross-Country Empirical Study*. Cambridge MA: MIT Press.

———. 2001. "Human Capital and Economic Growth." *American Economic Review* 91:12–17.

Barro R. J., and J. W. Lee. 1994. "Sources of Economic Growth." *Carnegie-Rochester Series on Public Policy* 40:1–46.

———. 1996. "International Measures of Schooling Years and Schooling Quality." *American Economic Review Papers and Proceedings* 86:218–223.

———. 2001. "International Data on Educational Attainment: Updates and Implications." *Oxford Economic Papers* 53:541–563.

Barro, R. J., and X. Sala-i-Martin. 2004. *Economic Growth*. Cambridge MA: MIT Press.

Becker, G. S. 1962. "Investment in Human Capital: A Theoretical Analysis." *Journal of Political Economy* 70:9–49.

————. 1964. *Human Capital: A Theoretical and Empirical Analysis with Special Reference to Education.* New York: Columbia University Press.

Becker, G. S., and B. R. Chiswick. 1966. "Education and the Distribution of Earnings." *American Economic Review* 56:358–369.

Becker, G. S., K. M. Murphy, and R. Tamura. 1990. "Human Capital, Fertility, and Economic Growth." *Journal of Political Economy* 98:S12–S37.

Benhabib, J., and M. M. Spiegel. 1994. "The Role of Human Capital in Economic Development: Evidence from Aggregate Cross-Country Data." *Journal of Monetary Economics* 34:143–173.

————. 2005. "Human Capital and Technology Diffusion." In P. Aghion, and S. Durlauf (Eds.), *Handbook of Economic Growth, Vol. 1A.* Amsterdam: North Holland.

Bernanke, B. S., and R. S. Gürkaynak. 2001. "Is Growth Exogenous? Taking Mankiw, Romer, and Weil Seriously," *NBER Macroeconomics Annual 2001.* Cambridge, MA: MIT Press.

Bils, M., and P. J. Klenow. 2000. "Does Schooling Cause Growth?" *American Economic Review* 90:1160–1183.

Blandy, R. 1967. "Marshall on Human Capital: A Note." *Journal of Political Economy* 75:874–875.

Bosworth, B. P., and S. M. Collins. 2003. "The Empirics of Growth: An Update." *Brookings Papers on Economic Activity* 113–179.

Caselli, F., G. Esquivel, and F. Lefort. 1996. "Reopening the Convergence Debate: A New Look at Cross-Country Growth Regressions." *Journal of Economic Growth* 1:363–389.

Cass, D. 1965. "Optimum Growth in an Aggregate Model of Capital Accumulation." *Review of Economic Studies* 32:233–240.

Chamberlain, G. 1982. "Multivariate Regression Models for Panel Data." *Journal of Econometrics* 18:5–46.

Coe, D. T., E. Helpman, and A. W. Hoffmaister. 1997. "North–South R&D Spillovers." *Economic Journal* 107:134–149.

Cohen, D., and M. Soto. 2007. "Growth and Human Capital: Good Data, Good Results." *Journal of Economic Growth* 12:51–76.

De la Fuente, A., and R. Doménech. 2006. "Human Capital in Growth Regressions: How Much Difference Does Data Quality Make?" *Journal of the European Economic Association* 4:1–36.

Dinopoulos, E., and P. Thompson. 1999. "Reassessing the Empirical Validity of the Human-Capital Augmented Neoclassical Growth Model." *Journal of Evolutionary Economics* 9:135–154.

Dowrick, S., and M. Rogers. 2002. "Classical and Technological Convergence: Beyond the Solow–Swan Growth Model." *Oxford Economic Papers* 54:369–385.

Durlauf, S. N. 1993. "Nonergodic Economic Growth." *Review of Economic Studies* 60:349–366.

Durlauf, S. N., and P. A. Johnson. 1995. "Multiple Regimes and Cross-Country Growth Behaviour." *Journal of Applied Econometrics* 10:365–384.

Easterly, W., and R. Levine. 1997. "Africa's Growth Tragedy: Policies and Ethnic Divisions." *Quarterly Journal of Economics* 112: 1203–1250.

Edwards, S. 1998. "Openness, Productivity and Growth: What Do We Really Know?" *The Economic Journal* 108:383–398.

Enke, S. 1960. "The Gains to India from Population Control: Some Money Measures and Incentive Schemes." *Review of Economics and Statistics* 42:176–177.

Fan, J. 1992. "Design-Adaptive Nonparametric Regression." *Journal of the American Statistical Association* 87:998–1004.

Fan, J., and I. Gijbels. 1996. *Local Polynomial Modeling and its Applications.* London: Chapman and Hall.

Fan, J., W. Härdle, and E. Mammen. 1998. "Direct Estimation of Low Dimensional Components in Additive Models." *The Annals of Statistics* 26:943–971.

Fan, J., and W. Zhang. 1999. "Statistical Estimation in Varying-Coefficient Models." *The Annals of Statistics* 27:1491–1518.

Fan, Y., and Q. Li. 1996. "Consistent Model Specification Tests: Omitted Variables, Parametric and Semiparametric Functional Forms." *Econometrica* 64:865–890.

———. 1999. "Root-N-Consistent Estimation of Partially Linear Time Series Model." *Journal of Nonparametric Statistics* 11:251–269.

———. 2003. "A Kernel-Based Method for Estimating Additive Partially Linear Models." *Statistica Sinica* 13:739–762.

Fan, Y., Q. Li, and T. Stengos. 1995. "Root-N-Consistent Semiparametric Regression with Conditional Heteroscedastic Disturbances." *Journal of Quantitative Economics* 11:229–240.

Forbes, K. J. 2000. "A Reassessment of the Relationship between Inequality and Growth." *American Economic Review* 90:869–887.

Galor O. 2005. "The Transition from Stagnation to Growth: Unified Growth Theory." In P. Aghion and S. Durlauf (Eds.), *Handbook of Economic Growth*. Amsterdam: North Holland.

Galor O., and O. Moav. 2002. "Natural Selection and the Origin of Economic Growth." *Quarterly Journal of Economics* 117:1133–1192.

Galor O., and D. N. Weil. 2000. "Population, Technology, and Growth: From the Malthusian Regime to the Demographic Transition and Beyond." *American Economic Review* 90:806–828.

Gemmel, N. 1996. "Evaluating the Impacts of Human Capital Stocks and Accumulation on Economic Growth: Some New Evidence." *Oxford Bulletin of Economics and Statistics* 58:9–28.

Gollin, D. 2002. "Getting Income Shares Right." *Journal of Political Economy* 110:458–474.

Gylfason, T. 1999. *Principles of Economic Growth*. New York: Oxford University Press.

Hall R. E., and C. I. Jones. 1999. "Why Do Some Countries Produce So Much More Output Per Worker than Others?" *Quarterly Journal of Economics* 114:83–116.

Hanushek, E. A., and D. Kimko. 2000. "Schooling, Labor Force Quality, and the Growth of Nations." *American Economic Review* 90:1184–1208.

Hanushek, E. A., and L. Woessmann. 2007. "The Role of School Improvement in Economic Development." *NBER Working Paper No. 12832*.

Härdle, W. 1990. *Applied Nonparametric Regression*. New York: Cambridge University Press.

Härdle, W., and O. Linton. 1994. "Applied Nonparametric Methods." In R. Engle, and D. McFadden (Eds.), *Handbook of Econometrics, Vol. 4*. Amsterdam: North Holland.

Hill, A., and E. King. 1995. *Women's Education in Developing Countries*. Baltimore: Johns Hopkins University Press.

Hirschman, A. O. 1958. *The Strategy of Economic Development*. New Haven, CT: Yale University Press.

Horvat, B. 1958. "The Optimum Rate of Investment." *Economic Journal* 68:747–767.

Islam, N. 1995. "Growth Empirics: A Panel Data Approach." *Quarterly Journal of Economics* 110:1127–1170.

Jones, C. I. 2002. *Introduction to Economic Growth*. New York: W. W. Norton.

Kalaitzidakis P., T. Mamuneas, A. Savvides, and T. Stengos. 2001. "Measures of Human Capital and Nonlinearities in Economic Growth." *Journal of Economic Growth* 6:229–254.

Keller, W. 2004. "International Technology Diffusion." *Journal of Economic Literature* 42:752–782.

Ketteni, E., T. Mamuneas, and T. Stengos. 2007a. "Nonlinearities in Economic Growth: A Semiparametric Approach Applied to Information Technology Data." *Journal of Macroeconomics* 29:555–568.

———. 2007b. "The Effect of Information Technology and Human Capital on Economic Growth." Unpublished manuscript, Department of Economics, University of Guelph, Ontario.

Kiker, B. F. 1966. "The Historical Roots of the Concept of Human Capital." *Journal of Political Economy* 74:481–499.

———. 1968. "Marshall on Human Capital: Comment." *Journal of Political Economy* 76:1088–1090.

King, R. G., and R. Levine. 1994. "Capital Fundamentalism, Economic Development and Economic Growth." *Carnegie-Rochester Conference Series on Public Policy* 40:259–292.

Klasen, S. 2002. "Low Schooling for Girls, Slower Growth for All? Cross-Country Evidence on the Effect of Gender Inequality in Education and Economic Development." *World Bank Economic Review* 16:345–373.

Klenow, P., and A. Rodríguez-Clare. 1997. "The Neoclassical Revival in Growth Economics: Has It Gone Too Far?" In B. S. Bernanke, and J. J. Rotemberg (Eds.), *NBER Macroeconomics Annual 1997*. Cambridge, MA: MIT Press.

Knowles S., P. K. Lorgelly, and P. D. Owen. 2002. "Are Educational Gender Gaps a Brake on Economic Development? Some Cross-Country Empirical Evidence." *Oxford Economic Papers* 54:118–149.

Koopmans, T. C. 1965. "On the Concept of Optimal Economic Growth." In *The Econometric Approach to Development Planning*. Amsterdam: North Holland.

Krueger, A. B., and M. Lindahl. 2001. "Education for Growth: Why and for Whom?" *Journal of Economic Literature* 39:1101–1136.

Larson, D. F., R. Butzer, Y. Mandlak, and A. Crego. 2000. "A Cross-Country Database for Sector Investment and Capital." *World Bank Economic Review* 14:371–391.

Lee, J. W., and R. J. Barro. 2001. "Schooling Quality in a Cross-Section of Countries." *Economica* 68:465–488.

Li, Q., C. Huang, D. Li, and T. Fu. 2002. "Semiparametric Smooth Coefficient Models." *Journal of Business and Economic Statistics* 20:412–422.

Li, Q., and J. Racine. 2006. *Nonparametric Econometrics: Theory and Practice*. Princeton, NJ: Princeton University Press.

Li, Q., and S. Wang. 1998. "A Simple Consistent Bootstrap Test for a Parametric Regression Function." *Journal of Econometrics* 87:145–165.

Linton, O. B., and J. P. Nielsen. 1995. "A Kernel Method of Estimating Structural Nonparametric Regression Based on Marginal Integration." *Biometrika* 82:93–100.

Liu, Z., and T. Stengos. 1999. "Non-Linearities in Cross-Country Growth Regressions: A Semiparametric Approach." *Journal of Applied Econometrics* 14:527–538.

Lucas, R. 1988. "On the Mechanics of Economic Development." *Journal of Monetary Economics* 22:3–42.

Mamuneas T., A. Savvides, and T. Stengos. 2006. "Economic Development and the Return to Human Capital: A Sooth Coefficient Semiparametric Approach." *Journal of Applied Econometrics* 21:111–132.

Mankiw, N. G., D. Romer, and D. N. Weil. 1992. "A Contribution to the Empirics of Economic Growth." *Quarterly Journal of Economics* 107:407–437.

Murphy, K., A. Schleifer, and R. Vishny. 1989. "Industrialization and the Big Push." *Quarterly Journal of Economics* 106:503–530.

Nehru, V., and A. Dhareshwar. 1993. "A New Database on Physical Capital: Sources, Methodology and Results." *Revista de Análisis Económico* 8:37–59.

Nehru, V., E. Swanson, and A. Dubey. 1995. "A New Database on Human Capital Stock in Developing and Industrial Countries: Sources, Methodology and Results." *Journal of Development Economics* 46:379–401.

Nelson, R. R., and E. S. Phelps. 1966. "Investment in Humans, Technological Diffusion, and Economic Growth." *American Economic Review* 56:69–75.

Pagan A., and A. Ullah. 1999. *Nonparametric Econometrics.* Cambridge, UK: Cambridge University Press.

Papageorgiou, C. 2003. "Distinguishing Between the Effects of Primary and Post-Primary Education on Economic Growth." *Review of Development Economics* 7:622–635.

Pritchett, L. 2001. "Where Has All the Education Gone?" *The World Bank Economic Review* 15:367–391.

Psacharopoulos, G. 1994. "Returns to Investment in Education: A Global Update." *World Development* 22:1325–1343.

Psacharopoulos, G., and H. A. Patrinos. 2002. "Returns to Investment in Education: A Further Update." *NBER Working Paper No. 2881.*

Quah, D. T. 1996. "Empirics for Economic Growth and Convergence." *European Economic Review* 40:1353–1375.

Ramsey, F. 1928. "A Mathematical Theory of Saving." *Economic Journal* 106:1045–1055.

Rebelo, S. 1991. "Long-Run Policy Analysis and Long-Run Growth." *Journal of Political Economy* 99:500–521.

Redding, S. 1996. "The Low-Skill, Low-Quality Trap: Strategic Complementarities between Human Capital and R&D." *Economic Journal* 106:458–470.

Robinson, P. 1988. "Root-N-Consistent Semiparametric Regression." *Econometrica* 56:931–954.

Romer, P. M. 1986. "Increasing Returns and Long-Run Growth." *Journal of Political Economy* 94:1002–1037.

———. 1990. "Endogenous Technological Change." *Journal of Political Economy* 98:S71–S102.

Savvides, A., and M. Zachariadis. 2005. "International Technology Diffusion and the Growth of TFP in the Manufacturing Sector of Developing Economies." *Review of Development Economics* 9: 482–501.

Schultz, T. W. 1960. "Capital Formation by Education." *Journal of Political Economy* 68:571–583.

———. 1961a. "Investment in Human Capital." *American Economic Review* 51:1–17.

———. 1961b. "Reply to Investment in Human Capital: Comment." *American Economic Review* 51:1035–1039.

———. 1962. "Reflections on Investment in Man." *Journal of Political Economy* 70:1–8.

Shaffer, H. G. 1961. "Investment in Human Capital: Comment." *American Economic Review* 51:1026–1035.

Silverman B. 1986. *Density Estimation for Statistics and Data Analysis.* New York: Chapman and Hall.

Spengler, J. 1977. "Adam Smith on Human Capital." *American Economic Review* 67:32–36.

Stock, J. H. 1989. "Nonparametric Policy Analysis." *Journal of American Statistical Association* 84:567–575.

Stone, C. J. 1977. "Consistent Nonparametric Regression." *Annals of Statistics* 5:595–620.

———. 1985. "Additive Regression and Other Nonparametric Models." *Annals of Statistics* 13:685–705.

———. 1986. "The Dimensionality Reduction Principle for Generalized Additive Models." *Annals of Statistics* 14:592–606.

Temple, J. 1999. "The New Growth Evidence." *Journal of Economic Literature* 37:112–156.

————. 2001. "Generalizations that Aren't? Evidence on Education and Growth." *European Economic Review* 45:905–918.

Topel, R. 1999. "Labor Markets and Economic Growth." In O. Ashenfelter and D. Card (Eds.), *Handbook of Labor Economics, Vol. 3C.* Amsterdam: North Holland, 2943–2984.

Vandenbussche, J., P. Aghion, and C. Meghir. 2006. "Growth, Distance to Frontier and Composition of Human Capital." *Journal of Economic Growth* 11:97–127.

Walsh, J. R. 1935. "Capital Concept Applied to Man." *Quarterly Journal of Economics* 49:255–285.

Weil, D. N. 2005. *Economic Growth.* Boston: Addison-Wesley.

Weisbrod, B. A. 1961. "The Valuation of Human Capital." *Journal of Political Economy* 69:425–436.

————. 1962. "Education and Investment in Human Capital." *Journal of Political Economy* 70:106–123.

Yatchew, A. 1997. "An Elementary Estimator of the Partially Linear Model." *Economics Letters* 57:135–143.

Index